100 THINGS PURDUE FANS SHOULD KNOW & DO BEFORE THEY DIE

Tom Schott
with Nathan Baird

TRIUMPH
BOOKS

Library of Congress Cataloging-in-Publication Data available upon request.

This book is available in quantity at special discounts for your group or organization. For further information, contact:

Triumph Books LLC
814 North Franklin Street
Chicago, Illinois 60610
(312) 337-0747
www.triumphbooks.com

Printed in U.S.A.
ISBN: 978-1-62937-690-5
Design by Patricia Frey
Photos courtesy of Purdue Athletics archives unless otherwise indicated

To Jane, August, and Sam—my home team; to Bobette, Debbie, and Steve—my family; to Tom Campbell and Tim Newton—my Boilermaker brothers; and to the memory of Joe Tiller—my friend.

—T.S.

Contents

Foreword

What an honor to be asked to write the foreword for a book that chronicles the top 100 things about Purdue athletics. And to be included as one of the chapters—I truly am humbled.

While there are accounts of great games and anecdotes about subjects pertaining to the University and the Greater Lafayette area, most of the stories in this book are about people. That's not surprising, especially to anyone who has been associated with the Boilermakers, because people are what make Purdue such a special place.

When I got word that I was selected for the Purdue Intercollegiate Athletics Hall of Fame, the first thing I thought of was all the people who had a role in helping me achieve my goal of playing college basketball. First and foremost, I am thankful for my parents, Glenn and Linda, for taking me from Valparaiso, Indiana, all over the country to play in AAU tournaments, and my poor brother, Dan, who got dragged along on most of those trips. At Purdue, I was incredibly fortunate to have outstanding coaches, awesome teammates, and great support staff. It honestly was the best five years of my life. You go to school, get to play basketball, try to figure things out and become an adult...all while having a lot of fun along the way. My only regret is not getting to the Final Four in 2010 after suffering my first knee injury. With guys like E'Twaun Moore, JaJuan Johnson, Chris Kramer, Lewis Jackson, and Keaton Grant, I truly believe we had a team that could have won the national championship.

Then I thought about all the legends who are synonymous with Purdue basketball: John Wooden, Rick Mount, Joe Barry Carroll, and Glenn Robinson, to name just a few. Those are the caliber of people every Purdue player strives to be, and to be put in a category with them as a Hall of Famer really is surreal. I consider myself extremely fortunate.

I absolutely loved playing basketball at Purdue. I loved playing at Mackey Arena. Our fans are the best in the country. They are incredibly passionate, incredibly knowledgeable, and they expect that every time you take the floor, you give elite effort. I love that about them. They really care, and they are completely invested in their team. It was a privilege and honor to play for them.

As an alum, I feel a tremendous sense of pride in our basketball program. I am so happy Matt Painter is finally getting the credit he deserves from a coaching standpoint. He is without a doubt one of the best coaches in all of college basketball. The program is in great hands. We have enjoyed a lot of success, but I think our best days are ahead of us.

People always ask me about Coach Painter and what it was like playing for him. He was tremendous throughout my whole experience, beginning with the recruiting process and continuing throughout my time at Purdue. He was great to play for and was always there for me. The best thing I can say about him is that he genuinely cares about his players, on and off the court, and how they do after they leave Purdue. Whether you are a current player or a former player, he wants what is best for you. When I got hurt playing in Italy in 2016, I came back to West Lafayette to rehab with the Purdue athletic trainers, and he invited me to live at his house for four or five months. He didn't have to do that, and I truly believe he would do it for any one of his guys who played for him. One of the first mornings I was there, he knocked on my bedroom door and said, "Rob, do you want breakfast? I'm making bacon-filled waffles if you're hungry." To me, that sums up the kind of person Coach Painter is—he would give the shirt off his back to anyone, and that is something all Purdue fans should know.

—Robbie Hummel

March 2020

Purdue Intercollegiate Athletics Hall of Fame Class of 2020

2019 USA Basketball Male Athlete of the Year

Introduction

When Triumph Books made the decision to add *100 Things Purdue Fans Should Know & Do Before They Die* to its successful lineup of titles, it made a smart choice by signing up Nathan Baird as author.

Nathan was an award-winning sports reporter for the Lafayette *Journal & Courier* for 14 years, primarily covering Purdue men's basketball while assisting with other sports. In August 2019, Nathan left Greater Lafayette to cover Ohio State football for Cleveland.com and, in doing so, did not feel he could continue writing this book.

That's when Josh Williams of Triumph contacted me and asked if I would be interested in completing the project. You bet. I eagerly accepted the offer. As expected, Nathan had done an excellent job laying the foundation and getting the project off the ground. Then I came in, wrapped up the construction, and added the finishing touches. Together, we played the roles of engineer and conductor wonderfully.

As for my story, I came to the Purdue athletics department in July 1990 on a 10-month internship...and stayed for 29½ years. Over those nearly three decades, I witnessed so many unforgettable events; most notably, the 1999 NCAA women's basketball championship and the 2001 Rose Bowl. More importantly, I made lifelong friendships with countless student-athletes, coaches, and administrators. It truly was a labor of love.

A compilation of the greatest Purdue vignettes easily could extend beyond 100, and I hope you agree with the ones we selected as the cream of the crop. Many of them are about events I observed firsthand and people I have known and worked with, while the remainder are tales that I had heard and required research to fill in the blanks. Whichever the case, recounting Purdue athletics history has been a longtime passion of mine, and having my name associated with *100 Things Purdue Fans Should Know & Do Before They Die* is a career highpoint.

Thanks for reading. Boiler Up!

—T.S.

1 What Is a Boilermaker?

It is one of the most unique nicknames in college sports. So unique, in fact, that many college sports fans—possibly even some Purdue followers—do not recognize the reference or its origins.

To find the answer, we must return to the 19th century, the infancy of Purdue football.

Imagine a time when Butler University, DePaul University, and Wabash College—all respected institutions of higher learning today, though none of them with a Division I football program—were considered the "Big Three" of college football in Indiana.

Purdue's first game in 1887—its only game of that season—was a 48–6 loss to Butler.

By 1891, however, fortunes were turning. Purdue traveled south to Crawfordsville to face Wabash. And a 44–0 victory earned the squad a new nickname.

The *Crawfordsville Daily Argus News* report of the game christened Purdue's team with a headline both partisan and hyperbolic: SLAUGHTER OF INNOCENTS. WABASH SNOWED COMPLETELY UNDER BY THE BURLY BOILER MAKERS FROM PURDUE.

The Lafayette *Sunday Times* embraced the derisive moniker: "As everyone knows, Purdue went down to Wabash last Saturday and defeated their eleven. The Crawfordsville papers have not yet gotten over it. The only recourse they have is to claim that we beat their 'scientific' men by brute force. Our players are characterized as 'coal heavers,' 'boiler makers' and 'stevedores.'"

Nicknames such as "Boiler Maker" referred to the blue-collar careers that many Purdue graduates pursued—at least in the eyes of those from a liberal arts college such as Wabash.

All-Time Purdue Big Ten Championships

Baseball
1909, 2012

Men's Basketball
1911, 1912, 1921, 1922, 1926, 1928, 1930, 1932, 1934, 1935, 1936, 1938, 1940, 1969, 1979, 1984, 1987, 1988, 1994, 1995, 1996, 2010, 2017, 2019

Women's Basketball
1991, 1994, 1995, 1997, 1999, 2001, 2002

Men's Cross Country
1916, 1941, 1943

Field Hockey
1977, 1978, 1979

Football
1918, 1929, 1931, 1932, 1943, 1952, 1967, 2000

Men's Golf
1950, 1953, 1955, 1956, 1958, 1959, 1960, 1964, 1965, 1967, 1971, 1981

Women's Golf
2000, 2006, 2008, 2009, 2010, 2013

Squash
1935, 1936, 1941, 1942

Women's Track & Field
1987 (outdoor), 1999 (outdoor), 2001 (indoor), 2017 (outdoor)

Women's Volleyball
1979, 1980, 1982, 1985

Wrestling
1942, 1945, 1948, 1949, 1950, 1954

Through 2019–20

2

In the fall of 1891, Purdue had added a working railroad engine to a newly established locomotive laboratory. For whatever reason, growing commitments to engineering education and agriculture brought mockery from opposing teams and fans.

Other nicknames directed Purdue's way included blacksmiths, cornfield sailors, foundry hands, grangers, pumpkin-shuckers, and railsplitters. Considering some of those options, it may be for the best that "Boilermakers" has stood the test of time.

The nickname perhaps is best visualized by the 18-foot bronze statue located between Ross-Ade Stadium and the Mollenkopf Athletic Center. Titled *The Boilermaker*, the statue depicts a 19th-century locomotive boilermaker working in a boiler room.

All-Time Purdue Big Ten Tournament Championships

Baseball
2012

Men's Basketball
2009

Women's Basketball
1998, 1999, 2000, 2003, 2004, 2007, 2008, 2012, 2013

Women's Soccer
2007

Women's Tennis
2012

Women's Volleyball
1982

Through 2019–20

2 John Wooden

Before his name became synonymous with unparalleled success as head coach at UCLA, John Wooden was a standout basketball player at Purdue.

Playing for head coach Ward "Piggy" Lambert, whom he credited with having the biggest influence on his career, Wooden was a three-time All-American and the 1932 National Player of the Year. The 5'10", 178-pound guard excelled as a scorer, ball-handler, playmaker, and defender.

Born in Hall, Indiana, Wooden and his family moved to Centerton and then Martinsville, where he attended high school and played for a state championship basketball team as a junior, sandwiched around two runner-up finishes. Wooden picked Purdue for its academic prowess, specifically in civil engineering.

"Everyone knows that Purdue is among the finest engineering schools in the nation," Wooden said. "People think I selected Purdue because I wanted to play for Mr. Lambert. They say that because that's the way many basketball players today make their college choice. When I was a student, we selected an area of study and matched it with a university."

The NCAA did not permit freshmen to play in Wooden's days, so he practiced and scrimmaged during the 1928–29 season. The following year, he teamed with 6'7" senior center Charles "Stretch" Murphy to give the Boilermakers a dynamic inside-outside combination. Purdue posted a 13–2 record and both losses came with Wooden sidelined due to a leg injury. The Boilermakers were 10–0 in Big Ten games to capture the conference championship.

As a senior, Wooden averaged a Big Ten-best 12.2 points per game in leading the Boilermakers to a 17–1 record and another conference crown. Purdue was named national champion by the Helms Athletic Foundation. Wooden earned the Big Ten Medal of Honor for demonstrating great proficiency in scholarship and athletics.

Following graduation, Wooden became a high school teacher and coach, first in Dayton, Kentucky, and then in South Bend, Indiana. Over 11 seasons, his teams compiled a 218–42 record, an .838 winning percentage. In 1934, Wooden came up with his definition of success: "Success is peace of mind which is a direct result of self-satisfaction in knowing you made the effort to become the best you are capable of becoming." While teaching and coaching, Wooden also played professionally for several years with the Hammond All-Americans, Indianapolis Kautskys, and Whiting All-Americans.

During an ensuing stint as a lieutenant in the U.S. Navy from 1943 to 1946, Wooden was slated to be deployed on the USS *Franklin* aircraft carrier in January 1945 on a mission in the South Pacific. But having undergone recent surgery to have his appendix removed, Wooden was not regarded healthy enough and was replaced by a fellow Purdue graduate, Fred Stalcup. In March 1945, the *Franklin* was attacked by a Japanese dive bomber in the Battle of Okinawa that killed hundreds, including Stalcup.

Following his military discharge, Wooden spent two years at Indiana State Teachers College (now Indiana State University) as athletics director, basketball coach, and baseball coach while also completing his master's degree.

On April 17, 1948, Wooden accepted an offer from UCLA to become its basketball coach. He had been expecting an offer from the University of Minnesota the same day, as well, but a major winter storm knocked out telephone service in Minneapolis, delaying the call. By the time that call came, Wooden had taken the UCLA job and, although he would have preferred Minnesota because of his Midwestern roots and Big Ten pedigree, he felt obliged to turn it down.

And so began an extraordinary 27-year career at UCLA. "The Wizard of Westwood," a nickname Wooden did not like, amassed a 620–147 record and an .808 winning percentage. The Bruins captured 10 national championships in a 12-year span, including

John Wooden was a three-time All-American and the 1932 National Player of the Year.

6

seven in a row from 1967 to 1973, and 19 Pac-10 titles. They put together unfathomable winning streaks of 88 overall games and 38 NCAA Tournament contests. From the 1966–67 to 1972–73 seasons, UCLA won 205 of 210 games. Wooden was a seven-time National Coach of the Year honoree.

In 1949, Purdue athletics director Guy "Red" Mackey offered Wooden the opportunity to return to his alma mater as head coach following the 1949–50 season. But the arrangement did not sit well with Wooden.

"Mackey wanted to let [Mel] Taube coach the 1949–50 team and then replace him with me—regardless of how well that Purdue team did," Wooden said. "I didn't like that method of doing business, and I told Mackey that. I decided that I would remain at UCLA. Did I want the Purdue job? Most definitely, but not under those conditions."

Wooden was a member of the inaugural Purdue Intercollegiate Athletics Hall of Fame class in 1994. He is one of merely four individuals enshrined in the Naismith Basketball Hall of Fame as a player (1960) and a coach (1973), along with Bill Sharman, Lenny Wilkens, and Tom Heinsohn. In 2003, Wooden received the nation's highest civilian honor when he was awarded the Presidential Medal of Freedom.

The Purdue athletics department established the John R. Wooden Leadership Institute in 2009 to accelerate the leadership development of Boilermaker student-athletes. Resources include the legendary Pyramid of Success, which highlights each of Wooden's 15 building blocks—behavioral traits—for a better life: industriousness, loyalty, alertness, initiative, enthusiasm, self-control, friendship, cooperation, intentness, confidence, skill, team spirit, poise, condition, and competitive greatness.

Speaking at the 60th annual dinner of the Greater Lafayette Chamber of Commerce in 1987, Wooden told the crowd, "This Hoosier is one who went away but never really left...My interests and heart will always be back home in Indiana." He also spoke of paying attention to the goings-on at Purdue. "Sure, I check the basketball and football scores, keep up on the accomplishments of the university, and thrill in the achievements of our astronauts."

Known for being humble and unassuming, Wooden was held in high esteem for his impeccable moral character. Twice, he was honored as Sportsman of the Year, by *The Sporting News* in 1970 and *Sports Illustrated* in 1972. Wooden died in 2010 at age 99.

3 Drew Brees

Drew Brees arrived at Purdue as a little-known quarterback. He left as one of the most decorated players in school history:

- He established two NCAA records, 12 Big Ten records, and 18 Purdue records.
- He was a two-time Heisman Trophy finalist, two-time Big Ten Offensive Player of the Year, and two-time first-team All-Conference selection.
- He won the 2000 Maxwell Award as the nation's most outstanding player and the *Chicago Tribune* Silver Football as the Big Ten Most Valuable Player.
- He was the 2000 Academic All-American of the Year.

A member of head coach Joe Tiller's first Purdue recruiting class, Brees served as Billy Dicken's understudy in 1997. Tiller and his staff, however, weren't completely confident in Brees, and they signed junior college signal-caller David Edgerton. But Brees emerged as the starter and carried the Boilermakers to heights not reached in more than three decades, capped with the 2000 Big Ten championship and just the second Rose Bowl appearance in school history.

In his fifth start, against Minnesota at Ross-Ade Stadium on October 3, 1998, Brees set school records for passing yards (522), total offense (524), and passing touchdowns (6) in just three quarters of a 56–21 victory. The following week at Wisconsin, he set an NCAA record by throwing 83 passes and tied the record with 55 completions.

Statistically, the 1998 season was Brees' best. He set school and conference marks for passing attempts (569), completions (361), yards (3,983), and touchdowns (39), as well as total offense (4,176).

But over the next two years, Brees became a complete player, cutting down his interceptions, improving his game management, and becoming a threat to run the ball. In 2000, Brees broke his own total offense record with 4,189 yards, leading the nation with an average of 358.1 per game. He completed 309 of 512 passes for 3,668 yards with 26 touchdowns and 12 interceptions, and rushed for 521 yards on 95 carries (5.5 average) with five touchdowns. He was voted team MVP by his teammates.

"Brees is to Tiller's wide-open offense what Laurence Olivier was to Hamlet. Nobody does it better," ABC announcer Brent Musburger said. "This is a young man who plays with talent, spirit, and heart. It's so much fun to talk to him because he has such a good attitude. You know, the smile—he lights it up. He's a delightful young man to be around."

Brees left Purdue holding Big Ten career records for passing attempts (1,678), completions (1,026), passing yards (11,792), passing touchdowns (90), and total offense (12,692).

"What Drew has done for Purdue is elevate our program from a national awareness standpoint," Tiller said. "He has created awareness of Purdue football all over the country."

9

There was more to Drew Brees than gaudy statistics. He was the ultimate student-athlete, majoring in industrial management, and was extremely generous with his time in the community. (Getty Images)

But there was more to Brees than gaudy statistics. He was the ultimate student-athlete, majoring in industrial management, and he was extremely generous with his time in the community. Among his honors, certainly the most fitting was the inaugural Socrates Award, presented in January 2000, recognizing the nation's finest athlete in terms of academics, athletics, and community service.

Brees was inducted into the Purdue Intercollegiate Athletics Hall of Fame in 2009 and the College Sports Information Directors Academic All-America Hall of Fame in 2016.

Since leaving Purdue, Brees has become one of the greatest quarterbacks to play in the National Football League, first with the San Diego Chargers (2001–05) and then with the New Orleans Saints (2006–present). He is a 13-time Pro Bowl selection and twice has been named Offensive Player of the Year.

On October 21, 2018, when the Saints beat the Baltimore Ravens 24–23, Brees joined Brett Favre and Peyton Manning as the only three quarterbacks to have a victory against all 32 current NFL teams.

Entering the 2020 season, Brees was the NFL career record-holder for passing yards (77,416), passing touchdowns (547), completions (6,867), completion percentage (.676), and total offense (75,268).

Brees was named the MVP of Super Bowl XLIV after leading the Saints to a 31–17 win over the Indianapolis Colts. He tied a Super Bowl record with 32 completions, the last a two-yard slant to Jeremy Shockey for the winning touchdown with 5:42 remaining. Brees finished 32 of 39 for 288 yards with two touchdowns and no interceptions.

Brees was honored as the 2006 Walter Payton NFL Man of the Year.

4 Gene Keady

For 25 seasons, Gene Keady was the face of Purdue men's basketball.

The head coach of the Boilermakers from 1980–81 to 2004–05, Keady is the winningest coach in school history with a record of 512–270, a snappy .655 winning percentage. His teams won 20 or more games 14 times and 25-plus on six occasions, including 29 victories in 1987–88 and 1993–94.

Keady engineered Purdue to six Big Ten championships (1984, 1987, 1988, 1994, 1995, and 1996) and three second-place showings (1983, 1990, and 1997) among 18 finishes in the top half of the league.

Purdue earned 17 NCAA Tournament berths, advancing to the Elite Eight in 1994 and 2000 and the Sweet 16 in 1988, 1998, and 1999.

Keady was named Big Ten Coach of the Year a record seven times (1984, 1988, 1990, 1994, 1995, 1996, and 2000) and National Coach of the Year on six occasions (1984, 1988, 1994, 1995, 1996, and 2000).

"It was a wonderful career, and I loved my time at Purdue," Keady said. "I was fortunate to coach in the Big Ten, in a state that loved basketball and at a school that stressed academics and had a great basketball tradition. The people I was surrounded by were great. I'm not sure how I could have topped my experience. Purdue was my type of school."

Throughout his career, Keady was renowned for his passionate sideline antics and cajoling and badgering of referees. He was also universally admired for getting the most out of his talent. He got his players to believe in and perform their roles, and successfully blended together the diverse personalities of each team. Keady preferred hard workers over blue chippers and never was afraid to raise his voice when necessary.

"Our practices were harder than the games. We got after it every day," Keady said. "I treated my players the way my dad treated me. He might have scolded me, but afterward he always explained to me why he did it."

The Boilermakers were equally as successful in the classroom as they were on the court. Nearly 90 percent of the seniors who stayed at Purdue for four seasons under Keady graduated.

"That would be my legacy," Keady said. "Earning your degree from a world-class university like Purdue is something you can always hold on to and use to provide a better life for your family."

Born and raised in Larned, Kansas, Keady was a four-sport athlete: baseball, basketball, football, track & field. After two seasons at Garden City Junior College, where he was an All-America quarterback, Keady went to Kansas State University. He played football two years while also competing in the 60-yard dash and shot put and playing baseball for one year apiece. In 1958, Keady was drafted by the Pittsburgh Steelers as a wide receiver in the 19th round of the NFL Draft. He went to training camp—where one of his teammates was former Purdue star quarterback Len Dawson—but was released.

Keady returned to Kansas and forayed into teaching and coaching, beginning at Beloit High School in 1959 and continuing at Hutchinson Junior College six years later. Then, in 1975, Keady was hired as assistant basketball coach at the University of Arkansas. He developed a strong reputation for being able to recruit, landing the famous "Triplets"—Sidney Moncrief, Ron Brewer, and Marvin Delf—who led the Razorbacks to the 1978 NCAA Final Four.

Keady served as head coach at Western Kentucky for the 1978–79 and 1979–80 seasons, sharing the Ohio Valley Conference championship his second year while compiling a 38–19 record.

When Purdue head coach Lee Rose departed for the University of South Florida after taking the Boilermakers to the 1980 Final Four, athletics director George King acted swiftly and hired Keady on April 11. Ironically, Keady was in attendance at Market Square Arena in Indianapolis when Purdue lost to UCLA in the national semifinals.

Keady's first two Purdue teams played in the NIT before the Boilermakers became a regular participant in the NCAA

The always passionate Gene Keady was named Big Ten Coach of the Year a record seven times and National Coach of the Year on six occasions. (Tom Campbell)

Tournament as well as perennial contenders for the Big Ten championship. The Boilermakers' back-to-back-to-back outright conference titles from 1994 to 1996 marked the first three-peat by a Big Ten school since Ohio State from 1960 to 1962. "Purdue put a man on the moon since," Big Ten commissioner Jim Delany said upon presenting the Boilermakers the 1996 championship trophy.

On December 6, 1997, Keady passed Ward "Piggy" Lambert as the Boilermakers' winningest coach with his 372nd victory, an 87–62 decision at Louisville. In recognition of the achievement, Mackey Arena's playing floor subsequently was dubbed Keady Court.

In Big Ten history entering the 2020–21 season, Keady ranks third in overall wins and Big Ten victories (265), trailing only Indiana's Bob Knight and Michigan State's Tom Izzo. Keady was 21–20 in games against Knight.

In addition to his triumphs on the collegiate level, Keady boasted a 22–2 record as head coach of four USA Basketball teams and won two gold medals. The first came at the 1979 National Sports Festival in Colorado Springs, Colorado, where he was observed by former Purdue basketball coach-turned-administrator Fred Schaus, who liked what he saw and recommended him for the Boilermakers vacancy a year later. Keady also won gold at the 1989 World University Games and as an assistant for the 2000 Dream Team at the Sydney Olympics.

Many of Keady's players and assistants went on to become successful head coaches. His coaching tree includes current Purdue coach Matt Painter, along with Bruce Weber, Cuonzo Martin, Steve Lavin, and Kevin Stallings.

"Gene is the master," Purdue athletics director Morgan Burke said in April 2004, when he announced that Painter would join the staff as head-coach-in-waiting for one season prior to Keady's retirement. "He has developed coaching talent that now populates college basketball from coast to coast. That Matt will get a year of seasoning with a floor general like Gene is an absolutely ideal situation."

After leaving Purdue, Keady spent the 2005–06 season as an assistant coach with the Toronto Raptors of the NBA. He later served as an assistant to Lavin at St. John's from 2010 to 2015. Keady now makes his home in Myrtle Beach, South Carolina, but regularly returns to West Lafayette, especially during basketball season to watch the Boilermakers.

Keady was inducted into the Indiana Basketball Hall of Fame in 2001, Purdue Intercollegiate Athletics Hall of Fame in 2010, and National Collegiate Basketball Hall of Fame in 2013. He received the 2007 John R. Wooden Legends of Coaching Award.

Joe Tiller

Joe Tiller ranks as one of the most beloved and popular figures in Purdue Athletics history.

Tiller served as the Boilermakers' head football coach from 1997 to 2008. The winningest coach in school history, he posted an 87–62 record, including 53–43 in Big Ten games. He was 10–2 in Old Oaken Bucket showdowns against Indiana. Tiller's 149 games coached are the most in Purdue annals.

Prior to Tiller's hiring in November 1996, Purdue football had played in a total of five bowl games. In the preceding 15 years, the Boilermakers managed merely a 54–107–5 record. Tiller introduced the spread offense to Purdue, featuring three, four, even five wide receivers and forcing defenses to cover the field from sideline to sideline. It was a radical change from the smash-mouth Big Ten style and, in the basketball-crazed state of Indiana, it was dubbed affectionately "basketball on grass."

The result was 10 bowl games, including the 2001 Rose Bowl, an average of more than seven wins per season, and a Big Ten championship in 2000. Tiller coached 53 Purdue players who went on to the National Football League, six All-Americans and two Academic All-Americans.

Tiller was recognized as the 1997 Big Ten and National Coach of the Year.

In addition to the Rose Bowl, the Boilermakers played in the 1997 Alamo, 1998 Alamo, 2000 Outback, 2001 Sun, 2002 Sun, 2004 Capital One, 2004 Sun, 2006 Champs Sports, and 2007 Motor City Bowls. Purdue was nationally ranked in the Associated Press poll for 80 weeks—tied with Jack Mollenkopf for the most under any coach in school history—including a high of No. 5 during the 2004 season.

"The respect Joe Tiller garnered from both his former players and the Purdue community speaks volumes for his contributions to the game and this university," current Purdue head coach Jeff Brohm said when Tiller died in 2017. "He molded together a blueprint for success for Purdue football and pursued his vision in a way that players and fans were able to embrace."

Tiller topped Jack Mollenkopf for the most wins by a Purdue coach with his 85th victory—a 32–25 verdict over Central Michigan at Ross-Ade Stadium on September 20, 2008.

Tiller served as head coach of the East team in the 2005 East-West Shrine Game and earned a 45–27 victory. He played for the West team in 1963 and became just the fifth individual to both play and coach in the Shrine Game.

From 1983 to 1986, Tiller was assistant head coach, defensive coordinator, and defensive line coach at Purdue under Leon Burtnett.

"Joe took a chance coming back to Purdue, and all Boilermakers, me in particular, are grateful," said Purdue athletics director Morgan Burke, who hired Tiller. "Joe was the best evaluator of talent I have ever seen. His dry wit endeared him to his players, and he knew how to coach and motivate them."

The charismatic Tiller endeared himself to Boilermakers fans everywhere with his sense of humor and humility.

The winningest football coach in Purdue history, Joe Tiller posted an 87–62 record, including 53–43 in Big Ten games. He was 10–2 in Old Oaken Bucket showdowns against Indiana. (Tom Campbell)

"People ask me about my legacy at Purdue, and I guess I see myself as a guy who came in and fit the place, and the place fit him—a man of the people," Tiller said. "I've always prided myself on being able to get along with anybody, whether they are a major donor or someone who comes to one game a year. I've tried to respect everybody, so I would like my legacy to be that I was a good guy who could also coach football."

In January 2008, Tiller was awarded the Order of the Griffin, one of Purdue's highest honors, given to individuals whose commitment to the university goes well beyond the call of duty, and whose strength and vision have greatly benefited the institution.

Tiller was inducted into the Indiana Football Hall of Fame in 2012 and the Purdue Intercollegiate Athletics Hall of Fame in 2013. Joe Tiller Drive, located immediately north of Ross-Ade Stadium, was named in his honor in 2015.

Tiller's 18-year head coaching record, including six seasons at Wyoming from 1991 to 1996, was 126–92–1, a .578 winning percentage.

There was much more to Tiller than football. He was devoted to God and the United States of America. His interests included antiques, art, cribbage, history, wildlife, and good food. He was a member of the Model A and Pioneer Car Club in Buffalo, Wyoming (where he lived in retirement), driving his 1929 Ford Model A in parades.

"Coach Tiller was an important person in my life and to so many other guys who played for him," said Drew Brees, who played quarterback for Tiller from 1997 to 2000. "He did so much more than teach us how to win. He taught us life lessons and how to be great leaders and men."

6 Rick Mount

A half century later, the numbers remain mind-boggling.

Rick Mount averaged 32.3 points per game over the course of his three-year Purdue basketball career from 1967 to 1970. His 2,323 total points—in merely 72 games—are the most in Boilermakers history and rank sixth in Big Ten annals behind five players who had four-year careers. (Freshmen were not eligible to play until 1972–73).

"The Rocket" topped the Big Ten in scoring each of his three seasons, averaging 28.4, 33.3, and 35.4 points before there was a 3-point shot. He scored in double figures in every game he played, including 30 or more points in 46 games, 40-plus on 13 occasions, and 50-plus three times. On January 28, 1970, Mount poured in 61 points, then an NCAA record and the Big Ten high-water mark to this day, draining a whopping 27 field goals and adding seven free throws against Iowa at Mackey Arena. Had the original 3-point line been in existence, his total would have been 74 points, as he made 13 baskets from beyond 19 feet, 9 inches.

"Rick, by far, was the greatest pure shooter I ever saw," Purdue head coach George King said of his 6'4" guard.

A three-time first-team all-conference honoree, Mount earned Big Ten Most Valuable Player honors and was a consensus All-American both his junior and senior seasons.

Purdue made its first-ever trip to the NCAA Tournament in 1969, and with a trip to the Final Four on the line, Mount hit arguably the biggest shot in Purdue history. It was a jump shot from the right corner—famously described as a "leaping lofter"—with two seconds remaining in overtime to give the Big Ten–champion Boilermakers a 75–73 victory over Marquette. Mount subsequently scored 36 points in the Boilermakers' national semifinal win over North Carolina before Purdue lost to UCLA in the championship game.

Mount matriculated to Purdue from Lebanon, Indiana, located 40 miles south of campus. He was named Indiana Mr. Basketball and the nation's best high school player in 1966 and became the

Rick Mount topped the Big Ten in scoring each of his three seasons, averaging 28.4, 33.3, and 35.4 points before there was a 3-point shot. He scored a Big Ten–record 61 points against Iowa on January 28, 1970.

first prep athlete to appear on the cover of *Sports Illustrated*. Mount initially committed to the University of Miami, but his townsfolk convinced him to stay closer to home. His initial Purdue game also marked the opening of Purdue Arena (later renamed Mackey Arena) on December 2, 1967. Mount hit the first shot he took and went on to score a game-high 28 points, but visiting UCLA pulled out a 73–71 win. Mount and the Boilermakers posted a 56–20 record during his career, including 33–3 at home.

An inaugural member of the Purdue Intercollegiate Athletics Hall of Fame in 1994, Mount was inducted into the Indiana Basketball Hall of Fame in 1992 and the National Collegiate Basketball Hall of Fame in 2017.

"You don't duplicate greatness," current Purdue head coach Matt Painter said. "There's never going to be another Rick Mount. You think there should be, but when someone is that good at something, there's only one of them."

Mount was selected with the first overall pick in the 1970 ABA Draft by the Indiana Pacers. The Pacers won the ABA championship in 1972, and Mount subsequently played for the Kentucky Colonels (1972–73), Utah Stars (1973–74), and Memphis Sounds (1974–75).

Boilermakers in the National Collegiate Basketball Hall of Fame

Player	Played at Purdue	Inducted
Charles "Stretch" Murphy	C1927–30	2006
John Wooden	G1929–32	2006
Rick Mount	G1967–70	2017
Terry Dischinger	C1959–62	2019

Coach	Coached at Purdue	Inducted
Ward "Piggy" Lambert	1916–17, 1918–46	2006
Gene Keady	1980–2005	2013

Despite his legendary status, Mount, a private person, became estranged from the basketball program as the years and decades passed. On January 2, 2016, fittingly in a game against Iowa, he made his first public return to Mackey in more than a quarter century. Fans received a bobblehead, and at halftime Mount was hailed on the court with a thunderous ovation that lasted nearly a minute.

"The Purdue fans are the best fans in the nation," Mount told the jazzed-up crowd. "This is the greatest place to play basketball: in West Lafayette, Indiana, at Purdue University. [Athletics director] Red Mackey told me before the dedication game in 1967 that he had a dream of filling this place. It came true. Look at these fans."

Mount's son, Richie, played for the Boilermakers in 1989–90 and for two games the following season before transferring to Virginia Commonwealth University.

Mount continues to make his home in Lebanon, and a three-mile stretch of Interstate 65 that passes through the town was named "Rick Mount Highway" in 2016. Additionally, a grain silo near mile marker 141 is bedecked in his honor, complete with these words: THE GREATEST SHOOTER THAT EVER LIVED.

7 Glenn "Big Dog" Robinson

Former Boilermakers guard Todd Foster vividly remembers his on-campus introduction to the player known as "Big Dog."

"They said, 'Here's your teammate. His name is Glenn Robinson,'" Foster said. "I'm like, 'This guy is my age? You sure he's not 28?'"

How good does a player need to be when he shared a number with John Wooden, yet is considered the greatest Boilermaker to wear that number?

Robinson arrived at Purdue with more hype than any player in a generation. The Indiana Mr. Basketball had averaged 21.6 points and 12.3 rebounds as a senior while leading Gary Roosevelt High School to the state championship.

McDonald's All-American. Parade All-American. Prior to his arrival, the baseline expectation was the 6'8" forward would establish himself as one of the all-time great Boilermakers.

Improbably, Robinson not only reached those lofty expectations, he exceeded them.

Gene Keady said he first saw Robinson as an eighth-grader, when the future Player of the Year accompanied some other players down to Purdue's summer camp. He immediately recognized the teen's size, skills and instincts. The aura of "Big Dog," however, grew from more than his basketball talents.

"He had a great competitive spirit," Keady said. "He was a guy you'd want with you in any kind of battle. You'd want him in a foxhole with you. And he was a great team guy. He was locked in."

Academically ineligible for his first year on campus, Robinson played only two seasons with the Boilermakers. But he left an indelible impression with his all-around ability and his desire to take over games.

Robinson's 24.1 points per game as a sophomore led the Big Ten. He posted 12 double-doubles and was a second-team All-American.

That was nothing, however, compared to Robinson's season-long dominance in 1993–94. Along with Cuonzo Martin, Porter Roberts, Matt Waddell, and Brandon Brantley, the Boilermakers rose to become one of the nation's elite teams.

Purdue opened its season by claiming the Great Alaska Shootout championship en route to winning its first 14 games.

Robinson, however, saved some of his greatest career highlights for a late-season run to the Big Ten championship.

Playing at No. 3 and conference-leading Michigan on March 6, Robinson's jumper at the buzzer gave the No. 9 Boilermakers a 95–94 victory. Robinson poured in a career-high 49 points a week later as Purdue clinched the league title with an 87–77 victory over Illinois.

Glenn Robinson's average of 30.3 points per game led the nation in 1993–94, and he became the first Big Ten player to surpass 1,000 points in a season.

"It's not like he was sitting down saying, I'm going to go out and try to do this," Martin said. "He was gifted, had a toughness level to him, and a competitive spirit to be the best.

"He simply played basketball. He's probably one of the smartest guys I played with because he took what defenses gave him."

The Boilermakers earned a No. 1 NCAA Tournament seed and advanced to the Southeast Regional in Knoxville, Tennessee. Robinson crushed Kansas with 44 points in an 83–78 victory that left the Boilermakers one game shy of that elusive Final Four berth.

However, Robinson was not at full strength for the Elite Eight matchup with Duke. At the time, the star's back injury was blamed on an in-game collision with Kansas star Greg Ostertag. Keady later learned the true source of the soreness.

"I found out like a year later that what happened was, one of our players and Glenn were wrestling in their hotel room the night before the Duke game, and Glenn wrenched his back," Keady told the *Indianapolis Star* in 2016. "They didn't have the guts to tell me, because they knew I'd kill him."

With Robinson limited, Purdue fell to national runner-up Duke 69–60. The Final Four remained elusive to Keady and the Boilermakers.

Robinson's 30.3 points per game led the nation that season, and he became the first Big Ten player to surpass 1,000 points in a season with 1,030. The unanimous Big Ten Player of the Year also won the Naismith Award and John R. Wooden Award. He was the first Boilermaker to win National Player of the Year honors since Wooden himself in 1932.

Robinson announced his intention to turn pro at a press conference in his hometown. The Milwaukee Bucks selected him with the No. 1 overall pick. Robinson made the NBA's All-Rookie team and was a two-time All-Star with the Bucks before helping the San Antonio Spurs win the 2005 NBA championship. He was inducted into the Purdue Intercollegiate Athletics Hall of Fame in 2006.

Robinson's son, Glenn III, starred in basketball at Michigan and hit a big shot at Mackey Arena to secure an overtime victory over the Boilermakers in 2014. Another son, Gelen, played defensive line for the Purdue football team from 2014 to 2017.

Cradle of Quarterbacks

Ask a casual fan which college football program has produced the most NFL quarterback starts and touchdown passes, and you would probably hear a long list of guesses before anyone mentioned Purdue.

The Boilermakers, however, can lay claim to both of those achievements. Certainly, a lot of the heavy lifting for that distinction is done by Drew Brees, who finished the 2019 season as the league's all-time leader in passing yards, passing touchdowns, completions, completion percentage, and total offense.

Brees, though, is only one of the 15 Boilermakers who have taken a snap under center in the NFL.

In the early 1970s, Purdue commissioned artist Keith Butz to create a poster commemorating seven of the greatest quarterbacks in program history. The first mention of the "Cradle of Quarterbacks" came later that decade, and over time the list has grown to recognize a dozen signal callers.

Three of them have been enshrined in the College Football Hall of Fame, and Brees will undoubtedly become the third member selected to the Pro Football Hall of Fame.

The members of the Cradle of Quarterbacks span more than seven decades and came from different playing styles and eras of football. Yet their common excellence helped define Purdue as an incubator for the most glamorous position in sports.

Bob DeMoss (1945–48)

Considered the patriarch of the Cradle of Quarterbacks, the Kentucky native wasted no time making an impression. He started from the first game of his freshman season and led the Boilermakers to four straight victories. Then came a signature moment in front of 73,585 in Columbus—racing out to a 28–0 lead at No. 4 Ohio State and rolling to a 35–13 victory.

DeMoss threw for 2,759 yards and 23 touchdowns in his playing career. After one season with the NFL's New York Bulldogs, DeMoss returned to Purdue to begin a long career as an assistant coach and administrator. He coached the Boilermakers to a 13–18 record from 1970 to 1972 and served as an assistant athletics director from 1973 to 1992.

Five of the other quarterbacks on this list were recruited and/or developed by DeMoss.

Dale Samuels (1950–52)

One of those DeMoss protégés was Samuels, a Chicago native who was the first in his family to attend college. Only one game into his career, he led Purdue to one of the signature victories in program history. With a 28–14 victory in South Bend on October 7, 1950, the Boilermakers snapped No. 1 Notre Dame's 39-game winning streak.

"In the middle to late '40s, if you were a betting person you didn't bet against Notre Dame, Joe Louis or the New York Yankees," Samuels told the Lafayette *Journal & Courier* in 2018. "Playing in South Bend, we were decidedly the underdogs. The way the coaches told it to us, we've got everything to gain and nothing to lose. Let's go get 'em."

What to do for an encore? While Samuels' records have since been overshadowed in the era of aerial attacks, in his day he set the Boilermakers standard for passing excellence.

No Boilermakers quarterback before him had thrown for 1,000 yards or 10 touchdowns in a season. Samuels quarterbacked Purdue to a second-place Big Ten finish in 1951 and a shared championship with Wisconsin in 1952.

Len Dawson (1954–56)

Dawson followed Samuels' lead, opening the 1954 season with a four-touchdown performance against Missouri. He followed with four more in an upset of top-ranked Notre Dame in South Bend. (The Fighting Irish winning streak at that time had grown to only 13 games.)

Dawson earned the nickname "Golden Boy" for those performances and threw 15 touchdown passes as a sophomore. While injuries held him back over his final two seasons, Dawson was still a first-round NFL Draft pick of the Pittsburgh Steelers.

Yet it was only after reconnecting with former Purdue assistant Hank Stram with the AFL's Dallas Texans in 1962 that Dawson found the path to his greatest acclaim. That franchise became the Kansas City Chiefs, and Dawson led them to three AFL championships and was Most Valuable Player of the Super Bowl IV victory over the Minnesota Vikings.

Dawson played professional football until age 40 and was elected to the Pro Football Hall of Fame in 1987.

When he left Purdue, Dawson's 3,325 passing yards and 29 touchdown passes both stood as school records.

Bob Griese (1964–66)

In 1987, this multi-sport star from Evansville, Indiana, was voted the All-Time Quarterback for the first 100 years of Purdue football.

If you have noticed a pattern on this list, victories over Notre Dame tend to springboard a quarterback to legendary status. As a junior, Griese led the Boilermakers to a 25–21 upset of No. 1 Notre Dame in 1965, which catapulted Purdue to No. 2 in the rankings.

One year later, Griese led Purdue to an 8–2 regular season record and an appearance in the Rose Bowl. The resulting 14–13 victory over USC remains Purdue's only Rose Bowl victory. Griese finished as the runner-up to Florida quarterback Steve Spurrier in Heisman Trophy voting.

Through the 2019 season, Griese remains among the Boilermakers' all-time leaders in completions (358, 11th), passing yards (4,541, 11th), passing touchdowns (28, 11th), completion percentage (.571, 12th), and passing efficiency (123.4, 14th).

Griese's winning reputation extended to the NFL, where he quarterbacked the Miami Dolphins to the league's only undefeated season in 1972. A College and Pro Football Hall of Famer, Griese went on to a long career broadcasting college football for ABC and ESPN.

Mike Phipps (1967–69)

Purdue's Rhodes Scholar signal-caller joined the club of Boilermakers greats who stamped their legacy with a victory over Notre Dame. Then he went out and achieved something none of the other great quarterbacks before him.

Phipps beat top-ranked and defending national champion Notre Dame in 1967, beat the No. 2 Irish as quarterback of the No. 1–ranked team a year later in South Bend, then led a win over the No. 9 Irish in 1969. No previous Boilermakers quarterback had overseen three consecutive victories over Notre Dame.

Phipps' 2,527 yards and 23 touchdowns passing in 1969 were team records at the time. He finished runner-up to Oklahoma running back Steve Owens for the Heisman Trophy by merely 154 votes, the closest Boilermaker ever to earn college football's most coveted award.

Gary Danielson (1970–72)

Danielson's 213 rushing yards against Washington in 1972 remain the most in a game for a Purdue quarterback. But like the other players on this list, Danielson made his name with his arm. In 1971, his 1,467 passing yards and 57.8 completion percentage both led the Big Ten.

Also like other Cradle members, Danielson too found a second career behind the microphone. He played 15 professional seasons in the NFL and World Football League before serving as a college football analyst for CBS and ESPN.

Danielson took a strong Purdue connection with him when he left school. His wife, Kristy, was also an alum, whose father, George King, served as head men's basketball coach and athletics director.

Mark Herrmann (1977–80)

While others on this list went on to greater professional success, none of them re-wrote the college football passing record books the way Herrmann did. Leading head coach Jim Young's era of success, Herrmann became the first college quarterback to throw for 9,000 career yards (after first becoming the first to throw for 8,000).

Herrmann saved some of his biggest performances for the biggest stage. He led Purdue to victories in the 1978 Peach Bowl, 1979 Bluebonnet Bowl, and 1980 Liberty Bowl and was named most valuable player of all three games.

After an 11-season NFL career, the College Football Hall of Famer returned to Indiana as a color commentator for Indianapolis Colts games.

Scott Campbell (1980–83)

Following Herrmann was no small task, but Campbell more than held his own. His first season as a starter, in 1981, included a 516-yard passing performance against Ohio State.

By the time he wrapped up his career in 1983 as the Boilermakers' team most valuable player, Campbell ranked second in passing only to Herrmann in Purdue and Big Ten history. He played six NFL seasons.

Jim Everett (1981–85)

The No. 3 overall pick in the 1986 NFL Draft, Everett may be best known nationally for his 12-year NFL career, including a Pro Bowl selection in 1990.

In West Lafayette, he is remembered as the strong-arm successor to Campbell who remains the only Purdue quarterback to defeat Notre Dame, Michigan, and Ohio State in the same season—doing so in 1984 and leading the Boilermakers to the Peach Bowl.

Everett's career pass efficiency rating of 132.7 remains the best in Purdue history for a minimum of 300 attempts. Despite playing only two full seasons, he ranks sixth in completions (572), seventh in passing yards (7,411), and seventh in passing touchdowns (43) through the 2019 season.

Drew Brees (1997–2000)

The lofty numbers piled up by this gunslinger from Austin, Texas, speak for themselves. Brees left the program as Purdue's all-time leader in touchdown passes (90), passing yards (11,792), and total offense (12,692), while ranking second in completion percentage and passing efficiency.

Brees is the only Purdue quarterback with multiple 500-yard games and the only one besides Everett with two or more 450-yard games (Brees has four). Brees threw for 300 or more yards seven times in 1999, a feat matched only by Everett in 1985. His 16 career 300-yard games are also a record.

Besides all the records, Brees also won, headlining head coach Joe Tiller's "basketball on grass" offense. He went on to establish himself as an all-time great in the NFL, as well, first with the San Diego Chargers and with his current team, the New Orleans Saints.

Kyle Orton (2001–04)

Brees passed the torch to Orton, who led Purdue to a bowl game as a freshman and repeated that feat in each of the next three seasons. He became only the 13th college football player ever to accomplish that distinction.

Orton ranks fifth in Purdue history with 9,337 passing yards and 63 touchdown passes.

Orton was selected by the Chicago Bears in the fourth round of the 2005 NFL Draft and subsequently played for the Denver Broncos (2009–11), Kansas City Chiefs (2011), Dallas Cowboys (2012–13), and Buffalo Bills (2014).

Curtis Painter (2005–08)

How many Purdue fans would know which quarterback holds both the school game and season passing yardage records? Brees, perhaps the obvious answer, held both until Painter surpassed him.

Painter's 3,985 passing yards in 2006 eclipsed Brees' previous mark by two yards and with the benefit of one more game. One year later, against Central Michigan in the Motor City Bowl, Painter threw for 546 yards in a 51–48 victory.

With wide receivers Dorien Bryant and Greg Orton and tight end Dustin Keller among his favorite targets, Painter assured Tiller's high-powered offense would continue its attack on the Big Ten. Painter's 11,163 career passing yards rank second to Brees.

The Indianapolis Colts drafted Painter in the sixth round of the 2009 NFL Draft. He also played for the Baltimore Ravens and the New York Giants in a five-year NFL career.

9 1967 Rose Bowl

Pick a cliché—"always a bridesmaid, never a bride" or "close but no cigar" —and it was apropos for Purdue football in the early-to-mid-1960s.

But the tide was about to turn.

The 1966 Boilermakers were talented with players like quarterback Bob Griese, end Jim Beirne, offensive tackle Jack Calcaterra, defensive halfback George Catavolos, defensive halfback John Charles, end Jim Finley, linebacker Chuck Kyle, defensive tackle Lance Olssen, fullback Perry Williams, and halfback-defensive back Leroy Keyes—undoubtedly the most gifted athlete ever at Purdue.

Off to a 3–1 start, the ninth-ranked Boilermakers visited Michigan on October 15 and won their fifth straight over the Wolverines, pulling out a 22–21 victory when junior linebacker Frank Burke, a 27-year-old married father of two, blocked a punt and recovered it for the game-winning touchdown. Next was No. 2 Michigan State in East Lansing, and the Spartans disposed of the Boilermakers 41–20. The loss virtually ended Purdue's chances of winning the Big Ten, but the Rose Bowl was still a possibility thanks to a Big Ten rule that prevented the same team from making repeat appearances. Michigan State had gone the previous year.

The Boilermakers had a crucial game the following week against Illinois at Ross-Ade Stadium, and things didn't look good as Griese threw five interceptions and the Fighting Illini led 21–10 through three quarters. But Griese redeemed himself with a pair of fourth-quarter touchdown passes, including the game-winner, a 32-yarder to Finley with 1:20 remaining, for a 25–21 victory. Said Griese, who bettered his own school record with 288 passing yards, "I knew I had to go out and make up for it [five interceptions] because up until then I was the goat. I had to prove that I'm a better passer than that."

A 23–0 victory at Wisconsin on November 5 improved the Boilermakers to 6–2 (4–1 Big Ten) with two games to play. A trip to Minnesota followed and Purdue posted its second straight

In their first trip to the Rose Bowl, the Boilermakers defeated USC 14–13 on January 2, 1967.

shutout 16–0, to all but formally clinch a Rose Bowl bid. Griese's 30-yard field goal in the first quarter would prove to be all the points Purdue needed on a snowy day in Minneapolis.

"This is the greatest day of my life," head coach Jack Mollenkopf said just after being carried off the field by his players. "You have to give the boys and the assistant coaches credit for that. They've done it. They've done everything. And they've done it the hard way."

Purdue put an exclamation point on the regular season with a 51–6 victory over Indiana at home on November 19 and accepted the school's first invitation to the Rose Bowl. The Boilermakers' opponent was the University of Southern California, which was coached by John McKay, who played halfback at Purdue in 1946 before transferring to the University of Oregon.

The Boilermakers took up residence at the Huntington-Sheraton Hotel in Southern California, and Mollenkopf, a tell-it-like-it-is guy, was an immediate hit with members of the Los Angeles media. Lafayette radio station WASK reported on December 23: "He may be the most popular coach to have appeared here. Middlewest writers who cover the Boilermakers week after week already know this, but when the hard core of the journalist world—the Los Angeles press— accepts a visiting coach with such idolist banners, Purdue can't miss."

The Rose Bowl was played on January 2 before the largest crowd ever to watch the Boilermakers—101,455. Purdue was a heavy favorite, but USC held its own, and the game came down to the final 2½ minutes. The Trojans scored a touchdown on a 19-yard pass from Troy Winslow to Rod Sherman to pull within a point at 14–13, and McKay opted to go for the win and not the tie. Winslow's two-point pass attempt was intercepted by Catavolos. After Purdue was stopped on its ensuing possession at the USC 43, the Trojans had one last chance, but with the goal posts at both ends already torn down, Winslow was sacked by junior tackle Fred Rafa to end the game.

"Sure, I'm satisfied with a one-point win," Mollenkopf said. "We wanted to come out here and win, and it was a great win for us."

Charles, who had been sidelined since late October with a separated shoulder, recovered a fumble that stymied a USC drive at the Purdue 9-yard line and recorded 11 tackles to be selected the game's most valuable player. End Bob Holmes recovered another fumble, and Burke blocked a field goal. Williams scored both touchdowns, from one and two yards out respectively.

Purdue finished with a 9–2 record and ranked seventh in the Associated Press poll. In Heisman Trophy voting, Griese, who set a school season record with 1,888 passing yards and was named the Big Ten MVP, finished second to University of Florida quarterback Steve Spurrier.

10 1969 Men's Basketball Final Four

The only men's basketball national championship banner you will see at Mackey Arena is from 1932. It hangs as the result of a vote of a panel of experts convened by the Helms Athletic Foundation and honors the 17–1 season compiled by John Wooden and his teammates.

The 1968–69 Boilermakers came oh-so-close to hanging another banner with an NCAA Tournament title.

Purdue entered that season with high expectations both inside and outside the program. Rick Mount had already begun the sensational shooting and dynamic play that would eventually make him the most prolific scorer in Boilermaker history. He had averaged 28.5 points the previous season while christening the newly opened Mackey Arena.

Head coach George King had to meld that once-in-a-generation talent alongside his returning co–Most Valuable Players. Herman Gilliam and Billy Keller had combined to average more than 30 points and almost 14 rebounds the prior season. The Boilermakers were talented inside and out, opening the season ranked No. 10 in the country and poised to make an assault on the Big Ten title.

If Purdue needed a measuring stick to judge its potential, it didn't need to wait long. UCLA had made the trip to West Lafayette for the 1967–68 season opener and beat Purdue 75–73 in the Mackey Arena opener. So the Boilermakers headed west for a rematch with the, at that point, two-time defending national champions.

Mount scored 33 points, but UCLA's own legend—7–2 center Lew Alcindor, later known as Kareem Abdul-Jabbar—posted 18 points and 20 rebounds. UCLA pulled away for a 94–82 victory. It would not be the last time the teams met that season.

The Boilermakers fell short of championship aspirations at Arizona State's Sun Devil Classic and the Rainbow Classic in Hawaii. But only a loss at Ohio State interrupted their march to the outright Big Ten championship.

Two victories over intrastate rival Indiana stood out in particular. In Bloomington on February 18, a pair of Gilliam free throws with four seconds left lifted Purdue to a 96–95 win. There was no such drama in the regular season finale at Mackey. Mount poured in 40 points while breaking the Big Ten's season scoring record, and a 120–76 victory sent the Boilermakers into the postseason with momentum.

Purdue opened the NCAA Tournament in the Big Ten footprint in Madison, Wisconsin. After receiving a first-round bye and knocking off Miami (Ohio), a tougher challenge against head coach Al McGuire and Marquette awaited. While not a true home game for the Warriors, the 100-mile proximity helped them amass a partisan crowd.

Larry Weatherford hit a pair of free throws with 19 seconds remaining to give Purdue a 63–62 lead. It needed only to defend the final possession to advance. But Marquette got the ball inside to center Ric Cobb, who was fouled with two seconds remaining.

Cobb made the first free throw, but missed the second. The Boilermakers secured the rebound to force overtime.

In the extra period, the season, as one might expect, hinged on Mount's heroics. He scored 26 points that night, though they came at a labored pace on 11 of 32 shooting.

With the score tied in the final seconds of the first overtime period, the ball reached Mount in the corner on Purdue's end. He recreated the shot at a park in his hometown of Lebanon during an interview with Tim Layden of *Sports Illustrated* in 2001.

"This was the shot against Marquette in '69," Mount said of the so-called "leaping lofter" with two seconds remaining that secured a 75–73 victory. "Two dribbles to my right, went up and hit it, and we went to the Final Four."

The outcome led some in the Boilermakers locker room to consider that perhaps this was a team of destiny.

"I just wouldn't bet against this club," King said after the game. "After this, I'd say anything can happen."

Moving on to the Final Four in Louisville, Mount backed up his buzzer-beater with 36 points in the national semifinals against North Carolina. Keller added 20 points in a 92–65 thrashing of North Carolina and legendary head coach Dean Smith.

"This is the best Big Ten team since Ohio State in the early 1960s," Smith said afterward, as recounted in *Boilermaker Basketball: Great Purdue Teams and Players* by Alan Karpick. "Nobody shoots like they do, and they were a better defensive team than we expected."

"We weren't looking ahead to anyone," King said.

On the other side of the bracket, fate nearly upended the Bruins' march to another title—and potentially the Boilermakers' chance at history. Few expected tiny Drake from the Missouri Valley Conference to derail mighty UCLA.

With under a minute to play, however, Dolph Pulliam's put-back basket cut the Bruins lead to one point. UCLA held on for an 85–82 victory—its lowest winning margin during its championship run under Alcindor.

Perhaps that woke up the Bruins, because they took full advantage of a Purdue team compromised by Keller and Gilliam playing through injuries. Mount missed 15 straight jump shots. He, Keller, and Gilliam combined to make only 18 of 67 field goal attempts (26.9 percent).

Alcindor posted 37 points and 20 rebounds, and the Bruins retained their crown with a 92–72 rout. UCLA improved to 91–2 over a three-year span—on its way to seven consecutive national titles and 10 in 12 seasons under Wooden, who first rose to fame as an All-American player at Purdue.

Gilliam and Keller both moved on to pro careers. Mount, Purdue's first Big Ten Most Valuable Player in 23 years, returned for one more record-setting season. But no Boilermakers team has returned to the national championship game.

11 Wooden Leads 1932 "National Champions"

On January 9, 1932, two legends left West Lafayette in a car for a road game at Illinois.

The coach, Ward "Piggy" Lambert, won 371 games and 11 Big Ten titles in his career. His passenger, a senior guard named John Wooden, would surpass his coach's accomplishments as the architect of the UCLA dynasty in the 1960s and '70s.

On that day, however, both player and coach ended up over-turned after Lambert's car hit a patch of ice. Wooden sustained cuts to his hand, which hampered his performance in the Boilermakers' 28–21 loss in Champaign.

It took an act of nature to derail Purdue that season. That loss proved to be the only one suffered by one of the great teams in school history.

Wooden, already recognized as a star, had help from Ray Eddy, Ralph Parmenter, and Harry Kellar. Lambert brought an up-tempo, pressure defense style to fuel fast breaks and wear opponents down.

After that loss at Illinois, only three teams played within even 10 points of the Boilermakers—none closer than a 26–23 home victory over Marquette. That run included a 42–29 victory at intra-state rival Indiana and a 34–19 home win over Illinois to avenge the lone defeat.

Wooden went into the final game against Chicago needing 15 points to break the Big Ten season scoring record that Indiana's Branch McCracken set two years earlier.

"From the tipoff, it was evident that Kellar had only one idea in mind—to help John set a new mark," Gordon Graham wrote in the Lafayette *Journal & Courier*. "John was not so willing to take all the honors, and the boys had to urge him to shoot unless he was absolutely open near the basket."

Wooden closed the season and his career with a dominant 21-point effort in a 53–18 home victory.

This era preceded the creation of postseason national tourna-ments and the Associated Press poll. Instead, national title teams were retroactively crowned by a vote of a panel convened by the Helms Athletic Foundation, beginning in 1936.

That panel chose Purdue as college basketball's best in 1931–32. The banner commemorating that title hangs in Mackey Arena alongside the program's growing collection of Big Ten championships.

12 The Origins of Purdue Football

Purdue football was born on October 29, 1887. On that date, a dozen Purdue students took the 60-mile railroad ride south to Indianapolis to play a football game against Butler College at Athletic Park in the northern part of the capital city.

A land-grant school, Purdue had been founded in 1869—the same year the first American football game was played between Princeton University and Rutgers University—but it took two decades before the sport found a permanent home in Indiana.

Leading up to that first game, Purdue called for volunteers to form its team. A 23-year-old by the name of Albert Berg, who lived across the Wabash River, was chosen as coach because it was believed he had some knowledge of the game from his days as a student at Princeton. He was hired at the rate of $1 per lesson. But Berg was a deaf mute, brought on by childhood spinal meningitis, and he had merely one week to prepare the squad of 12 men. No wonder Butler, which had organized its first team a year earlier, won 48–6. The game was described by author and playwright George Ade, an 1887 Purdue graduate, as "a low comedy reproduction of the Custer massacre at Little Big Horn."

J.B. Burris, from Cloverdale, Indiana, was captain and is credited with selecting yellow-orange (old gold) and black as the team's colors, patterned after powerful Princeton. J.M. Sholl, the quarterback, scored Purdue's first touchdown (worth four points at the time) in the first half.

Some 37 years later, as part of the Ross-Ade Stadium dedication festivities, Berg had the following sentiments read on his behalf: "On account of my inability to hear and my ability to talk only to a limited extent…my instruction was mainly by imitation of my own

Purdue Football Milestone Wins

No.	Opponent	Score	Date	Head Coach
1	DePauw	34–10	November 16, 1889	George Reisner
100	Wabash	26–0	October 4, 1913	Andy Smith
200	at Carnegie Tech	7–6	October 31, 1936	Noble Kizer
300	at Washington	13–6	September 23, 1961	Jack Mollenkopf
400	Ohio State	27–16	October 14, 1978	Jim Young
500	Indiana	52–7	November 21, 1998	Joe Tiller
600	Nevada	24–14	September 24, 2016	Darrell Hazel

playing. The way the boys caught on and improved would have delighted and encouraged any coach. They were a willing and loyal lot, full of pep and college spirit, and the foundation, I am sure, was then and there laid for Purdue's subsequent gridiron success."

A one-game season was it for Purdue in 1887, and with no volunteers signing up the following fall, there was no football in 1888. But after the one-year hiatus, the sport returned and has been played ever since by those who eventually would be called "Boilermakers."

13 The Origins of Purdue Basketball

The first documented men's basketball game played by Purdue students occurred early in 1897. The precise date is unknown but believed to have been in January or February.

The Purdue team played host to a group from the Lafayette YMCA in the Military Hall and Gymnasium—referred to as the "Old Gym"—an armory that doubled as a place for students to keep physically fit in the winter, although it lacked heat.

Six basketball teams were formed: one from each of the under-graduate classes, one for postgraduates, and one for faculty. Games were played on Saturday nights.

(According to Alan Karpick in the book *Boilermaker Basketball: Great Purdue Teams and Players*, the first basketball contest at Purdue "against an outside opponent probably was a women's game," as ladies from the university played citizens prior to the Saturday evening intraschool scrimmages.)

A group of players from the six teams was assembled for the contest against the YMCA. It was organized by C.H. Robertson and coached by F. Homer Curtis. Robertson was joined in the starting lineup by A.W. Anderson, Rodney Hitt, E.W. Morey, and Bob Treat. The YMCA team captain was Ray Ewry, who would go on to win 10 Olympic gold medals from 1900 to 1908.

Purdue won 34–19, the first of more than 1,800 victories achieved since.

A 23–19 loss to the Crawfordsville YMCA concluded the inaugural season.

Games against outside competition did not return until December 1899, when the Lafayette YMCA got revenge with a 16–11 win at the Old Gym. Alpha Jamison, who had completed his second season as football coach, coached the basketball squad, which also was captained by a football player, John Miller.

Purdue Men's Basketball Milestone Wins

No.	Opponent	Score	Date	Head Coach
1	Lafayette YMCA	34–19	1897	F. Homer Curtis
500	at Louisville	55–51	December 8, 1945	Ward "Piggy" Lambert
1,000	Minnesota	74–59	February 5, 1981	Gene Keady
1,500	Iowa	66–63	February 16, 2005	Gene Keady
1,750	Iowa	89–67	December 28, 2016	Matt Painter

In the winter of 1900–01, Purdue played 12 games and won them all, including the first two matchups against Indiana, 20–15 on March 1 in Bloomington and 23–19 on March 15 at the Old Gym. Jamison coached—or, more aptly, administered—the team, and it was led by captain Henry Wallace "Dutch" Reimann, who is broadly regarded as the "father of Purdue basketball."

Over the next four seasons, Purdue had three head coaches and played 13 games in 1903–04 without one. The first sign of stability came in 1905–06, when C.B. Jamison came from Rose Polytechnic Institute to begin a three-year tenure at the same time the Boilermakers joined the fledgling Western Conference (later the Big Ten). The team's first conference game was a 34–14 loss to Wisconsin on January 20, 1906. Fittingly, the first conference win came against Indiana on February 10, a 27–25 nail-biter at home.

14 Governor's Cup

Purdue and Indiana have competed against one another athletically as far back as November 4, 1891, when Purdue won a football game 60–0 at the Lafayette YMCA Park.

The two schools, located 115 miles apart, first squared off in basketball on March 1, 1901, and Purdue won 20–15 in Bloomington.

In 1925, the Old Oaken Bucket was introduced as a traveling trophy for football, and similar awards followed for women's volleyball (Monon Spike) in 1981, women's basketball (Barn Burner Trophy) in 1994, and women's soccer (Golden Boot) in 2002.

Since 2001–02, the two schools have conducted an all-sports competition. It was originally known as the Titan Series until

2004, when it was renamed the Crimson & Gold Cup. It became the Governor's Cup in 2013.

Points are awarded to the winning team in each of the schools' 20 shared sports. If the two teams do not meet during the regular season, the higher finisher at the Big Ten Championship is the point winner. In the case of ties, both teams get half a point.

In 18 years of competition through 2018–19, Purdue has captured the title seven times and Indiana nine times. Two years have ended in a tie. The Boilermakers won three consecutive crowns in 2013–14 (12–8), 2014–15 (10–9), and 2015–16 (12.5–7.5). Purdue's 12.5 points in 2015–16 are tied for the most ever by either school (also Indiana in 2008–09).

Purdue president Mitch Daniels, formerly the governor of Indiana, pays close attention to the standings each year.

"I have told [athletics director] Mike Bobinski, 'This is not negotiable,'" Daniels said. "I don't want to face my IU friends if we don't come away with the Governor's Cup."

To the chagrin of all Purdue fans, the Boilermakers came up short in two of Bobinski's first three years on the job.

15 2001 Rose Bowl

On September 30, 2000, the 24th-ranked Purdue football team lost at Penn State 22–20, thanks in large part to two botched punt attempts, and saw its record drop to 3–2. The normally unflappable Drew Brees showed his frustration afterward, saying, "This is a team game and we lose as a team, but if we want to have a chance to compete in this league and be Big Ten champions or win on the road, we need to clear some things up. We need to take pride, whether it's on offense, defense, or special teams."

The situation looked bleaker the following week when the Boilermakers trailed No. 6 Michigan 28–10 after two quarters at Ross-Ade Stadium. But a halftime speech by head coach Joe Tiller that focused on believing turned the tables, and the Boilermakers rallied for a 32–31 victory. Travis Dorsch, who missed a potential game-winning 32-yard field goal with 2:11 left, nailed a 33-yarder with four seconds remaining to cap the amazing comeback and start a memorable month of October.

Joe Tiller (left) and Drew Brees celebrate the Boilermakers' 41–13 win over intrastate rival Indiana on November 18, 2000, which sent Purdue to the Rose Bowl. (Tom Campbell)

After a 41–28 victory at No. 17 Northwestern on October 14, the Boilermakers traveled to Wisconsin and beat the Badgers 30–24 in overtime. Defensive tackle Craig Terrill blocked a 58-yard field goal attempt by Vitaly Pisetsky, and cornerback Ashante Woodyard picked up the ball and raced 36 yards for the overtime touchdown.

Next was a home date with No. 12 Ohio State on October 28. The Boilermakers led 24–21 before Brees threw his fourth interception of the game, leading to the Buckeyes taking a 27–24 advantage with 2:16 to go. But Brees went back to work and 21 seconds later hooked up with wide receiver Seth Morales, his fourth option on the play, for a 64-yard touchdown strike that will be etched in the memories of Boilermakers fans for a long time. "I'm still in shock about what happened at the end," Brees said afterward. "It's weird how things work out."

With a four-game winning streak, Purdue traveled to Michigan State on November 11 and was outplayed in a 30–10 loss. But thanks to Iowa upsetting Northwestern 27–17, the Boilermakers could still dream of a Big Ten championship and the Rose Bowl. All they needed was to beat Indiana at home in the regular season finale, and they did 41–13 to finish with an 8–3 overall record. Running back Montrell Lowe rushed for 208 yards on a school-record-tying 38 carries and scored four touchdowns. Purdue, Michigan, and Northwestern shared the conference title with 6–2 records, and the Boilermakers got the Rose Bowl invitation by virtue of beating both the Wolverines and the Wildcats. The capacity-plus crowd of 69,104 spilled onto the field in a jubilant postgame celebration.

"It's been a long time coming, but it's been worth the wait," Tiller said of the 33-year Big Ten championship drought and 34-year Rose Bowl dry spell. "We always say we have to sniff the roses as we go through life, and Purdue has a chance to do that now."

In their second Rose Bowl in school history, the Boilermakers faced fourth-ranked Washington, and the Huskies won 34–24 in

Pasadena, California, on New Year's Day 2001. The game was tied at 17 early in the third quarter before Washington pulled away. Some 35,000 Purdue fans were among the crowd of 94,392.

16 Rondale Moore's Phenomenal Freshman Year

Jeff Brohm does not hold back when talking in glowing terms about Rondale Moore.

Heading into the 2018 season, the Purdue head coach anticipated big things from the freshman wide receiver and return specialist, and knows precisely why he proved prophetic.

"Clearly, Rondale is an unbelievable talent, but his work ethic, attention to detail, and desire to be great set him apart," Brohm said. "He does everything right and represents our program and the university in a first-class fashion. We believed he would be a difference-maker, we put a lot on his plate, and he made an impact on everything."

College football observed what Brohm forecast, and Moore wound up as the first true freshman consensus All-American in the country since Oklahoma running back Adrian Peterson in 2004 and the first Big Ten freshman (true or redshirt) so recognized since freshmen became eligible in 1972.

Moore was a first-team All-American as an all-purpose player by the Associated Press and the Football Writers Association of America and a second-team selection as an athlete by The Sporting News. He also garnered All-America honors from CBS Sports, ESPN, and *Sports Illustrated*.

Moore won the Paul Hornung Award (most versatile player in college football) and the Paul Warfield Award (nation's top receiver) and was a semifinalist for the Maxwell Award (nation's outstanding player) and the Biletnikoff Award (nation's outstanding receiver). He was the National Freshman of the Year by CBS Sports.

The diminutive Moore stands 5'9" and 175 pounds but is super strong and lightning-fast. He squatted 600 pounds during the summer of 2018 (becoming a social media sensation) and has been timed in the 40-yard dash in 4.33 seconds. Moore is a humble superstar, preferring to speak about anything but himself.

"I'm probably the most nonchalant guy when it comes to attention," Moore said. "I don't get into statistics and all that. I'm just excited to play the game. I try not to get too high or too low and just focus on the next play. I know I can keep getting better and improve on some things."

Moore became the first non-junior or senior Purdue player to earn first-team All-American honors, the first by any Boilermaker since defensive end Ryan Kerrigan was a unanimous selection in 2010 and the 21st consensus All-American in school history (including the legendary Leroy Keyes twice).

"Everybody is ready to hang up his All-America banner except him," quarterback David Blough said. "He just loves playing football. He loves figuring out what he is supposed to do and then doing it to the best of his ability. His knowledge of the game and the intricacies of playing wide receiver are remarkable for a true freshman. But the best part about him is his humility and unselfishness."

A native of New Albany, Indiana, Moore led the nation with 114 receptions, the second-most in a season by a Big Ten player. Chris Daniels of Purdue holds the record with 121 in 1999. Moore topped the conference with 1,258 receiving yards (10th nationally and second in school history) and 12 receiving touchdowns (tied for eighth nationally and tied for fourth in school history) and ranked second with a school-record 2,215 all-purpose yards (fourth nationally) and 14 total touchdowns (tied for eighth in school history). Moore boasted seven 100-yard receiving games, tied for the most in a season in Purdue annals and tied for fifth on the career list.

The last Purdue player to lead the Big Ten in receptions was Keith Smith (91) in 2009, and the last to lead the country was running back Rodney Carter (98) in 1985. The only other Boilermaker to lead the country was tight end Dave Young (67) in 1980.

Moore possessed the football 180 times and averaged 12.3 yards per touch. He had 33 plays of 20 or more yards, including a 76-yard touchdown rush and a 70-yard scoring reception. Moore was the Boilermakers' third-leading rusher (21 carries for 213 yards, 10.1 average) and topped the team in kickoff returns (33 for 662 yards, 20.1 average) and punt returns (12 for 82 yards, 6.8 average).

Even more impressive: he achieved a 3.81 grade-point average during the fall semester, the sixth-highest in the program, and aspires to earn his degree in selling and sales management.

Moore earned two major Big Ten honors—the Richter-Howard Receiver of the Year and the Thompson-Randle El Freshman of the Year. He was the first Boilermaker to be recognized as the Big Ten's best receiver and the fifth to be selected the top freshman. He was named Big Ten Newcomer of the Year by the Associated Press.

Moore earned first-team All-Big Ten honors as a wide receiver by the coaches and media, becoming the first Purdue player at that position so honored since Smith in 2009.

Moore was named first-team return specialist by the coaches and second-team by the media, and he earned Big Ten Freshman of the Week honors four times—following games against Northwestern, No. 23 Boston College, No. 2 Ohio State, and Indiana.

In his first collegiate game, Moore set the Purdue game record with 313 all-purpose yards against Northwestern on August 30— the fifth-most in the country during the 2018 season. The previous mark of 312 all-purpose yards was held by Otis Armstrong in his last collegiate game against Indiana on November 25, 1972. Moore amassed his yardage total on merely 18 touches, while Armstrong needed 34.

The bounty of awards and gaudy numbers have lifted the Boilermakers in their return to eminence under Brohm.

"Rondale put his trust in our program and this university to help him achieve his goals when he had other great opportunities and options," Brohm said. "When you get a special player like him, it helps you attract more special players. The fact that he had so much success as a true freshman should be a clear indication of the endless possibilities at Purdue. He will continue to have a positive effect on and off the field."

17 Stephanie White

Before she scored her first basket at Mackey Arena, Stephanie White was a phenomenon in the state of Indiana. Growing up in West Lebanon, a 45-minute drive southwest from Purdue, White made headlines at Seeger High School en route to becoming the state's all-time leading scorer, being named Indiana's Miss Basketball and earning national player of the year honors in 1995.

On the night White set the state career scoring record, January 19, 1995, the game was moved from the Turkey Run High School gym (capacity 1,700) to Fountain Central's gym (capacity 2,800) to accommodate the anticipated crowd. More than 4,000 fans filled every nook and cranny to witness history.

In the second edition of his book *Hoosiers: The Fabulous Basketball Life of Indiana* (published in 1995), author Phillip M.

Hoose has a cover drawing of Indiana basketball's Mount Rushmore, and the figures he picked were Larry Bird, Bob Knight, Oscar Robertson, and White.

White was labeled "the most highly regarded and sought-after recruit in the nation." With childhood dreams of becoming an astronaut and attracted to its aviation program and proximity to home, White took her 2,869 prep points, still the fourth-most ever by a Hoosier State girl, and star power to Purdue.

Despite playing for three head coaches, White enjoyed a decorated collegiate career. It was capped in fairy-tale fashion. As a senior, the 5'11" guard/forward led the Boilermakers to the 1999 national championship, received the Wade Trophy as the country's best player, and was selected as the Academic All-American of the Year. She earned Big Ten Player of the Year and Female Athlete of the Year honors, as well, after averaging 20.2 points, 5.4 rebounds, and 4.5 assists per game.

"You definitely can't determine Stephanie's impact by her statistics alone," Purdue head coach Carolyn Peck said. "On the court, she is a lot like Magic Johnson because she makes everyone else on the floor so much better. She has all the intangibles, and that helps everyone out there. She is a fierce competitor and a winner. The leadership she provides and the example she sets are what set her apart from other great players. I wouldn't trade her for anyone."

The road wasn't always smooth for White, who had thoughts of giving up basketball after her first year at Purdue. But she stuck it out and never missed a game in her four seasons, starting all 127 of the Boilermakers' contests and averaging 34.6 minutes played.

After White's freshman campaign, during which she averaged 10.8 points, head coach Lin Dunn was dismissed and replaced by Nell Fortner. Subsequent player transfers left the Boilermakers with three returning players for the 1996–97 season, but they still managed to share the Big Ten championship and play in the NCAA Tournament. Then Fortner departed to become head coach of the

USA Basketball Women's National Team. Peck, one of Fortner's assistants, was tabbed to take over the program and, led by White's 20.6 points per game, Purdue won the 1998 Big Ten Tournament and advanced to the Elite Eight of the NCAA Tournament. That summer, Peck was hired as head coach and general manager of the expansion Orlando Miracle of the WNBA. But after some strong cajoling by White and classmate Ukari Figgs, Peck agreed to stay at Purdue for the highly anticipated 1998–99 season that concluded with a 62–45 victory over Duke in the national championship game. The Boilermakers went 34–1 overall, including 16–0 in the Big Ten.

"I came here expecting to play with a great program and reach new levels," said White, who was inducted into the Purdue Intercollegiate Athletics Hall of Fame in 2006 and the College Sports Information Directors Academic All-America Hall of Fame in 2017. "It wasn't exactly the path I envisioned, but here we are, and we're stronger because of it."

On the Boilermakers' career lists, White ranked second in assists (578), third in points (2,182), sixth in steals (277), and 15th in rebounds (667) through the 2019–20 season. She recorded the first triple-double in school history with 20 points, 11 rebounds, and 10 assists against Indiana on January 22, 1999. White's popularity pushed Purdue's season attendance average from 4,664 the year before she arrived to 9,681 her senior season—then a program record and still the second-biggest figure.

"Stephanie's personality and her character allowed fans to get close to her," said Mike Carmin, who covered White throughout high school and college for the Lafayette *Journal & Courier*. "She never turned down an autograph, never had a frown on her face, and always recognized the faithful fans who followed her career."

White was selected with the 21st pick in the 1999 WNBA Draft by the Charlotte Sting. She subsequently played for the Indiana Fever for four seasons, including three under Fortner, before becoming an assistant coach with the Chicago Sky and then the Fever. White served as head coach of the Fever for the 2015 and 2016 seasons, leading the team to the WNBA Finals her first year, before becoming the head coach at Vanderbilt. A communication major at Purdue, she has also spent time as a college basketball analyst for ESPN and the Big Ten Network.

18 Jack Mollenkopf

Jack Mollenkopf's tenure as head football coach at Purdue is rightfully hailed as the "Golden Years."

From 1956 to 1969, the Boilermakers put together the greatest sustained run of success in school history.

Mollenkopf was Stu Holcomb's line coach from 1947 to 1955. Gordon Graham, sports editor of the Lafayette *Journal & Courier*, likened the Holcomb-to-Mollenkopf transition to the one 26 years earlier from Jim Phelan to Noble Kizer. "Kizer had been much the same howling, hard-driven line coach under Phelan that Mollenkopf has been under Holcomb.... Players instinctively like leaders who push them on to great things, provided the man is fair. Noble was and Mollenkopf is."

Mollenkopf patrolled the sidelines longer than any coach before or after him and produced an 84–39–9 overall record (.670 winning percentage), which included a 57–32–5 mark in Big Ten games. He is second-winningest coach in school history, behind Joe Tiller (87 victories).

Mollenkopf guided the Boilermakers to their only Rose Bowl victory on January 2, 1967 (14–13 over USC), and a Big Ten tri-championship in 1967. Purdue finished second in the Big Ten twice (1959 and 1966) and third on four occasions (1964, 1965, 1968, and 1969).

In addition, the Boilermakers were nationally ranked for 80 weeks—tied with Joe Tiller for the most under any head coach—including the No. 1 spot the first five weeks of the 1968 season.

"Jack the Ripper" was 11–2–1 against Indiana and 10–4 against Notre Dame.

A total of 14 players were named All-Americans under Mollenkopf. Moreover, a Boilermaker finished in the top three in Heisman Trophy balloting four consecutive seasons: quarterback

Under head coach Jack Mollenkopf from 1956 to 1969, Purdue football put together the greatest sustained run of success in school history.

Bob Griese second in 1966, halfback Leroy Keyes third in 1967 and second in 1968, and quarterback Mike Phipps second in 1969. It took a while to get things revved up, however, and disgruntled Purdue students called to "Fire Fat Jack" midway through his tenure. But after going 4–4–1 in 1962, the Boilermakers averaged seven wins over Mollenkopf's final seven seasons.

A prominent figure on the sidelines of postseason All-Star games, Mollenkopf served as head coach of the 1958, 1959, and 1960 Blue-Gray games; 1962 and 1963 East-West Shrine games; 1964, 1967, and 1970 Hula bowls; 1968 All-American Bowl; and 1969 North-South Shrine Game.

On January 7, 1970, while in Honolulu to coach in the Hula Bowl, Mollenkopf announced his retirement via a telephone conference call. The fact that he would reach the Purdue Board of Trustees' established retirement age of 65 on July 1 had led to speculation about his future. Mollenkopf could have requested a waiver but opted against pursuing it.

"It has been a great honor, privilege, and opportunity for me to serve at Purdue University these past 23 years, and especially the last 14 years as head football coach," Mollenkopf said. "The most difficult part in reaching the decision I have is disassociating myself from the hundreds of young men that I have enjoyed coaching and helping in their development into manhood.

"I hope my years of labor at Purdue have contributed to her football quality, tradition, and image. My fondest dream is that she grow ever stronger in the years ahead."

Mollenkopf, who succumbed to intestinal cancer on December 4, 1975, at age 72, was inducted into the College Football Hall of Fame in 1988 and was a member of the inaugural class of the Purdue Intercollegiate Athletics Hall of Fame in 1994. The Mollenkopf Athletic Center, which houses Purdue's indoor practice facility, was named in his honor in 1990.

Hank Stram played under Mollenkopf in 1947 and served as an assistant alongside him from 1948 to 1955 before going on to a Pro Football Hall of Fame head coaching career. "Jack earned the right to be regarded as one of the great college coaches during his 14 years as head coach at Purdue," Stram said. "He had a great capacity of getting the most out of his players. He was very tough and very demanding, and believed in discipline. Yet, his players not only respected him, they loved him."

19 The Opening of Mackey Arena

Ask an opposing player about the experience of playing a game at Mackey Arena, and he or she will typically come back to one word: loud.

"It's like they've got a microphone with everybody's voice in there," Northwestern guard Bryant McIntosh said in 2017. "Everything's jumbled up in there, so you can't really hear anything."

That auditory advantage came by design. In 2016, while naming Mackey the fourth-toughest road environment in the Big Ten, ESPN referred to the arena as a "concrete dungeon of noise." What the bowl lacks in cutting-edge frills it makes up for by being simply one of the most intimidating destinations for opponents— and one of the league's best home-court advantages.

"That place was insane," said Purdue All-American Joe Barry Carroll, who played from 1976 to 1980. "I can't imagine anyone I played with [in the NBA] had a better college experience than I did in Mackey Arena. Some nights it felt like they were going to blow the roof off that place, because they love Purdue basketball."

When ground broke on what was then called Purdue Arena in 1965, its circular structure and domed roof made it the "first of its kind among collegiate sports facilities." It took more than two years and $6 million to build the facility that replaced Lambert Fieldhouse as the home of Boilermakers basketball.

The arena opened December 2, 1967, with the return of former Boilermakers great John Wooden as the head coach of defending national champion UCLA. The Bruins and Lew Alcindor edged Purdue 73–71. The standing room only-crowd of 14,400 also witnessed the debut of another legend: Rick Mount.

A year later, the arena was home to a team that rolled all the way to the national championship game before again falling to Wooden, Alcindor, and the Bruins.

Guy "Red" Mackey served as athletics director for 29 of his 45 years associated with Purdue. He died in 1971, and in March of the following year, the arena was renamed in his honor.

Women's basketball began playing at Mackey Arena in 1975. A quarter-century later, the Boilermaker women marched to what remains Purdue basketball's only NCAA Tournament championship.

A series of upgrades and renovations led up to Mackey Arena's rededication in November 2011. The concourse has been refurbished to include exhibits recognizing Purdue's basketball history.

The upgrades also included expanded sports medicine and strength & conditioning facilities and a practice court named for former basketball players Brian and Danielle (Bird) Cardinal. Premium seating and club areas were also added in the arena.

Mackey has a seating capacity of 14,222, with a total capacity (including non-ticketed individuals) of 14,804.

Through the 2019–20 season, more than 10 million fans had watched a game at Mackey Arena. Men's basketball boasted better than an .800 winning percentage over nearly 800 games played there. Purdue ranked in the top 20 nationally in attendance each of the last five seasons.

20 Take a Ride on the Boilermaker Special

A university with a unique nickname needs a distinctive mascot.

Hello, Boilermaker Special. The mascot is a replica of a Victorian-era locomotive, exemplifying the engineering heritage of the university, as well as brute force. It is presumed to be the largest, fastest, heaviest, and loudest collegiate mascot.

In the 1890s, Purdue became a leader in the research of railroad technology and remained so until the 1930s, when the industry switched from steam-powered to diesel-electric locomotives.

Israel Selkowitz, a sophomore pharmacy student, is credited with proposing the idea of a mascot in 1939. The campus newspaper, the *Exponent*, endorsed the idea, and alumni provided financial support to get the project off the ground. Paul Hoffman, president of the Studebaker Corporation in South Bend, Indiana, donated a chassis to the university, and W.H. Winterrowd, president of the Purdue Alumni Association and vice president of Baldwin Locomotive Works in Pennsylvania, built the superstructure for the mascot.

On September 11, 1940, the first Boilermaker Special was presented to the student body at a convocation in the Hall of Music. University president Edward Elliott assigned the Reamer Club, a student spirit organization, to maintain and operate the Special.

Since then, there have been four additional versions of the Boilermaker Special, revealed in 1953, 1960, 1993, and 2011. Wabash National, a semi-trailer manufacturer in Lafayette, took the lead in providing materials and labor for the most recent update, which included replacing the engine, transmission, and chassis. The current Special, which was dedicated on September 3, 2011, at halftime of the Purdue-Middle Tennessee football game at Ross-Ade Stadium, features the original bell and whistle.

Despite being the fifth iteration, the current Special is known as VII because IV and VI (and now VIII) were used for versions of the Xtra Special, a scaled-down version built on a golf cart that can be used indoors.

The word *Special* pays homage to the extra trains that were operated in addition to regularly scheduled ones; those that transported Purdue athletic teams to road games were known as "Boilermaker Specials."

A replica of a Victorian-era locomotive, the Boilermaker Special is presumed to be the largest, fastest, heaviest, and loudest collegiate mascot.

The Special appears at all home football games and travels to away contests. Each fall, its cowcatcher is adorned with hats of opponents the football team has defeated. The Special accompanied the Boilermakers to the 2001 Rose Bowl (Pasadena, California) and the 2017 Foster Farms Bowl (Santa Clara, California), although it was shipped—the only times it has not been driven to an event. Two Reamer Club students, who undergo extensive training, serve as pilot and co-pilot. The Special can reach a speed of 75 mph.

The Reamer Club—described as "a group of highly dedicated and spirited students devoted to bettering Purdue University"—offers free rides on the Special on the Fridays before home football games from noon to 3:00 PM, originating from in front of Stewart Center. The Special also can be requested for private events.

21 Mike Alstott

Only one Purdue football player has amassed 2,500 rushing yards and 1,000 receiving yards over the course of a career.

It's Mike Alstott, the Boilermakers' multifunctional fullback from 1992 to 1995. He is Purdue's all-time leader with 3,635 rushing yards to go with 1,075 receiving yards.

Purdue head coach Jim Colletto said of "A-Train" late in his senior season, "He is a guy who is fast enough to run away from people. He's a pass-receiver who rarely, if ever, drops a football. And when he's not running or catching, he's blocking full speed for our tailbacks. His work ethic is phenomenal. I've never seen him loaf one minute. We have to force him to rest. He is, as they would say, the real deal."

Despite being a productive 6'1", 205-pound tailback at Joliet (Illinois) Catholic High School, most colleges recruited Alstott as a fullback-to-be, and he picked Purdue because the Boilermakers planned to run a split-back offense where the fullback was involved more than as a blocker.

As a freshman against third-ranked Michigan on Halloween 1992, Alstott recorded the first of his Purdue career-record 16 100-yard rushing games. A star was born, and Alstott subsequently emerged as the focal point of the Boilermakers' offense, as a relentless runner and reliable receiver.

With his weight up to 236 pounds, Alstott was the first sophomore in school history to be named team Most Valuable Player after rushing for 816 yards, including 171 at Minnesota on October 9, 1993, and catching a career-high 30 passes.

In 1994, Alstott became Purdue's first 1,000-yard rusher since Scott Dierking in 1976, finishing with 1,188 yards, the second-most ever by a Boilermaker. He reached the 100-yard plateau in four games, including a pair of monster performances, 183 against Minnesota on October 8 and 181 at Michigan State on November 12. Alstott, who scored 14 of Purdue's school season-record 36 rushing touchdowns, repeated as team MVP.

Alstott fully intended on returning to Purdue for his senior season but still went through the process of having the NFL's College Advisory Committee evaluate his draft prospects. The report projected Alstott as a third-round pick, reinforcing his decision to stay in West Lafayette. To prepare for the 1995 campaign and for an eventual professional career, Alstott made headlines over the summer when he and defensive lineman Jayme Washel took turns pushing Alstott's Jeep Wrangler 100 yards on the parking lot north of Ross-Ade Stadium—doing so twice a week, eight times each, for a month.

"It's a combination of speed and power," Alstott said. "It's like driving linebackers back with the angle of your body and the short choppy steps you have to take."

At the same time, the Purdue sports information department was hyping Alstott as a Heisman Trophy candidate. Only four fullbacks had won the award bestowed on college football's outstanding player and none since Earl Campbell of the University of Texas in 1977.

Spurred by a school-record nine 100-yard rushing games, Alstott broke Otis Armstrong's Purdue season mark with 1,436 yards on 243 carries, a robust 5.9-yard average. Alstott saved his best for last, roughing up Indiana for 264 yards, 12 shy of Armstrong's school standard, on 25 carries in a 51–14 victory in Bloomington on November 24. He had runs of 24, 59, 62, and 35 yards and played only until early in the fourth quarter with the game's outcome decided.

"The guy's incredible," Washel said. "Some of the runs he makes, I don't know how he does it. He just appeared out of nowhere in a couple of those piles. I think he's got one of those magic cloaks that makes him disappear or something."

Alstott concluded his career as the Boilermakers' all-time leader in rushing yards, all-purpose yards (4,710), rushing touchdowns (39), and total touchdowns (42). The only three-time team MVP in school annals, he earned All-American honors as a senior while finishing 11th in the Heisman race.

Purdue legend Leroy Keyes, who was the Boilermakers' running back coach during Alstott's senior season, said Alstott was "truly one of the greatest fullbacks to ever put on a football uniform. Not only at Purdue, but in college history."

Alstott's exploits, however, were not enough for the Boilermakers to reach a bowl game. They posted a 14–27–3 record over the course of his four years. Purdue came close in 1995, going 4–6–1 with four losses by a touchdown or less.

Alstott produced an outstanding 12-year NFL career, all with the Tampa Bay Buccaneers after being selected in the second round (No. 35 overall) of the 1996 draft. While becoming the face of the franchise, Alstott scored a Buccaneers-record 71 touchdowns (58 rushing and 13 receiving) while ranking second with 5,088 rushing yards. He was a six-time Pro Bowl selection, scoring three touchdowns in the 2000 game. Tampa Bay won Super Bowl XXXVII 48–21 over the Oakland Raiders, and Alstott's two-yard touchdown plunge in the second quarter was the first by a former Purdue player in a Super Bowl.

Alstott was inducted into the Purdue Intercollegiate Athletics Hall of Fame in 2006 and the Indiana Football Hall of Fame in 2014. He entered the Buccaneers' Ring of Honor in 2015.

22 Robbie Hummel

If Marques Johnson had decided to play basketball at Purdue, Robbie Hummel never would have become a Boilermaker. Head coach Matt Painter frankly told Hummel as much. Johnson wound up going to Tennessee, so Hummel was offered a scholarship and accepted it.

"The rest, you could say, is history," said Hummel, who was part of a highly touted recruiting class with JaJuan Johnson, E'Twaun Moore, and Scott Martin. "Purdue checked all the boxes for me: I liked Coach Painter and the staff, the program was trending forward, and I knew I would get a great education. Obviously, I'm glad it all worked out."

From 2007 to 2012, Hummel developed into perhaps the best all-around players ever to wear a Purdue uniform. To wit: the versatile 6'8" forward from Valparaiso, Indiana, is the lone player in school history with 1,500 career points, 800 rebounds, and 250 assists. On the Boilermakers' all-time lists through the 2019–20 season, he ranked fifth in rebounds (862, 6.8 per game), sixth in free throw percentage (.841), seventh in 3-pointers (216), and 10th in points (1,772—14.0 per game). Rounding out his numbers were 268 assists, 132 steals, and 112 blocked shots.

But there was more to Hummel than glitzy statistics. He was a nice guy with a sparkling image and a work ethic to match. As much as he was a prototype player, he was a model citizen. His popularity on campus and across the county was off the charts. Fittingly, Hummel won the Senior CLASS Award in 2012 as the outstanding men's basketball senior student-athlete in the nation. He also received the Big Ten Medal of Honor for demonstrating great proficiency in scholarship and athletics, following his father, Glenn, who won the award as a University of Illinois tennis player in 1976.

"Rob has been everything you can want as a person, as a player, as a student," Painter said late in Hummel's career. "I like guys who come early, who stay late, that love the game of basketball. I am biased toward those guys, but I'm also biased toward those habits, how guys carry themselves. Those are the things that you need to be successful."

Hummel was a second-team All-American in 2010. He earned first-team All-Big Ten honors in 2008, 2010, and 2012—the first three-time Purdue honoree since Rick Mount from 1968 to 1970—and was the 2009 Big Ten Tournament Most Valuable Player for the champion Boilermakers.

"I had so much fun playing basketball at Purdue," said Hummel, a member of the Purdue Intercollegiate Athletics Hall of Fame class of 2020. "I was fortunate to play on some very good teams with some great coaches."

The Hummel story can't be fully told without mention of the two torn anterior cruciate ligaments he suffered in his right knee. The first came February 24, 2010, at Minnesota with the third-ranked Boilermakers viewed as a legitimate Final Four team.

Without Hummel, they were knocked out in the South Regional semifinals. Eight months later, on the first day of practice for the 2010–11 season, Hummel tore the ACL again and missed the entire campaign.

"It was a long road," said Hummel, who dealt with a stress fracture in his back as a sophomore. "There were times I thought I wouldn't make it. But I have a great family and great friends, plus the wonderful support system at Purdue, which helped me

Robbie Hummel is the lone player in Purdue men's basketball history with 1,500 career points, 800 rebounds, and 250 assists. (Tom Campbell)

get through everything. I probably gained a better perspective on things and an appreciation for basketball."

Hummel was selected in the second round (No. 58 overall) of the 2012 NBA Draft by the Minnesota Timberwolves. After spending a season in Spain, he played for the Timberwolves in 2013–14 and 2014–15 before going back overseas to play in Italy and Russia for two years. In October 2017, Hummel, who had taken part in a National Basketball Players Association initiative called Sportscaster U., opted to begin a second career as a color commentator for BTN and ESPN. His experience, knowledge and ability as an orator made him a natural, and he quickly became highly regarded.

"I came to hate playing overseas," Hummel said. "I couldn't do it anymore. It was hard to be by yourself, away from your family, in a country where a lot of people don't speak the same language you do. It was a very lonely experience, and I was burned out.

"I decided to pursue announcing, and I absolutely love it. It's the best thing I could be doing right now. You get to sit courtside and watch high-level basketball. It's not work, and it's really fun."

When he retired from professional basketball, Hummel figured he was finished playing competitively. But a friend, Craig Moore, who played against Hummel at Northwestern, introduced him to the 3-on-3 game. Hummel was skeptical at first but got hooked and wound up leading his USA Basketball team to the gold medal at the World Cup in Amsterdam in June 2019. He earned tournament MVP honors and subsequently was named the USA Basketball Male Athlete of the Year.

Meanwhile, 3-on-3 has become an Olympic sport, and Hummel should be a member of the first-ever United States team, which will play in Tokyo in the 2021 Games, postponed a year due to the COVID-19 pandemic.

23 Leroy Keyes

Leroy Keyes was a football megastar for the Boilermakers from 1966 to 1968.

A two-time unanimous All-American, Keyes finished third and second in Heisman Trophy voting his junior and senior seasons, respectively. (UCLA quarterback Gary Beban and USC running back O.J. Simpson were Nos. 1 and 2 in 1967, and Simpson won in 1968.)

A 6'4", two-way player with speed and strength, Keyes set Purdue career records for touchdowns (37), points (222), and all-purpose yards (3,757). He was voted the All-Time Greatest Player as part of the 100-year anniversary of Purdue football in 1987 and was an inaugural member of the Purdue Intercollegiate Athletics Hall of Fame in 1994. He was inducted into the College Football Hall of Fame in 1990, Rose Bowl Hall of Fame in 2010, and Indiana Football Hall of Fame in 2014.

"The great thing about Leroy was that he did so many things," said Bob DeMoss, an assistant coach for the Boilermakers when Keyes played. "When you play both offense and defense, can run, catch and throw the ball, there's not much left."

Keyes primarily played defensive back as a sophomore, when the Boilermakers defeated USC in the Rose Bowl. The following season, he moved to halfback (while continuing to play some defense) and scored 19 touchdowns (13 rushing and six receiving) to set the still-existing Purdue record and led the nation with 114 points. He was honored as the Big Ten Most Valuable Player as Purdue shared the conference championship. As a senior, Keyes became the first Boilermaker to rush for 1,000 yards in a season and was selected to the 1968 East-West Shrine Game. In his final game as a Boilermaker, Keyes scored three fourth-quarter touchdowns to propel Purdue to a 38–35 Old Oaken Bucket Game win over Indiana.

"If Leroy doesn't get the Heisman Trophy, they ought to blow it up," Purdue head coach Jack Mollenkopf said midway through the 1968 season.

Leroy Keyes was voted the All-Time Greatest Player as part of the 100-year anniversary of Purdue football in 1987 and was an inaugural member of the Purdue Intercollegiate Athletics Hall of Fame in 1994.

Nicknamed "The Golden Mr. Do-Everything," Keyes' career statistics included 2,094 rushing yards, 80 receptions, eight touchdown passes (among 12 completions), four interceptions, and a 25.8-yard kickoff return average. He also handled kickoff duties. It is no wonder the rallying cry was, "Give the ball to Leroy."

More than 50 years after he played, Keyes remains the Purdue career record-holder for rushing average (5.88 yards per carry). He ranks third in total touchdowns, fifth in rushing touchdowns (29), sixth in points, ninth in all-purpose yards, and 11th in rushing yards.

Keyes did some of his best work in his three games against Notre Dame. His 95-yard fumble return on September 24, 1966, in South Bend remains the longest in Purdue history. In the 10th-ranked Boilermakers' 28–21 victory over the top-ranked Fighting Irish on September 30, 1967, at Ross-Ade Stadium, Keyes caught a touchdown pass and preserved the win with an interception. Finally, on September 28, 1968, in a showdown of No. 1 squads (Purdue by the Associated Press and Notre Dame by United Press International), Keyes accounted for three touchdowns (two rushing and one passing) while doing a yeoman's job defending Notre Dame All-American receiver Jim Seymour for the second year in a row as the Boilermakers prevailed 37–22 in South Bend.

"I always figured if you beat Notre Dame, the pope would know about it," Keyes said. "I was surprised that I never got a call from the pope."

Purdue owes a debt of gratitude to Marv Levy, the Pro Football Hall of Fame coach, for Keyes winding up in West Lafayette. While Keyes was attending Carver High School in Newport News, Virginia, Levy was coaching at the College of William and Mary and knew Burnie Miller, who had just been hired the recruiting coordinator at Purdue.

"Marv told Burnie about me, and Burnie came out and asked all the coaches of the schools I played against whether they thought I could play Big Ten football," Keyes said. "They all said that I could, so Burnie invited me out for an official visit. The telling point was meeting coach Mollenkopf. He was a no-nonsense coach who told it like it was, and I appreciated his honesty. Everything seemed like a perfect fit for me at Purdue."

Keyes' time in college coincided with the radical and tumultuous times that existed throughout the United States. The pied piper of Purdue did not shy away from voicing his opinion about football or events of the day.

"I think my legacy will be that I was a good guy who stood up for my beliefs," Keyes said. "There were stances we all had to take. I was always upbeat and had a smile on my face. I may not have won the Heisman, but how you carry yourself and how people react and respond to you is more important than a trophy."

Boilermakers in the College Football Hall of Fame

Players	Played at Purdue	Inducted
Elmer Oliphant, HB	1911–13	1955
Alex Agase, OL	1943	1963
Cecil Isbell, HB	1935–37	1967
Bob Griese, QB	1964–66	1984
Chalmers "Bump" Elliott, HB	1943–44	1989
Leroy Keyes, HB	1966–68	1990
Mike Phipps, QB	1967–69	2006
Mark Herrmann, QB	1977–80	2010
Otis Armstrong, RB	1970–72	2012
Dave Butz, DT	1970–72	2014
Rod Woodson, DB	1983–86	2016

Coaches	Coached at Purdue	Inducted
Andy Smith	1913–15	1951
Jim Phelan	1922–29	1973
Jack Mollenkopf	1956–69	1988
Jim Young	1977–81	1999
William Dietz	1921	2012

The Philadelphia Eagles selected Keyes with the third overall pick of the 1969 NFL Draft. A running back and safety, he played for the Eagles from 1969 to 1972 and for the Kansas City Chiefs in 1973 before injuries curtailed his career. He had six interceptions and three fumble recoveries in 1971.

A desegregation specialist for the Philadelphia school district for 16 years, Keyes returned to Purdue as running backs coach under Jim Colletto in 1995 and 1996. Keyes subsequently served as an administrative assistant for football under Joe Tiller from 1997 to 1999 and then as a member of the John Purdue Club staff until his retirement in 2011.

24 Carsen Edwards

One of the best recruiting decisions in recent Purdue history was made when one of the Boilermakers' commitments changed his mind.

C.J. Walker, a point guard from Indianapolis, had pledged to Matt Painter's 2016 class in October 2014. Six months later, however, Walker backed out, citing the desire to find a better fit for his playing style.

So Purdue jumped back in to recruit players from whom its attention had been diverted. One of them was a high-scoring guard from Texas. Carsen Edwards originally hoped to stay closer to home for his college basketball career. But he saw an opportunity at Purdue—a strong academic school, a playing style that fit his skills, and an atmosphere that felt like home.

When Edwards committed in August 2015, Purdue saw him as a possible point guard of the future with a higher scoring potential than typically seen at that position.

By the time he arrived in West Lafayette the next summer, however, it became increasingly clear that despite his 6'0" height, Edwards' dynamic scoring ability would best serve the Boilermakers when playing off the ball.

Over the next two seasons, Painter and Edwards felt one another out as to how the guard's shooting bravado and highlight-reel dunking ability could fit within the framework of a talented, veteran lineup. Along the way, Edwards hinted at his scoring capacity while striving for a more efficient approach in which to deliver it.

Everything came together in a breakthrough night at Illinois on February 22, 2018.

The Boilermakers were playing their second straight game without senior forward Vincent Edwards—a four-year starter and one of the Big Ten's most versatile players. A 19-game winning streak had ended 10 days earlier, and a three-game losing skid ensued. Purdue needed to keep winning to stay in the Big Ten title race and keep pushing for a high NCAA Tournament seed.

Carsen Edwards (no relation to his older teammate) simply took over. He scored 27 points in the game's first 26-plus minutes. He showed off both his deep perimeter shooting range and his ability to get to the rim by slamming home a pair of impressive dunks.

Many of his drives, however, resulted in contact from Illinois defenders. He punished them by making 14 of 16 attempts at the free throw line. Edwards needed only 19 field goal attempts to score 40 points. He became the first Boilermaker to reach that threshold since Glenn Robinson in 1994, and the first Big Ten player to do so in league play since Brandon Paul of Illinois in 2012.

No Purdue guard had scored 40 since Rick Mount's legendary 61-point performance against Iowa in 1970.

After the game, teammate P.J. Thompson called Edwards "a born scorer." But none of the Boilermakers had ever seen their young star put everything together on the same night.

"Not to this extent, where every possession he was getting a bucket and he was that hot," senior guard Dakota Mathias said after the game. "It was probably one of the best performances that I've seen."

Edwards went on to earn first-team All-Big Ten honors while leading Purdue to a Big Ten Tournament championship game appearance and a return trip to the Sweet 16. He was named the Jerry West Award winner as the nation's top shooting guard.

Edwards repeated that 40-point performance the following season at Texas, celebrating his only collegiate game in his home state. In that December 2018 game, however, the outburst could not lift Purdue to victory in a 72–68 loss.

In three seasons, Carsen Edwards scored 1,920 points—seventh in Purdue men's basketball history. He was a second-round draft pick of the Boston Celtics in the 2019 NBA Draft. (Tom Campbell)

The rest of the 2018–19 regular season could be described as a bit of a roller-coaster ride for Edwards, who remained a major scorer but struggled at times with streaky shooting. He repeated as a first-team All-Big Ten selection and was a consensus second-team All-American, then saved his best for last.

In the Boilermakers' NCAA Tournament second-round and Elite Eight games, Edwards blistered the nets for a career-high 42 points against both Villanova and eventual national champion Virginia. In between, he scored 29 against Tennessee, and he was named the Most Outstanding Player of the South Regional, becoming the first player to win that honor despite not being a member of the winning team since Steph Curry of Davidson in 2008.

In four tournament games, Edwards averaged 34.8 points, the most by any player since 1990 and tied for the ninth-most ever.

"To me, it was like he was playing Pop-a-Shot," Painter said. "He just got into one of those rhythms, and he felt really good about himself. What the whole nation got to see we saw in practice a lot. Even when he was not shooting at a high percentage during the season, he always would come back to practice and shoot the ball well. I always felt that when he lands on two feet, the ball is going in the basket. When he lands on one foot, it doesn't go in as much.

"He had similar games, but to be able to string them together like he did and get on that kind of run, especially in those type of games, he showed a lot of growth. When we did a good job setting him up and did a good job making good decisions, we executed at a high level."

Edwards left Purdue after three seasons and 1,920 points—seventh in program history—and was a second-round draft pick of the Boston Celtics in the 2019 NBA Draft.

25 Ross-Ade Stadium

After David Ross graduated from Purdue, he went on to patent 88 inventions and founded four companies related to his lifelong passion for engineering. Then the Lafayette native turned his attention to giving back to his alma mater. His efforts to raise donations from other alumni were instrumental in the building of the Purdue Memorial Union.

George Ade also grew up not far from Purdue in Kentland, Indiana. After college, he began a newspaper career that took him to the *Chicago Morning News* and *Chicago Record*. There he gained widespread acclaim as a columnist, humorist, and playwright.

Those two alums joined forces, and finances, to spearhead the construction of the football stadium that bears their names.

Prior to that gift, Purdue football played at Stuart Field, a 5,000-seat stadium on the site of what is now the Elliott Hall of Music.

Ross and Ade announced at a September 6, 1922, reception for Purdue president Edward Elliott that they had purchased a 65-acre dairy farm to be used as the site of a new football stadium and other athletic facilities.

Construction began June 2, 1924. Purdue held the dedication game for Ross-Ade Stadium on November 22, 1924, beating intrastate rival Indiana 26–7. The stadium originally featured a cinder track around the field and a seating capacity of 13,500—and another 5,000 in standing-room-only capacity.

The cinder track was removed in 1957. By then a series of additions and expansions had pushed the seating capacity beyond 50,000. The peak capacity of 69,200 came in 1970, and the largest crowd to see a game at Ross-Ade—71,629—came November 22,

1980, against Indiana. That was 56 years to the day, and with the same opponent, as the stadium's first game.

As of 2020, seating capacity sat at 57,282. One reason for the drop was the removal of 6,100 seats in 2014 and the building of a patio area in the south end zone that replaced dated bleachers taken out of Lambert Fieldhouse.

A number of renovations have helped modernize the stadium—most notably a $70 million project from 2001 to 2003. Permanent lighting was installed in 2017. The Big Ten required all of its programs to be able to host more late afternoon and evening games to better accommodate television network preferences.

The Boilermakers played six night games in their first three seasons with permanent lights, including a 49–20 crushing of No. 2 Ohio State in 2018.

A brick facade at field level and a new sound system were also installed in 2018, followed by a ribbon board at the north end in 2019.

To further enhance the fan experience, a new video board at the south end of Ross-Ade was put in for the 2020 season. It is one of the largest in the country for college football, measuring 150 feet, 4 inches wide by 56 feet, 9 inches high. Those measurements are more than four times bigger than the previous board (68 feet by 31 feet), which debuted in 2007.

From the upper floors of the Shively Media Center—the press box and suites located on the west side of the stadium—one can look out over the northern portion of campus and the tops of the trees in the adjacent neighborhoods.

26 Old Oaken Bucket

Since 1925, the Old Oaken Bucket has been presented to the winner of the annual Purdue-Indiana football game

The Chicago alumni groups of both schools came up with the idea for a traveling trophy, and Russell Gray of Purdue and Clarence Jones of Indiana were given the task of finding an appropriate object. They recommended that "an old oaken bucket would be a most typical trophy from this state and should be taken from a well somewhere in Indiana." Purdue's Fritz Ernst and Indiana's Whiley J. Huddle found the fabled bucket, in a bad state of repair and covered with moss and mold, on the Bruner farm between Kent and Hanover in southern Indiana.

The Bruner farm was settled in the 1840s, and family lore suggests the bucket might have been used by Confederate General John Hunt Morgan and his soldiers during their incursion into Indiana in 1863 during the Civil War.

George Ade, distinguished humorist from Purdue, and Harry Kurrie, president of the Monon Railroad, representing Indiana, formally presented the Old Oaken Bucket in 1925. The Boilermakers and Hoosiers subsequently battled to a 0–0 tie on November 21 at Ross-Ade Stadium, resulting in an "I-P" link being attached to the bucket.

Purdue has dominated the rivalry, and the bucket was adorned with 60 "P" links, 32 "I" links, and two additional "I-P" links entering the 2020 season. The Boilermakers have been victorious in 15 of the last 23 showdowns, dating to the arrival of Joe Tiller as head coach in 1997. Tiller went 10–2 against the Hoosiers, including a 62–10 shellacking in his final game on November 22, 2008.

In 1947, the Boilermakers suffered their fourth straight loss to Indiana, and Purdue fans were growing restless. First-year head coach Stu Holcomb, a newcomer to the rivalry, didn't understand what all the fuss was about. "We didn't put that much importance on the Indiana game," he admitted. "We actually believed that when we upset Ohio State we gave our fans a successful season. But if victory over Indiana is what they want, that's what they'll get. Indiana never will beat us again." Pretty heady talk, but Holcomb was true to his word. He beat the Hoosiers the eight remaining times he faced them through 1955.

Then, under head coach Jack Mollenkopf, Purdue went 11–2–1 against Indiana from 1956 to 1969.

The all-time series between Purdue and Indiana dates to 1891, with the Boilermakers boasting a 74–42–6 advantage through 2019, and the schools have played every year since 1920.

Throughout its history, the bucket has been kidnapped by partisans from both schools—a couple of times missing so long that it was given up as lost, only to turn up mysteriously just before or after the game.

Among the notable games:

November 20, 1926: The Boilermakers jumped to an early 7–0 lead when left halfback "Cotton" Wilcox scampered 56 yards around the right end for a touchdown. Purdue tacked on 10 more points in the second quarter and cruised to a 24–14 victory at Ross-Ade. Unfortunately, the Boilermakers did not immediately receive the Old Oaken Bucket for their triumph because it had been stolen from Purdue's gymnasium two days prior to the game.

November 21, 1931: Playing for a share of the Big Ten championship, intrastate rivals Purdue and Indiana were tied 0–0 at the half in Bloomington. The first two quarters may have been slow, but the defensive struggle did not last long. Right halfback Jim Purvis opened the second half with a 77-yard touchdown run, and Purdue scored twice more in the third quarter for a sure-handed 19–0 win. The victory gave Purdue a 9–1 overall record and a conference tri-championship with Michigan and Northwestern.

November 19, 1932: Purdue's dominant play prevented Indiana from executing a single offensive snap in the first quarter. The Hoosiers had the ball three times in the opening frame, but were so deep in their own territory they elected to punt the ball away on the first play of each series. Left end Paul Moss caught five passes for 168 yards and two touchdowns for the Boilermakers, scoring from 63 and 60 yards. The 25–7 victory in West Lafayette capped a 7–0–1 season and a share of the Big Ten championship with Michigan.

November 21, 1936: After a scoreless first half, Purdue and Indiana traded touchdowns at a frenzied pace in the second half and, when the dust settled, six touchdowns were scored in all. The game wound up deadlocked at 20 apiece at Ross-Ade. Fullback Cecil Isbell threw three touchdowns in the game and led Purdue on a riveting 77-yard scoring drive that tied the game in the closing minutes.

November 20, 1943: Purdue's bend-but-don't-break defense prevented Indiana from scoring on first-and-goal a staggering five times, and a 7–0 win in Bloomington preserved a perfect 9–0 record and share of the Big Ten championship with Michigan. A first-quarter 38-yard touchdown pass from quarterback Sam Vacanti to right end Frank Bauman proved to be the winning score.

November 22, 1952: Trailing 16–14 in the fourth quarter, quarterback Dale Samuels tossed a nine-yard touchdown pass to halfback Rex Brock that put the Boilermakers up for good en route to a 21–16 win at Ross-Ade. The win gave Purdue a 4–1–1 conference record and a share of the Big Ten championship with Wisconsin.

Brock was the key to Purdue's victory, scoring two touchdowns and rushing for 83 yards on just 12 carries.

November 23, 1968: In his final collegiate game, All-America halfback Leroy Keyes gave his hometown fans a virtuoso performance in a 38–35 comeback win. Purdue trailed 28–17 in the fourth quarter before Keyes exploded for three touchdowns, including a 56-yard reception for the game-winning score. Keyes finished the day with 140 rushing yards on 28 carries and three touchdowns, and 149 receiving yards on six catches and a score. It was the second time in his career he amassed more than 100 yards rushing and receiving in the same game.

November 25, 1972: All-America halfback Otis Armstrong rushed for a school-record 276 yards on 32 carries and three touchdowns, including a 53-yard touchdown run on the final carry of his collegiate career as the Boilermakers rolled to a 42–7 win in West Lafayette. With Purdue leading 14–7 at the half, Armstrong opened the third quarter with a thrilling 71-yard touchdown scamper. Armstrong finished with a Big Ten record 3,315 career rushing yards.

November 22, 1986: Two-time All-America defensive back Rod Woodson made his first career start at running back, his high school position, and led Purdue with 93 yards rushing and 67 yards receiving in his final collegiate game. He also recorded 10 tackles, one pass breakup, and one forced fumble on defense while returning three punts and two kickoffs. The Boilermakers edged the Hoosiers 17–15 at Ross-Ade.

November 25, 1989: Larry Sullivan kicked a 32-yard field goal with 2:51 left in the game to give Purdue a 15–14 victory at Memorial Stadium. The Boilermakers trailed 14–3 in the fourth quarter before scoring 12 unanswered points. Quarterback Eric Hunter, who led the Boilermakers with 184 yards passing and 38 positive rushing yards, sparked Purdue's comeback with a 20-yard touchdown pass to wide receiver Calvin Williams early in the fourth quarter.

November 24, 1995: All-America fullback Mike Alstott rushed for a career-high 264 yards on 25 carries and three touchdowns in his final game as a Boilermaker. Alstott broke Armstrong's school record for rushing yards in a season, finishing with 1,436 yards. The Boilermakers rode Alstott to a 51–14 blowout of the Hoosiers in Bloomington.

November 18, 2000: At 6:53 PM EST, Purdue saw both a 33-year Big Ten championship and Rose Bowl drought come to an end with a 41–13 victory at Ross-Ade. The Boilermakers scored first and didn't look back, leading 20–7 at halftime and 34–7 after three quarters. Running back Montrell Lowe ran wild, gaining 208 yards and scoring four touchdowns. Quarterback Drew Brees completed 20 of 29 passes for 216 yards with one touchdown. Defensively, free safety Stuart Schweigert came up with two interceptions.

November 20, 2004: It was a record-setting day in a 63–24 win in West Lafayette. The 63 points were the Boilermakers' most since a 91–0 win over Rose Polytechnic Institute on November 17, 1912. Purdue established a Big Ten record with 763 yards of total offense. Wide receiver Taylor Stubblefield became the NCAA career receptions leader with his 301st catch, a seven-yarder from quarterback Kyle Orton late in the first quarter. Orton set a school record with 530 yards of total offense while tying records with 522 yards passing and six passing touchdowns. Defensively, end Rob Ninkovich tied the school standard with four sacks.

November 22, 2008: Hollywood's finest writers and producers could not have scripted it any better. Joe Tiller's final game as Purdue football coach was striking and vivid. The Boilermakers scored on their first 10 possessions (eight touchdowns and two field goals)—before running out the clock to end the game—and dismantled Indiana 62–10 at Ross-Ade. Quarterback Curtis Painter completed 38 of 54 passes for 448 yards and five touchdowns to five different receivers. Purdue amassed a season-high 596 yards of total offense and limited the Hoosiers to 214 yards. The 52-point margin of victory was the Boilermakers' most-lopsided win over Indiana since 1893.

27 "Spoilermakers"

A biting wind whipped across campus October 20, 2018, marking the first truly Big Ten Saturday of the season.

Something besides the wind also stirred that day in West Lafayette. It began that morning, when ESPN aired a profile of Tyler Trent, a Purdue student stricken with terminal cancer whose story had touched the football program, the campus, and the community.

Trent planned to attend that night's game against Ohio State—ranked No. 2 in the nation behind a high-powered passing offense. Most expected Purdue, which had opened the season 0–3 before winning three straight, to fall back to earth against the Buckeyes.

Instead, the Boilermakers summoned their most inspired performance in years. The 49–20 seismic crushing played out in front of a stunned national television audience, putting Purdue head coach Jeff Brohm's resurgent team in the spotlight.

"I don't think I've been part of a day like that," Brohm said afterward. "It did have every aspect to it. From the atmosphere to the game to the win to Tyler Trent and everything he's been going through. I don't know what more you could ask. It involved everything and a reason for all of it."

That jaw-dropping victory was the first of its kind under Brohm. However, it extended a long tradition of Purdue teams that found a way to break through against heavily favored or highly ranked opponents in high-profile games.

It even earned the program a nickname: "Spoilermakers."

Purdue has beaten the No. 1 team in either the Associated Press or United Press International poll seven times each. (Some teams were not ranked No. 1 in both polls, so that equates to more than seven victories.) Only Miami, Notre Dame, Alabama, and Oklahoma have more victories over top-ranked opponents.

Yet as former *Indianapolis Star* sports editor and columnist Bob Collins noted in *Boilermakers: A History of Purdue Football*, some Purdue players and fans considered the Spoilermakers moniker a curse as much as an achievement.

More often than not—especially in the rivalry with Notre Dame—those season-making victories were followed by season-breaking defeats.

October 7, 1950: Notre Dame brought a 39-game winning streak into this meeting in South Bend. Purdue, undaunted, jumped out to a 21–0 lead. Neil Schmidt, a halfback who had been knocked out of the game against the Fighting Irish a year earlier with a knee injury, totaled 155 yards and a touchdown. Purdue 28, Notre Dame 14.

The win vaulted the Boilermakers to No. 9 in the rankings. They dropped out of the rankings a week later after a loss to Miami, which began a six-game losing streak.

October 24, 1953: Purdue opened the season 0–4, while Michigan State outscored opponents 115–34 and extended its winning streak to 28 games. However, Tom Bettis stepped up to lead a stifling performance from the Boilermakers defense at Ross-Ade Stadium. Dan Pobojewski, a Michigan State transfer who had not been listed on Purdue's depth chart before the season, scored on a one-yard touchdown run in the fourth quarter. Purdue 6, Michigan State 0.

Those Boilermakers won only one other game—a 30–0 victory over Indiana in the season finale.

October 2, 1954: Boilermakers fans were intrigued by Len Dawson after the quarterback passed for 185 yards and four touchdowns in a season-opening 31–0 victory over Missouri. They were sold a week later when he torched the Fighting Irish for 213 yards and four more touchdowns. That win in South Bend snapped another Notre Dame winning streak, this one at 13 games. Purdue 27, Notre Dame 14.

Now ranked No. 5 in the nation, the Boilermakers tied Duke 13–13 the following week, then lost three of their next five.

October 19, 1957: The Boilermakers couldn't break through a tough early schedule and took an 0–3 record into this road game. This turned out to be the only game all season in which Michigan State allowed more than 14 points. The Big Ten office later apologized for a blown referee call that negated a Spartans touchdown after Purdue had built a 14–0 lead. Purdue 20, Michigan State 13.

Three different polls went on to crown the Spartans national champions. Including that upset in East Lansing, Purdue won five of its last six games but went 0–3 against other ranked teams.

October 15 and November 12, 1960: In true Spoilermakers fashion, Purdue played five top-12 teams, beat two of them, and still finished with only a 4–4–1 record.

It had already been an up-and-down season before Purdue hosted Ohio State, ranked No. 1 in the UPI poll, on October 15. The Boilermakers opened with a 27–27 tie against No. 8 UCLA, went to South Bend for a 51–19 whooping of No. 12 Notre Dame, then suffered its not-so-unusual letdown with a 24–13 loss at unranked Wisconsin.

Ohio State came to West Lafayette having allowed seven total points in three games. Purdue running back Willie Jones broke through for his first career touchdown, then a second, then a third. Purdue 24, Ohio State 21.

Purdue had another chance at a top-ranked team with an October 22 trip to AP No. 1 Iowa, but fell short 21–14. It had lost three straight games and dropped out of the rankings when it traveled to Minnesota on November 12.

Despite those ups and downs, the Boilermakers nearly had a say in deciding the national championship picture. Jim Tiller's fumble recovery in the end zone put the game-clinching touchdown on the board. Purdue 23, Minnesota 14.

That was the only regular season loss the Golden Gophers suffered en route to the Rose Bowl. While they lost that game to Washington, they were still named national champion by four outlets, including the AP and UPI polls.

Purdue won the Old Oaken Bucket game for the 13th straight time the following week.

September 25, 1965: At the time, the 61,921 fans who watched this clash with Notre Dame at Ross-Ade represented the biggest football crowd in state history. Five lead changes and a virtuoso performance by quarterback Bob Griese—19 of 22 passing for 284 yards—set up a thrilling ending. Gordon Teter's three-yard touchdown run lifted the Boilermakers. Purdue 25, Notre Dame 21.

UPI ranked Purdue No. 1 the following week. The Boilermakers responded by blowing a 14–0 lead in a 14–14 tie with SMU at the Cotton Bowl. They finished the season unranked in the AP poll.

September 30, 1967: Does this sound familiar? Defending national champion Notre Dame had won 11 straight games when it visited Ross-Ade. Leroy Keyes burned the Fighting Irish both at flanker and halfback. He also played defense, recording the fourth and final interception of Notre Dame quarterback Terry Hanratty. Purdue 28, Notre Dame 21.

Purdue took a 6–0 record into the Old Oaken Bucket Game, but fell 19–14 when Indiana forced a fumble on a goal line stand with under seven minutes to play.

The Boilermakers opened the 1968 season ranked No. 1 in the AP poll and spent four weeks there—including a 37–22 win at Notre Dame—before a 13–0 loss at No. 4 Ohio State.

November 6, 1976: Purdue rode a three-game losing streak into this home game. Michigan, by contrast, had outscored its first eight opponents 352–58. But on this day, head coach Alex Agase's crew got the best of Bo Schembechler and the Wolverines. Rock Supan—a free safety who had only been a placekicker for only a few weeks—made a 23-yard field goal with under five minutes to play to give the Boilermakers a two-point lead. Michigan drove inside the Purdue 20-yard line, stalled at the 19, and settled for a Bob Wood 37-yard field goal try that sailed wide left. Purdue 16, Michigan 14.

The Boilermakers ended with a 5–6 record after losing to Indiana at home 20–14.

Notre Dame was ranked No. 1 in both 1989 and 1990 when it recorded lopsided victories over the Boilermakers. Purdue has not played a top-ranked team since.

28 Matt Painter

When athletics director Morgan Burke brought in former Purdue player Matt Painter to serve as head-coach-in-waiting behind Gene Keady, it allowed for a seamless transition between two eras of winning for the men's basketball program.

Painter, a hard-nosed Boilermakers guard from 1989 to 1993, returned to his alma mater in April 2004 following a successful season as head coach at Southern Illinois.

A decade and a half later, Painter has established himself as one of the top coaches in the country. He has led the Boilermakers to three Big Ten regular season championships (2010, 2017, and 2019), as well as the 2009 Big Ten Tournament title. Purdue has appeared in 12 NCAA Tournaments, advancing to the Sweet 16 five times and the 2019 Elite Eight.

Painter ranked third in school history in wins through the 2019–20 season with 337, trailing only College Basketball Hall of Famers Keady (512) and Ward "Piggy" Lambert (371). In Big Ten annals, Painter ranked tied for eighth (with Ohio State's Thad Matta) in overall victories and 10th with 167 conference wins.

Possessing an acute basketball mind and a quick wit, Painter has earned four Big Ten Coach of the Year awards, tied for the third-most in conference history since its inception in 1974 behind Keady (seven) and Bob Knight of Indiana (five).

Painter was voted by his peers as the National Association of Basketball Coaches National Coach of the Year in 2019, taking a team that started 6–5 to the Big Ten championship and NCAA Elite Eight.

"When your peers recognize you, I think they respected the job that our staff did from where we were at the beginning of the year,"

Painter said. "Coaches know how tough it is to be in a rut and to get out of that rut and achieve some level of consistency. We were able to do it, win the Big Ten and come close to the Final Four. It's a team award anytime someone receives an individual award."

Other Painter notables:

- He has averaged 22.5 wins per season at Purdue. Not counting his first transitional season (a 9–19 record), the average is 23.4 victories over the last 14 seasons.
- His average of 11.1 Big Ten wins per season is the fifth-most in conference history.
- The Boilermakers won a school-record 30 games, including a 19-game winning streak, during the 2017–18 campaign.

29 Bob Griese

At Rex Mundi High School in Evansville, Indiana, Bob Griese described himself as "a baseball player first and a basketball player second who just happened to play football."

But a tremendous work ethic under the tutelage of assistant coach Bob DeMoss enabled Griese to rise from seventh on the depth chart as a freshman to become one of the Boilermakers' premier quarterbacks from 1964 to 1966.

"I didn't know what I was doing until Purdue came and offered me a scholarship," said Griese, who also played basketball for the Boilermakers for one season. "That gave me an opportunity to make something of my life. Purdue opened the door, and I walked through it."

After beating out Doug Holcomb, son of former Purdue head coach Stu, for the starting position as a sophomore, Griese made his debut against Ohio University at Ross-Ade Stadium on September 26, 1964. He scored two touchdowns, kicked both extra points, and added a field goal to account for all the scoring in 17–0 victory. A star was born.

On their way to a 5–1 start, the Boilermakers edged fifth-ranked Michigan 21–20 in Ann Arbor on October 17. Griese threw three touchdown passes and kicked three extra points.

Griese continued his evolution in 1965 and burst onto the national scene against top-ranked Notre Dame at Ross-Ade on September 25. He completed 19 of 22 passes (86.4 percent) for a school-record 283 yards and three touchdowns as the sixth-ranked Boilermakers earned a 25–21 victory. The Fighting Irish led 21–18 with 5:20 remaining when Griese led Purdue on a four-play, 67-yard touchdown drive that was capped by a three-yard dive by Gordon Teter. Notre Dame coach Ara Parseghian called Griese's performance "sensational." "We tried everything," he added. "We used zone defenses, man for man and an exceptional rush. We were tenths of a second from getting him sometimes, but we only got him once. He was fantastic."

Griese kicked a 35-yard field goal with 55 seconds left to beat Michigan 17–15 in Ann Arbor on October 16, 1965. That year, Griese set six school game records and six season marks, including 1,719 passing yards, en route to being named a consensus All-American.

"Bob has great leadership qualities, and his athletic poise and confidence is to be envied by every coach who sees him play," Purdue head coach Jack Mollenkopf said.

As a senior, Griese broke his own school season record with 1,888 passing yards while becoming the first Purdue signal-caller to complete 60 percent of his passes (.601). He repeated as an All-American, was named the Big Ten Most Valuable Player, and finished as runner-up for the Heisman Trophy to Florida quarterback Steve Spurrier. Additionally, Griese received the Big Ten

Boilermakers in the Pro Football Hall of Fame

	Played/Coached in NFL	Inducted
Len Dawson, QB	1957–75	1987
Bob Griese, QB	1967–80	1990
Hank Stram, Coach	1960–74, 1976–77	2003
Rod Woodson, CB-S	1987–2003	2009

Medal of Honor for demonstrating great proficiency in scholarship and athletics and the Varsity Walk Award for bringing national attention to Purdue.

And, oh, by the way, Griese took the Boilermakers to the Rose Bowl for the first time.

"When we knew we were going to the Rose Bowl, I left like I was leading the entire Purdue contingent to the Promised Land, which was Pasadena," said Griese, who engineered the Boilermakers to a 14–13 win over USC. "It was incredible. The overriding factor was that we were taking part in something no one else had. We were the first, and there's something to be said for that."

Seemingly always cool and composed under fire, Griese left Purdue the career leader in passing attempts (627), completions (358), and yards (4,541), and was second with 28 touchdowns. He also was tops with 4,983 yards of total offense and 191 points scored.

Griese was selected by the Miami Dolphins with the fourth-overall pick in the 1967 NFL Draft and enjoyed a stellar 14-year professional career. Described by owner Joe Robbie as the "cornerstone of the franchise," Griese led the Dolphins to three consecutive Super Bowls (VI, VII, and VIII), winning Super Bowl VII over the Washington Redskins 14–7 to cap the only perfect season in NFL history and Super Bowl VIII over the Minnesota Vikings 24–7. Griese made eight appearances in the Pro Bowl, and his No. 12 jersey became the first Dolphins number to be retired in 1982.

A popular college football television analyst following his playing days, Griese was an inaugural member of the Purdue Intercollegiate Athletics Hall of Fame in 1994. Already enshrined in the College Football Hall of Fame in 1984 and the Pro Football Hall of Fame in 1990, Griese was the first Boilermakers alumnus to be inducted into all three shrines. He since has been joined by defensive back Rod Woodson.

Griese's son, Brian, played quarterback at Michigan from 1995 to 1997 and for 11 seasons in the NFL. He played on Rose Bowl and Super Bowl championship teams and, like his father, went on to a successful broadcasting career.

30 Terry Dischinger

Terry Dischinger was a scoring and rebounding machine for Purdue men's basketball.

From 1959 to 1962, Dischinger averaged 28.3 points and a school-record 13.7 rebounds per game. His totals of 1,979 points and 958 rebounds rank sixth and second in school history, respectively.

And nearly 60 years after playing his last game at Purdue, Dischinger remains the school career leader with 54 double-doubles—in 70 games played. How consistent was the 6'7", 190-pound center? He recorded 18 double-doubles in each of his three seasons.

His year-by-year numbers are eye-popping:

1959–60: 26.3 points and 14.3 rebounds
1960–61: 28.2 points and 13.4 rebounds
1961–62: 30.3 points and 13.4 rebounds

Dischinger owns the top three season rebounding averages in Purdue annals and three of the top nine scoring averages. He led the Big Ten in scoring all three seasons, one of only four players in conference history to do so.

There have been seven 30-point, 20-rebound games by Boilermakers all-time, and Dischinger has three of them, topping 40 points twice. He also has the most 20-point, 20-rebound performances (six) and the most 30-point, 10 rebound efforts (24).

"He had the most phenomenal pivot moves under the basket that you ever did see," the Lafayette *Journal & Courier* recalled in 1984. "He was an amazing player. Here was this tall, slim kid who had the quickness and speed of most guards, and that's how he managed to survive both offensively and defensively against big guys under the basket."

Dischinger holds the school record for most free throws made (713) and attempted (871), both by a considerable margin, while shooting with 81.9 percent accuracy from the line.

All the numbers added up to Dischinger being a three-time consensus All-American, earning second-team honors as a sophomore and first-team recognition as a junior and senior. He suitably was a member of the inaugural class selected for the Purdue Intercollegiate Athletics Hall of Fame in 1994.

A native of Terre Haute, Indiana, Dischinger was selected for the 1960 U.S. Olympic team, which won a gold medal in Rome after winning its games by an average of 42 points. The squad included all-time greats Oscar Robinson, Jerry Lucas, and Jerry West, and Dischinger, at age 19, was the fourth-leading scorer at 11.8 points per game.

"The first thing that comes to mind is that it was like a fairy tale or a dream," Dischinger said. "The Olympics were the highest mark of my athletic career. Especially with that team. For years, we were acclaimed the greatest team ever assembled. All our guys were such good all-around basketball players."

After Purdue, Dischinger was selected with the first pick of the second round (No. 8 overall) in the 1962 NBA Draft by the Chicago Zephyrs. He was named the 1963 Rookie of the Year and enjoyed a nine-year professional career that included stints with the Baltimore Bullets (1963–64), Detroit Pistons (1964–65, 1968–72), and Portland Trail Blazers (1972–73) and three All-Star games. He did not play in 1965–66 and 1966–67 while serving as a captain in the U.S. Army during the Vietnam War.

While stationed in Honolulu—where he played and coached basketball and was named Most Valuable Player of the Hawaiian League—Dischinger decided he wanted to practice dentistry after his basketball career concluded.

Dischinger, who majored in chemical engineering at Purdue, enrolled at the University of Tennessee Dental School in Memphis in 1968 and took classes during the NBA offseason. He ultimately settled in Lake Oswego, Oregon, as an orthodontist.

"I think Purdue has been the foundation of my life outside of the values which my parents raised me on," said Dischinger, who also played baseball as a senior. "The education and sports background from Purdue have been the foundation of everything else I've done in my life."

In 2019, Dischinger was inducted into the National Collegiate Basketball Hall of Fame.

31 Ryan Kerrigan

Joe Tiller liked players with "high motors." The Purdue head coach really liked Ryan Kerrigan.

Unheralded out of Muncie, Indiana, Kerrigan was the epitome of a self-made player. He possessed a tremendous work ethic and desire, and that combination led him to becoming one of the best players in the country.

Kerrigan played for the Boilermakers from 2007 to 2010. A member of the Den of Defensive Ends, he is the Purdue career record-holder with 14 fumbles forced, ranks tied for second with 33.5 sacks and is fifth with 57.0 tackles for loss.

As a senior, Kerrigan was a unanimous All-American, the Big Ten Defensive Player of the Year, and the Big Ten Defensive Lineman of the Year after leading the country with 26.0 tackles for loss (third-most in school history). Kerrigan also recorded 12.5 sacks among his 70 total tackles and five fumbles forced that season. He served as a captain and was selected team Most Valuable Player.

Kerrigan led the country with seven fumbles forced his junior season to go with 66 tackles, including 18.5 for loss and 13 sacks (tied for fourth in school history). He earned first-team All-Big Ten honors as a junior and a senior.

An education major, Kerrigan was a second-team Academic All-American his junior season and a three-time Academic All-Big Ten honoree. He earned the Big Ten Outstanding Sportsmanship Award as a senior.

Kerrigan was selected with the 16th pick of the 2011 NFL Draft by the Washington Redskins. A four-time Pro Bowl selection (2012, 2016, 2017, and 2018) at linebacker, he started the first 139 games of his nine-year professional career before an injury forced him to the sideline on December 1, 2019. It ranked as the fourth-longest streak among active NFL players. Entering the 2020 season, Kerrigan had 90 sacks to rank second in Redskins' annals behind only Dexter Manley with 91.

"I can't even begin to express how much he's meant to this organization, what he's contributed, what he means to his teammates and the type of pro that he is day in and day out," Redskins interim head coach Bill Callahan said to Redskins.com in 2019. "He's a consummate pro as you just watch him around the facility, in the meeting room, on the field. There's no better example of what a pro should be in the NFL than Ryan Kerrigan."

Kerrigan is tremendously active in the community. In 2013, he launched Ryan Kerrigan's Blitz for the Better Foundation, which provides opportunities, support and resources to children and families in need in the Washington metropolitan area. He was the Redskins' Walter Payton Man of the Year in 2015.

32 "Boiler Up"

To bring more enthusiasm to football games at Ross-Ade Stadium, Arnette Tiller came up with the phrase "Boiler Up" in 1997, the first year her husband, Joe, was head coach of the Boilermakers.

"I grew up hearing Cowboy Up, which can mean all the good things that being a cowboy represents, adopt a tough approach to a situation or simply to quit whining," Arnette said. "When we arrived at Purdue, they had been in the doldrums for a long time, and the fans were uninvolved to say the least. We needed to come up with something to get them engaged. I thought Boiler Up was the perfect thing to be said."

Arnette met with the Purdue cheerleaders to figure out how best to integrate Boiler Up into their cheers, ultimately settling on *Boiler up, clap, clap.* "And we were off," she said. "Thank God there was a lot to cheer about, so there were ample opportunities for the students to get involved, and then the rest of the fans joined in."

For his part, Joe Tiller began adding the inscription Boiler Up! to every autograph he signed and continued doing so throughout his successful 12-year tenure, during which he became the winningest football coach in Purdue history while leading the Boilermakers to 10 bowl games.

At the same time, Arnette purchased an authentic train whistle that was mounted on the video board at the south end of Ross-Ade. Members of the Reamer Club student group would blow the whistle after every Purdue touchdown.

There were plenty of reasons to Boiler Up and blow that whistle in 1997, as the Boilermakers, spurred by their high-octane passing offense, won nine games, beginning with a 28–17 upset of 12th-ranked Notre Dame on September 13 and ending with a 33–20 victory over Oklahoma State in the Alamo Bowl. They averaged 33 points per game, then the second-most ever by a Purdue team. Football was enjoyable again, and Arnette described every win as Christmas morning.

Boiler Up earned a permanent spot in the Boilermakers lexicon, and fans universally greet one another by exclaiming the byword. The hashtag #BoilerUp is used regularly with social media posts campus wide. Boiler Up even has been incorporated into the Purdue fight song, *Hail Purdue*, following the phrase, "Thus we raise our song anew."

What Arnette didn't know at the time of Boiler Up's origin was that in the days of steam-powered locomotives, when the fireman got the fire in the coal box hot enough for the engine to run, he would exclaim, "Boiler's up!"

33 David Boudia

When sports fans nationally think of Purdue, their minds inevitably turn to some of the all-time basketball and football greats who have played for the Boilermakers.

In recent years, however, some of the most accomplished Purdue athletes on the world stage have trained and competed in the building now known as the Morgan J. Burke Aquatic Center.

Under the tutelage of coach Adam Soldati, the Purdue diving program has attracted some of the top divers from around the nation. Through the 2019–20 season, the five-time NCAA Coach of the Year's tenure has included 12 NCAA champions, 50 All-Americans, and four Olympic medalists.

One diver stands out in that impressive haul of international accomplishments: David Boudia.

The Texas native once declared he had been "petrified" to attempt a dive from the 10-meter platform. Yet it has become the event with which he is most associated.

At the 2012 London Olympics, Boudia teamed with Nicholas McCrory to win bronze in synchronized 10-meter platform diving. It was the first men's diving medal for the United States since 1996.

However, Boudia's solo attempt in the event almost ended in the preliminaries, where he sat in 18th place. A strong third-place finish in the semifinals, however, propelled him into the finals.

Britain's Tom Daley delighted the home crowd by taking the lead going into the final round. Boudia responded by nailing his back 2 ½ somersault with 2 ½ twists and received a score of 102.60. When China's Qiu Bo—the defending world champion—scored 100.80 with the same dive, Boudia had a gold medal with a total score of 568.65.

"This is so surreal," Boudia said in the *Indianapolis Star.* "I can't believe I'm an Olympic champion. It was all about perspective, knowing God was in control and having that peace knowing whatever happens, happens."

Boudia became the first U.S. diver to win gold since 2000, the first U.S. man to win gold since 1992, and the first to win in the 10-meter platform event since 1988.

Four years later, at the 2016 Olympics in Rio de Janeiro, Boudia partnered with another Boilermaker—Steele Johnson—to take silver in the synchronized 10-meter platform event. Attempting to defend his individual title in that event, Boudia won bronze.

Among his other career accolades, Boudia is a 20-time USA Diving national champion and seven-time USA Diving Athlete of the Year (2008, 2010–15).

Following speculation about his future, Boudia announced in October 2017 that he would attempt to qualify for the 2020 Olympics in Tokyo. However, after suffering a concussion in practice in February 2018, Boudia decided to alter the event in which he specialized. He left the 10-meter platform behind to focus on 3-meter springboard.

With only a few healthy weeks in which to prepare, Boudia won the U.S. Nationals championship in 3-meter in May 2019, moving on to the FINA World Championships and keeping another Olympic dream alive, even if he will have to wait until 2021 to see it through.

"It's freaky up there, and I now realize after 15 years up there that it is pretty scary," Boudia said of the 10-meter dives. "At the same time, I don't think I would have been able to have a career on springboard.

"I don't know what I'm capable of down there. Making this switch is perfect for where I was in my career."

34 Mount's 61 Points Against Iowa

March 2, 1970, could have been one of the crowning games in the Rick Mount era of Purdue basketball.

Iowa came to Mackey Arena with a two-game lead on the Boilermakers in the Big Ten race, with two games remaining. The game easily should be remembered as the night Mount's league-record 61 points gave Purdue another chance at sharing the championship.

Instead, the game is remembered for an abundance of fouls, including a technical on the crowd that resulted in a six-point possession for the Hawkeyes in their eventual title-clinching 108–107 victory.

Mount, already the top scorer in Purdue and Big Ten history, came out blistering. His first five field goals accounted for all the Boilermakers' scoring in an early 10–6 lead.

Mount soon had to carry the load, however, with many of his fellow starters mired in foul trouble. Purdue was called for 20 fouls in the first half. Tyrone Bedford accounted for four of them, and three others starters were hit with three apiece.

"Iowa just played a hell of a game, and I'd rate it as strong as the club we took to the NCAA tourney last year," Purdue head coach George King said in the Lafayette *Journal & Courier*, referring to the Boilermakers' national runner-up squad of 1969.

"It's just a shame we had to have these kinds of people work a game this important."

Purdue fans apparently shared their coach's frustration, such that the referee had to warn them a technical foul would be assessed if any more paper or debris were thrown onto the playing floor.

With Purdue up 70–67 in the second half, Iowa's Steve Calabria scored while being fouled by Steve Longfellow. Someone threw a wad of paper on to the floor. The officials followed through with their threat and assessed a technical foul.

Calabria made his and-one and one technical free throw. The Hawkeyes also retained possession, and Glenn Vidnovic's basket completed the one-possession 6–0 run for a three-point Iowa lead.

"The crowd tested the officials, and the officials turned on the crowd," Iowa coach Ralph Miller said in the *Journal & Courier*. "It's ridiculous. Debris thrown on the floor can hurt a player— theirs as well as ours.

"It was a nice time, for us, for it to happen,"

Yet with 3:40 to play, Purdue still held a 101–92 lead. King tried a 3–2 zone to protect his players from their still-building foul trouble. The Hawkeyes, however, kept coming.

Fred Brown hit a pair of baskets back-to-back to cut the Boilermaker lead to 103–100. Starters Bob Ford and Beford fouled out within seven seconds of one another.

Iowa later went ahead when John Johnson sank a baseline jumper for a 106–105 advantage. Vidnovic hit a pair of free throws with 10 seconds left to ice it in the pre–3-point era.

Mount made 27 of 47 shots from the field and 7 of 8 at the free throw line. The last bucket came when he drove the length of the court before the final buzzer. That provided little solace as he summed when asked about his record day in the locker room after the game.

"But we lost," Mount said.

35 "Big Dog's" Biggest Game

In mid-March 1994, fewer teams were hotter than Purdue, and no player was on a roll comparable to Glenn Robinson.

Entering a March 13 game against Illinois at Mackey Arena, the Boilermakers had won four games in a row and eight of their last nine. Robinson had scored 30 or more points in five straight games en route to leading the NCAA in scoring with a 30.3 average.

That day against the Fighting Illini, though, Purdue and "Big Dog" both reached new heights.

Robinson did a little bit of everything in a 87–77 victory. He made 18 of 26 shots from the field—including five 3-pointers—and was 8 of 10 from the free throw line for a career-best 49 points. He grabbed five rebounds and swiped five steals.

In the final minutes, Robinson missed the front end of a 1-and-1 and fumbled away a fast-break chance. Those small gaffes, after the outcome had been decided, kept him from recording only the seventh 50-plus point performance in school history.

"We've never had a player impact the Big Ten like he did," Illinois coach Lou Henson said after the game. "He's great."

Robinson twice went on personal streaks of double-digit points. The second one—a 13–0 run—came after Illinois had pulled within two points. He scored on an alley-oop slam, on another gravity-defying close-range shot in which he hung in their air long enough to draw a foul, and on a 3-pointer with two minutes left to push the Purdue lead to 10 points.

Purdue scored 47 second-half points, and 32 of them came from Robinson.

"It was a great time to get into the zone," Robinson said. "I've been waiting on one of these kind of games since I first started my career at Purdue."

After the game, Purdue was awarded the No. 1 seed in the NCAA Tournament Southeast Regional.

Robinson's Purdue career lasted four more games. He led the Boilermakers to the Elite Eight, where they fell to Duke 69–60.

36 Rod Woodson

Rod Woodson, who was inducted into the Purdue Intercollegiate Athletics Hall of Fame in 2003, the Pro Football Hall of Fame in 2009, and the College Football Hall of Fame in 2016, is one of only two Boilermakers to be a member of all three shrines. Quarterback Bob Griese is the other.

A native of Fort Wayne, Indiana, Woodson played for the Boilermakers from 1983 to 1986. As a senior, he was a consensus All-American and runner-up for the Jim Thorpe Award. He was a first-team All-Big Ten selection his sophomore, junior, and senior seasons, one of only four players in school history to be honored three times.

Woodson tied the Purdue career record with 11 interceptions (since broken and now tied for third) and owned the record for interceptions returned for touchdowns with three (also since broken and now second). Likewise, he established the Purdue mark for solo tackles with 320 (now second); he also ranks fourth in total tackles (445) and ninth in pass breakups (29). Woodson left Purdue as the career leader with 1,535 kickoff return yards, which now ranks fifth.

"Without a doubt, Rod is the most extraordinary athlete that I was associated with during my playing days at Purdue and in the NFL," said Calvin Williams, who was Woodson's teammate in 1985 and 1986.

In his final collegiate game on November 22, 1986, Woodson played both ways in the Boilermakers' 17–15 Old Oaken Bucket victory over Indiana. He started at tailback and rushed for a team season-high 93 yards on 15 carries while catching three passes for 67 yards. At his usual cornerback position, he recorded 10 tackles, one pass breakup, and one forced fumble. He also returned three punts for 30 yards and two kickoffs for 46 yards. In all, Woodson appeared in an astounding 137 plays, approximately 90 percent of the game.

In his final collegiate game on November 22, 1986, against Indiana, Rod Woodson appeared in an astounding 137 plays, approximately 90 percent of the game.

"I've seen a lot of football, and I've never seen a young man play a game like that," head coach Leon Burtnett said afterward. "If he's not the best player in this conference, I don't believe I've seen him. I wouldn't trade anybody in the country for Rod Woodson."

In the 1987 NFL Draft, the Pittsburgh Steelers picked Woodson with the 10th overall pick. He played defensive back for 17 seasons with the Steelers (1987–96), San Francisco 49ers (1997), Baltimore Ravens (1998–2001), and Oakland Raiders (2002–03). He retired with 71 interceptions, the third-most in NFL history, a then-league-record 1,483 interception return yards, a league-record 12 interception returns for touchdowns, and 32 fumble recoveries. Woodson was selected to 11 Pro Bowls, and, in 1994, he was one of only five active players to be selected to the NFL's 75th Anniversary Team. In 2019, Wooden was named one of the NFL's 100 greatest players of all-time.

Woodson is one of only 10 players in NFL history to reach the Super Bowl with three different teams: XXX with the Steelers, XXXV with the Ravens (a 34–7 win over the New York Giants), and XXXVII with the Raiders. He was the 1993 NFL Defensive Player of the Year.

Woodson became just the 62nd individual elected to the Pro Football Hall of Fame in his first year of eligibility, and he was the fourth individual with Purdue ties to be enshrined, following quarterback Len Dawson (1987), Griese (1990), and running back and assistant coach Hank Stram (2003).

Woodson also ran track at Purdue and twice earned All-America honors in the hurdles. He was a five-time Big Ten champion and still boasts school records in the 60- and 110-meter hurdles.

Following his retirement from the NFL, Woodson worked as an analyst for the NFL Network and Big Ten Network from 2003 to 2011. He spent the 2011 season as the Raiders' cornerbacks coach before resuming his broadcasting career with Westwood One as a college football analyst in 2012 and 2013. Woodson interned with the Steelers in training camp in 2013 and participated in the Bill Walsh Minority Coaching Fellowship Program with the Denver Broncos during the 2014 offseason. Woodson returned to Oakland as assistant defensive backs coach in 2015 and subsequently was promoted back to cornerbacks coach in 2017.

1943 Boilermakers

The World World II effort took hundreds of thousands of young men from their homes and everyday lives. As you might expect, it affected college attendance and athletic participation on campuses, including at Purdue. Many colleges discontinued their football programs. The effects also were felt at the professional level, with the Philadelphia Eagles and Pittsburgh Steelers temporarily combining to form the "Steagles" for the 1943 season.

Certainly, such a toll was a small price to pay in the greater context. However, the 1942 Purdue football team was hit especially hard. They won only one of their nine games—a 7–6 victory at Northwestern—and were shut out five times and outscored 179–27 overall. Many of that team's starters, including future NFL Hall of Famer Hank Stramm, were headed for active military duty in the offseason.

Yet a year later, the war effort helped lift Purdue football to one of its greatest seasons.

Purdue had previously served as a training site for the Armed Services. Beginning in July 1943, it became the home to the V-12 Navy College Training Program. Over 1,200 sailors and marines lived in Cary Quadrangle and campus fraternities.

The Army did not allow its personnel to compete in intercollegiate athletics. The Navy and Marines, however, had no such restrictions. So 26 Marines and nine sailors bolstered the Boilermakers' 1943 roster.

Some of these servicemen resumed careers at Purdue that had begun at other schools. Alex Agase was an All-American right guard at Illinois—one of a dozen former Fighting Illini to join the Boilermakers. He gained some renown for scoring four touchdowns in a game at Minnesota in 1942—becoming only the second college guard to accomplish the feat.

Lou DeFilippo had been an All-American lineman at Fordham. One of Agase's Illini teammates, fullback Tony Butkovich, also enlisted in the Marines and converted to Purdue colors.

Behind those talented linemen, Butkovich enjoyed a breakout season for a Purdue team that quickly stormed up the national rankings. A 3–0 start vaulted the Boilermakers to No. 7 in the Associated Press poll. After a 30–7 victory at Ohio State, a 28–7 home victory over Iowa, and a 32–0 blanking at Wisconsin, Purdue had the No. 2 team in the nation. It grabbed a record five interceptions in that last game—a testament to owning one of the nation's stoutest defenses.

Butkovich led the nation in rushing that season, totaling 833 yards on 142 carries (5.9 average) with 16 touchdowns—still tied for the school record. In the documentary *Perfect Warriors* about the 1943 season, written and directed by Cory Palm, the story goes that head coach Elmer Burnham called for an onside kick late in that lopsided win over Wisconsin to get the ball back so Butkovich could score again and break the Big Ten's season scoring record.

But that rout of Wisconsin was Butkovich's last game as a Boilermaker. He and eight teammates, including Agase, were called up to active duty by the Marines. They shipped out to Parris Island, Texas, the next day, missing the final two games of the season.

Purdue, however, kept winning. Sam Vacanti's touchdown pass to Babe Dimancheff with 38 seconds remaining beat Minnesota 14–7. Vacanti's early touchdown pass to end Frank Bauman a week later—and the defense's fourth shutout—gave the Boilermakers a 7–0 victory over Indiana for the Old Oaken Bucket and a share of the Big Ten title.

No other team that played as many games as Purdue finished with an undefeated record. However, the Boilermakers only ranked fifth in the final AP poll, and they received merely 12 of over 130 first-place votes cast.

Notre Dame, which took a 9–0 record and the No. 1 ranking into the final week, finished No. 1 despite losing to Great Lakes Navy in its finale. Purdue had beaten the same Great Lakes Navy team to open the season. The Irish received 86 first-place votes.

Iowa Pre-Flight—another team with a Naval connection—Michigan, and Navy also finished ahead of Purdue in the poll. Purdue did not play Michigan that season, and the teams shared the conference championship with 6–0 records.

A relatively soft schedule may have hurt the Boilermakers' cause for a higher ranking. Minnesota was the only other opponent to post a winning record besides Great Lakes Navy. Purdue outscored opponents 214–55 over nine games—an average margin of victory of almost 18 points per game.

Agase again earned All-American recognition, then fought in the battles of Okinawa and Iwo Jima, earning a Purple Heart for wounds sustained in action. After the war, he returned to Illinois to complete his collegiate football career.

Agase spent six seasons in the NFL before beginning a coaching career that included head coaching tenures at Northwestern and Purdue.

Butkovich also was an All-American, despite missing those final two games. In April 1945, he was killed in action at Okinawa.

Other notable players from that team included Dick Berwagen, an offensive lineman who was named to four Pro Bowls as well as the NFL's All-Decade team for the 1950s. Dimancheff returned to lead the team in rushing in 1944 and was named first-team All-Big Ten. Halfback Bump Elliott went on to coach Michigan to a Rose Bowl championship and spent 21 years as Iowa's athletics director.

Cecil Isbell took over for Burnham as head coach in 1944, leading Purdue to a 5–5 record.

That 1943 season remains the most recent undefeated season in Purdue football history.

38 Ending Notre Dame's 39-Game Winning Streak in 1950

Purdue football suffered its third straight losing season in 1950, as the Boilermakers posted a 2–7 record.

One of the wins, however, was historic: 28–14 over No. 1–ranked Notre Dame in South Bend on October 7, snapping the Fighting Irish's 39-game unbeaten streak. The victory marked Purdue's first ever over a top-ranked team and led to the nickname "Spoilermakers."

Sophomore quarterback Dale Samuels had a coming-out party with 151 yards passing and two touchdowns, a 35-yarder to halfback Neil Schmidt just before halftime that gave Purdue a 21–0 advantage and a 56-yarder to senior halfback Mike Maccioli in the fourth quarter. The 5'9" Samuels benefitted from a new forma-tion—the moving pocket—in which he would roll out instead of dropping back and having his vision blocked by tall linemen.

"Purdue was beautifully prepared for this game, much better than we were," Notre Dame head coach Frank Leahy said. "I enjoy the pressure a winning streak builds up, but if we had to lose I'm happy it was to our wonderful friends and rivals from Purdue."

When the Boilermakers returned home, they were greeted at the Big Four Train Station downtown with a crowd so large that the mile-long-plus bus trip back to campus was wall-to-wall people. Those who witnessed the event say the only bigger celebration the city has ever seen was after the Japanese surrendered to end World War II.

What followed, though, was a six-game losing streak for Purdue, snapped with a 13–0 victory over Indiana in the season finale on November 25. Samuels became the first quarterback in school history to pass for 1,000 yards (he finished with 1,076) and throw 10 touchdown passes.

In 1952, Samuels led the Boilermakers to a Big Ten co-championship (with Wisconsin). His career totals of 259 completions, 3,161 passing yards, and 27 passing touchdowns still rank in the top 20 on Purdue lists. Samuels was a perfect 3-for-3 in games against intrastate rival Indiana.

Samuels essentially proved to be a lifelong Boilermaker. He was selected in the third round of the 1953 NFL Draft by his hometown Chicago Cardinals but never played professionally. Samuels had two coaching stints at Purdue, from 1960 to 1963 under Jack Mollenkopf and from 1970 to 1972 under Bob DeMoss. Samuels served as associate director of the Purdue Alumni Association in 1968 and 1969; administrative assistant to head football coaches Alex Agase, Jim Young, and Leon Burtnett from 1973 to 1979 and 1981 to 1982; and associate athletics director from 1983 until his retirement in 1995. He also provided football color commentary on WASK radio in Lafayette for five seasons (1977–81). Samuels was inducted into the Purdue Athletics Hall of Fame in 2001.

One of Samuels' most-significant accomplishments as an administrator was overseeing the development and construction of the Mollenkopf Athletic Center, which opened in 1990 featuring the largest indoor practice facility of its kind in the nation. Three decades later, it continues to be a focal point for player development and recruiting and ties in niftily with the Kozuch Football Performance Complex.

"I can't imagine there is a football program in the country with better facilities than what we have at Purdue," Samuels said. "When I think back to my freshman year in 1949 and then walk through the facilities now, it's just amazing what has been done. Having said that, bricks and mortar are one thing, but it is the people that make the difference, and Purdue is special because of the people. Always has been, always will be."

In 1992, Samuels introduced the W flag at Ross-Ade Stadium to signify a Boilermaker win. He got the idea from the Chicago Cubs, who have flown a W flag at their home ballpark, Wrigley Field, following victorious games since the late 1930s.

"I took the idea to Jim Colletto (the Boilermakers' head coach from 1991 to 1996), and he agreed to it," Samuels said. "We opened the 1992 season with a big victory over nationally ranked California, the flag went up atop the scoreboard and the fans liked it. I am very appreciative that the tradition has continued over the years."

39 E'Twaun Moore

No one has played more in a Purdue men's basketball uniform than E'Twaun Moore.

In 140 games, Moore was on the court for a school-record 4,517 minutes, an average of 32.3 per contest. And, oh, he was productive, scoring 2,136 points, the third-most in school annals, trailing only Rick Mount (2,323) and Joe Barry Carroll (2,175).

Moore, whose 136 games started are tops among all Boilermakers, ranked third in 3-point field goals (243), fourth in total field goals (780), sixth in steals (164), and 12th in assists (400) through the 2019–20 season.

Moreover, Moore became merely the third player in Big Ten history to record 2,000 points, 500 rebounds (611), and 400 assists in a career, following Steve Smith of Michigan State and Talor Battle of Penn State.

Gary Parrish of CBSSports.com described Moore thusly: "He's merely one of the most consistent performers in the nation and among the most well-rounded players in conference history."

Moore earned second-team All-Big Ten honors as a freshman and sophomore and first-team glories as a junior and senior. The organizational leadership and supervision major was a second-team Academic All-American in 2010 and a third-team All-American in 2011.

On February 20, 2011, Moore poured in a career-high 38 points to lead the Boilermakers to a 76–63 victory over No. 2 Ohio State at Mackey Arena.

Throughout his career, Moore played without bravado—a trait he traces to his growing up in a challenging East Chicago, Indiana, neighborhood.

"I think it's just my personality, not to be too flashy," Moore said in a 2010 interview with *Gold & Black Illustrated*. "Sometimes growing up, especially where I come from, if you do too much talking and hollering, people look at you as cocky or arrogant. When I score, I've always looked at it like, 'Okay, that's something I was supposed to do.'"

Purdue earned NCAA Tournament berths each of Moore's four seasons, advancing to the Sweet 16 in 2009 and 2010. Furthermore, Moore was a member of the Boilermakers' 2009 Big Ten Tournament title team and the 2010 regular season championship squad. Moore and classmate JaJuan Johnson won a school-record 107 games.

As a prep senior, Moore led East Chicago Central High School to the Class 4A state championship, scoring 28 points in the title game. One of his teammates was Kawann Short, who went on to play football at Purdue and became an All-Pro performer with the Carolina Panthers.

Moore was selected in the second round (No. 55 overall) of the 2011 NBA Draft by the Boston Celtics and subsequently has played for the Orlando Magic (2013–14), Chicago Bulls (2015–16), and New Orleans Pelicans (2017–20). Moore started 80 of 82 regular season games and all nine playoff contests for the Pelicans in 2017–18.

Since 2012, Moore has returned to his high school during the summer to conduct a youth basketball camp.

"One thing we want to do is help give these kids a lesson on life," Moore said. "Getting a good education is important. As for basketball, we want them to enjoy themselves.

"There aren't that many guys from my city the kids can look up to who are doing positive things. Hopefully me playing basketball and doing it at a high level can give them inspiration to do the same thing, or to do something even better."

40 Breakfast Club

Noon Eastern Time remains the traditional kickoff time by which many college football fans set their watches every fall.

In West Lafayette, however, gameday starts much earlier. It is called Breakfast Club—a tradition that began in the 1980s around the time the movie of the same name was released. While that film centered on a day in the life of high schoolers sequestered in the library for punishment, the Purdue gameday version of Breakfast Club promotes expression and revelry and mingling between students, alumni, and fans.

Above all, Breakfast Club is known for one thing: costumes. The more outrageous, outlandish and/or clever, the better—though it is important to retain a certain homemade quality. Groups of friends often coordinate their costumes around a theme. From pop culture favorites to the borderline risqué to just plain bizarre, the dress-up tradition is one of the most unique in the Big Ten if not in all of college football.

Police and barricades are present to monitor the situation and direct the flow of participants. Bars open at 7:00 AM, and many of them offer specials catering to the occasion. Festivities typically last through 10:00 AM or so, when Breakfast Clubbers head over to Ross-Ade Stadium to meet up with their tailgates or find somewhere to continue partying.

The Breakfast Club tradition goes on hiatus at the end of football season but returns each spring for the Purdue Grand Prix.

Of all of the traditions associated with Purdue sports, arguably none is as visceral or authentic as this morning wake-up routine.

41 Den of Defensive Ends

With its history of Super Bowl-winning and Hall of Fame passers, Purdue is known throughout college football as the Cradle of Quarterbacks.

Perhaps less known is the Boilermakers' reputation for terrorizing quarterbacks on the other side of the ball. In 2004, Tom

Schott coined the phrase "Den of Defensive Ends" to describe the program's prolific ability to turn out pass rushers.

The tradition ramped up under head coach Joe Tiller, and nine Purdue defensive ends were selected in the NFL Draft from 1999 to 2015. A select group of a dozen players have been inducted into the Den of Defensive Ends, including eight who reached the Pro Bowl and four who played for Super Bowl champions.

Leo Sugar (1949–51)
Sugar's Boilermaker career culminated in consensus All-American and first-team All-Big Ten honors as a senior. He played in two Pro Bowls in his nine-year NFL career.

Lamar Lundy (1954–56)
The first Black star athlete at Purdue, the 6'7" Lundy earned most valuable player honors in both basketball and football as a senior in 1956. With the NFL's Los Angeles Rams, he teamed with Rosey Grier, Deacon Jones, and Merlin Olson on the "Fearsome Foursome" defensive front.

Keena Turner (1976–79)
The converted tight end led Purdue in tackles for loss in three straight seasons. In his final two seasons alone, Turner recorded 48 takedowns in the backfield. He moved again, to outside linebacker, to help the San Francisco 49ers win four Super Bowls.

Chike Okeafor (1994–96, 1998)
The West Lafayette native opened his career at linebacker, leading Purdue in tackles as a sophomore. After Tiller's arrival and a one-year suspension for off-field issues, Okeafor returned as a defensive end. His 10-year NFL career included a 2008 Super Bowl trip with Arizona.

Rosevelt Colvin (1995–98)

A multi-sport star at Indianapolis' Broad Ripple High School, Colvin twice earned All-Big Ten honors. He holds the program's career sacks record with 35. He earned a spot on the Chicago Bears' All-Decade team, then won two Super Bowls with the New England Patriots.

Akin Ayodele (1999–2001)

After beginning his career at Coffeyville Community College in Kansas, Ayodele made an immediate impact by leading the Boilermakers in sacks his first two seasons. Purdue's Most Valuable Player in 2001 went on to a nine-year NFL career.

Shaun Phillips (2000–03)

Another converted tight end, Phillips caught a couple of touchdown passes in his Boilermakers career. He ranks among Purdue's all-time leaders in sacks (33.5, tied for second) and tackles for loss (60.5, third). His 11-year NFL career included a Pro Bowl selection with San Diego in 2010 and a Super Bowl appearance with Denver in 2013.

Ray Edwards (2003–05)

Edwards' Boilermakers career peaked with eight sacks and an honorable mention All-Big Ten selection in 2004. He made a bigger impact in the NFL with the Minnesota Vikings and Atlanta Falcons, where he recorded 224 tackles and 33 sacks over seven seasons.

Rob Ninkovich (2004–05)

Though he played only two seasons at Purdue after transferring from Joliet Community College, Ninkovich's 16 sacks rank in the career top 10. While he didn't start until midway through his senior season, he earned Most Valuable Player honors with team highs of 17 tackles for loss and eight sacks. He recorded 425 tackles and 46 sacks in his 131-game NFL career, winning a pair of Super Bowl rings with the New England Patriots.

Anthony Spencer (2004–06)

As a senior, the Fort Wayne native became the fourth defensive end named team Most Valuable Player in the first decade of Tiller's tenure. He ranks in the Boilermakers' career top 10 in both sacks (21) and tackles for loss (44). A first-round pick of the Dallas Cowboys, he made the Pro Bowl in 2010 as the only NFL player with 90-plus tackles and double-digit sacks.

Cliff Avril (2004–07)

Avril didn't convert to defensive end until his junior season, then went on to record the majority of his 35 career tackles for loss and 13 sacks. He helped the Seattle Seahawks win a Super Bowl title in 2013 and repeat as AFC champion the next season and went to the Pro Bowl in 2016.

Ryan Kerrigan (2007–10)

The Muncie native developed into one of the most fearsome defensive players in the Big Ten. As a senior, he was Purdue's first unanimous All-American since 1980. Only Colvin has more career sacks than Kerrigan's 33.5, and he holds two of the top five season sack efforts in team history.

42 Caleb "Biggie" Swanigan

From 2015 to 2017, the most dangerous place in the Big Ten was the space between a missed shot bouncing off of the rim and Caleb Swanigan.

"Every single rebound's a competition with nine other players on the floor," said Swanigan, Purdue's 6'8", 250-pound frontcourt star. "It's not just the other team. It's everybody. You've just got to get the ball."

Wait, nine other players?

"There's no teammates when you rebound," Swanigan said. "You've just got to get the ball."

In his two-year Purdue career, Swanigan put on a rebounding clinic throughout the Big Ten. His 436 rebounds as a sophomore in 2016–17 crushed the previous school record, and his 12.5 per-game average ranked fifth behind three seasons from Terry Dischinger and one from Wilson Eison.

The list of Boilermakers who have averaged a career double-double is both impressive and brief. After Don Beck (1953–55), Dischinger (1960–62), and Dave Schellhase (1964–66), no one—not Rick Mount, not Glenn Robinson—accomplished the feat until Swanigan's 14.4 points and 10.4 rebounds.

Yet Swanigan's story was a remarkable one long before he became the 2016 Big Ten Player of the Year and a consensus first-team All-American.

Swanigan weighed 360 pounds in middle school—an affliction for which he carries the nickname "Biggie" to this day. Drugs and other problems hovered around his family life. He spent time in homeless shelters.

When Swanigan was in eighth grade, his brother, Carl, reached out to a family friend to give his brother a chance. Roosevelt Barnes played baseball, basketball, and football at Purdue. That last sport gave him the most recognition, as Barnes reached the NFL with the Detroit Lions before beginning a career as a sports agent.

Barnes agreed to take in Swanigan, and at first the two clashed. Barnes imposed the discipline that had been missing in Swanigan's life. As the weight melted off, the teenager's basketball talent began to break through.

"Legend has it that his daddy, his biological father, was a 6'8", 400-pound point guard that could shoot with his left and his right hand," Barnes said of Carl Swanigan Sr., whose court skills earned him the nickname "Big Smooth."

"And his older brother, Carl Jr., had a tremendous basketball IQ, too. Biggie's been blessed with that."

Within a few years, Swanigan became one of the highest rated high school prospects in the nation. He earned Indiana Mr. Basketball honors in 2015 while leading Homestead to the Class 4A state championship. At the time, he had not yet chosen a college destination. When he made that choice in April, he first committed to another Big Ten program—Michigan State.

Within a few weeks, however, he backed out of that pledge and ultimately chose Purdue. He started immediately and formed an imposing frontcourt duo with 7-footer A.J. Hammons. They helped lead the Boilermakers to the 2016 Big Ten Tournament championship game.

As a freshman, Swanigan developed a reputation for both his relentless work ethic outside of games and his snarling disposition during them. He nearly departed for the NBA after one season, working out for teams and going through the evaluation process.

Swanigan learned that not only did he need to show scouts and front office personnel improved skills on the court; he also needed to show them he could lift a team.

"I'm trying to focus on helping my team, so they can see maybe I can help their team," Swanigan said in June 2016.

Did he ever.

Swanigan devoured teams throughout his sophomore season. He posted a Big Ten–record 28 double-doubles, including four 20–20 performances. His 32-point, 20-rebound domination of Norfolk State represented only the seventh 30–20 game in program history.

Swanigan averaged 18.5 points, 12.5 rebounds, and 3.1 assists. To become only the eighth player to lead the Big Ten in scoring and rebounding, the future first-round draft pick of the Portland Trail Blazers worked on his physique, refined his perimeter shot, and become more reliable in all facets.

With Swanigan's production setting the foundation, Purdue won its first Big Ten championship since 2010 and first outright title since 1996. The Boilermakers also broke a string of back-to-back first-round NCAA Tournament exits by advancing to the Sweet 16.

"I knew I would have to step my role up immensely," Swanigan told the Big Ten Network after being announced as Player of the Year. "With me doing that, I knew we could do some damage."

Purdue Pete

Who is Purdue Pete?

The costumed unofficial mascot of Purdue Athletics, Pete started out as an unnamed barrel-chested, mallet-wielding boilermaker symbol for University Book Store in 1940. Art Evans, an artist from California, created the caricature, which appeared originally as "The Boilermaker" on notebooks.

Four years later, the editors of the Purdue yearbook, the *Debris*, asked University Book Store owner Doc Epple if they could use the logo on that year's cover. Permission was granted, and when the editors asked Epple if the character had a name, he said Pete, "out of the blue," according to legend.

The 1948 *Debris* ran a photograph of the first known human Pete, but it wasn't until 1956 that he became a bona fide mascot. Larry Brumbaugh was selected "to inspire fans at home football games." He donned a sweater with a P on it over football shoulder pads with black pants and a 36-pound head created from papier-mâché, plaster apiarist, and chicken wire. The head sported a giant grin.

Since it debuted in 1956, the shape, size, and look of the Purdue Pete head has undergone six changes. Pete is the costumed unofficial mascot of Purdue Athletics.

The original head was lost in October 1962 when it blew out of the back of the Boilermaker Special on the way back from a football game at Iowa.

Since then, the shape, size, and look of the Pete head has undergone six changes. It was first made of fiberglass in 1976, weighing nearly 50 pounds. By that time, the Purdue athletics department had unveiled a new Pete logo, drawn by campus artist Keith Butz, that was "aimed to present a fierce, more competitive, tough-minded Purdue Pete to the world."

From 1980 to 1983, the significantly lighter 10-pound Pete head featured a mean look with a frown that tended to scare younger fans. A construction hardhat replaced the longstanding little square cap in 1983, when a smile returned to his face. The current version, designed and created by students in the aeronautical engineering technology department, has been around since 1989. It is made of composite materials and weighs five pounds. Although Pete's standard outfit is football-themed, he does adapt for other events (i.e. basketball jersey and shorts for a basketball game or even a tuxedo for a formal affair).

Steve Solberg, who has served as Purdue's spirit coordinator and head cheer/mascot coach since 2009, said, "When you think of a Boilermaker, you should think of Purdue Pete. He is somebody who is tough and has a certain swagger about him. But as a mascot, he has to be friendly, so he has to strike that balance. I would say his character has evolved over the years in terms of trying to make him more family friendly with how he acts around children versus adults."

At halftime of the 2011 Purdue football spring game, a new full-body suit Pete mascot was introduced and met with overwhelming disapproval. The traditional Pete was swiftly reinstated.

One student portrayed Pete each year until 1978, when a second one was selected to provide greater visibility while taking into consideration the time commitment. Currently, five students play the role and perform at all football games and all home men's and women's basketball and volleyball games (plus postseason tournaments). In addition, Pete makes appearances at other athletics events as well as around campus, throughout the Greater Lafayette community, and beyond. Whatever the event, Pete is not permitted to speak.

In 2014, Pete was a landslide winner of a *Chicago Tribune* poll of the best Big Ten mascot, receiving 74 percent of the more than seven million votes cast.

"It is really amazing to me how much our fans love Pete," Solberg said, "and how much they really just want to get a picture with him or a high-five."

From 1997 to 2007, Pete had a sidekick, Rowdy, a nearly 10-foot-tall inflatable mascot made of parachute material who had a childish look about him and represented a future Boilermaker.

44 Paint Crew

When Matt Painter succeeded Gene Keady as head men's basketball coach in 2005, the student section at Mackey Arena known as the Gene Pool needed a new name.

Meet the Paint Crew, a classy and colorful band of some 2,800 students who enthusiastically cheer on the Boilermakers while trying to wreak havoc on the opposition. A pregame fact sheet with intel about visiting players is distributed prior to each game to guide the appropriate harassing. The Paint Crew is collectively dubbed "the official sixth man" and is widely regarded as the premier student section in the country.

Paint Crew membership, which is regularly sold out, comes with benefits; most notably, entry into Mackey for games 15 minutes before other students, all of whom sit (make that stand) in general admission seating. A lottery determines the order in which Paint Crew members can enter.

Students are located at both the north and south ends of Mackey—in sections 4, 5, 13, 14, 104 to 107, and 114 to 116—so there is an equal dose of cheering and pestering throughout every game. Before tipoff, one end shouts, "Whose house?" and the other end replies, "Our house!"

For marquee games, like Indiana and Michigan State, Paint Crew members camp out the night before so those who are most dedicated get the best seats. Painter and his players regularly deliver pizza and hot chocolate to the campers. In the case of particularly cold temperatures, the athletics department requires the Paint Crew to move its campout inside.

Paint Crew members must wear either their issued T-shirt or a black Purdue basketball jersey. Themed costumes are acceptable on occasion, but "no red Purdue shirts or red of any kind will be permitted in the lower bowl under any circumstances." Signs are allowed—and encouraged—as long as they are in good taste.

Five students make up the executive board and govern the Paint Crew. Its forthright guideline: "Every member of the Paint Crew represents the Paint Crew and more importantly Purdue University. Please conduct yourself in a manner that represents Purdue University and the Paint Crew as a first-class institution and spirit group."

With the Paint Crew leading the charge, the noise inside Mackey can be downright deafening. During the Boilermakers' 86–75 Big Ten championship–clinching victory over Indiana on February 28, 2017, the boisterous cheers escalated to an arena-record 122.3 decibels (by comparison, a rock concert generally is 108 to 114 decibels).

45 Jeff Brohm

From the moment Mike Bobinski was hired as Purdue's 14th athletics director August 9, 2016, his mission was clear: find some way to turn around the Boilermakers football program.

The team was in the fourth year of Darrell Hazell's tenure as coach—one which had yielded only six victories in the first three seasons. By midseason, Bobinski decided a change had to be made. Hazell was dismissed after a 3–3 start, and the Boilermakers lost their final six games.

While a nationwide search began for a new head coach, Bobinski already had a candidate in the back of his mind. He remembered watching Louisville beat Michigan State in the 1993 Liberty Bowl. More specifically, he remembered the gutsy quarterback who led the Cardinals to that victory despite two steel pins and a steel plate in the index finger of his throwing hand.

That quarterback, Jeff Brohm, had risen through the coaching ranks following an NFL career and was three years into a successful tenure at Western Kentucky University.

On December 5, 2016, Purdue introduced Brohm as its new head coach.

"He is a coach who already has achieved tremendous success and, at the same time, has incredible upside," Bobinski said when announcing the hire. "His reputation and record of accomplishment as an innovative offensive coach and developer of quarterbacks is second to none. That pedigree, combined with his commitment to developing the complete student-athlete and doing so with integrity makes him a perfect fit for Purdue University."

Coincidentally, Purdue's 2017 season opener came against Brohm's alma mater, Louisville, at Lucas Oil Stadium in Indianapolis.

The Cardinals were ranked No. 16 in the country and led by the defending Heisman Trophy winner, Lamar Jackson, at quarterback. The Boilermakers impressed in a losing effort, leading 14–10 at halftime before falling 38–35. However, a tone had been set for a new standard.

Purdue beat Ohio 44–21 on the following Friday night to give Brohm his first victory. The real eye-opener, however, came the following week at Missouri. The Boilermakers had struggled to win any games of consequence on the road over the previous four seasons. But they went in to Columbia and routed the Tigers—a Southeastern Conference program that would play in a bowl later that season—35–3.

Ups and downs followed, but considering the malaise of the previous four seasons and modest expectations going into the season, a 4–6 record after six games seemed encouraging.

More thrills were yet to come.

Purdue went on the road November 18 and upset Iowa 24–15. A week later, the Boilermakers beat Indiana 31–24 to secure the Old Oaken Bucket and bowl eligibility for the first time since 2012.

An invitation to the Foster Farms Bowl to face Arizona sent Purdue in search of its first postseason victory since the 2011 Little Caesars Pizza Bowl. The Boilermakers dominated much of the first half. Gregory Phillips caught a pair of touchdown passes, and Spencer Evans' 26-yard field goal just before halftime gave Purdue a 31–14 lead.

Arizona stormed back, with quarterback Khalil Tate throwing three consecutive touchdown passes to account for 21 unanswered points. The third, with only 3:21 remaining, gave the Wildcats a 35–31 lead.

Purdue had one final answer. Elijah Sindelar, who had taken over sole starting quarterback duties when David Blough suffered an injury late in the season, led an eight-play, 75 yard drive. It culminated in a 38-yard touchdown pass to Anthony Mahoungou—a native of France who spent most of his career as a backup before emerging as a productive weapon in the back half of his senior season.

With a 38–35 win, Purdue finished the season 7–6—only two fewer victories than it had managed in the previous four seasons combined. Brohm's debut was generally regarded as one of the best turnaround jobs in college football that season.

That feat was even more impressive when it was learned, following the bowl victory, that Sindelar had played the final two games of the regular season—and the bowl game—with a torn knee ligament.

Brohm coached Purdue to another 6–6 regular season and bowl berth in 2018, when the Boilermakers recovered from an 0–3 start to finish in a tie for third place in the Big Ten West Division. Along the way, they knocked off three ranked opponents: No. 23 Boston College, No. 19 Iowa, and No. 2 Ohio State—a 49–20 victory that should endure as one of the most memorable ever in Purdue football history.

Bobinski had to fight to keep Brohm after both of his first two seasons. In December 2018, Louisville came after one of its favorite alums with an offer to take over the Cardinals. Brohm declined, and Purdue rewarded him with an extension that made him one of the highest-paid coaches in the nation.

46 2012 Big Ten Baseball Champions

Chicago Cubs faithful lived for generations with the year 1908 burned into their consciousness. Some fans went their entire lives knowing that was the last time their beloved team won a World Series championship without seeing them break the streak.

Purdue baseball fans endured a less-publicized drought, but one nearly as lengthy. In 1909, three years after joining the Big Ten, the Boilermakers won the conference championship. More than 100 years passed before the program won another. Purdue became a regular participant in the Big Ten Tournament under coach Dave Alexander in the 1980s. In 1987, with future major leaguer Archi Cianfrocco in the lineup, Alexander guided the Boilermakers to their first NCAA Tournament appearance.

Purdue experienced another prolonged run of success after one of Alexander's former players, Doug Schreiber, took over the program in 1999. He led the team to three runner-up Big Ten finishes and several conference tournament appearances. The Boilermakers maintained that level of competitiveness despite playing at Lambert Field, which despite its stellar playing surface and professional dimensions, had no lighting and limited seating.

After a successful 2011 season with a young nucleus of talent, Purdue originally hoped to move into a new stadium for the 2012 season. Construction delays prevented that from happening, so Lambert Field's final season coincided with a breakthrough 103 years in the making.

Purdue entered the 2012 season with a loaded lineup. Third baseman Cameron Perkins, a California native who played at Southport High School in suburban Indianapolis, still holds the state season batting average record. Another in-state product, Westfield's Kevin Plawecki, had emerged as one of the country's best catching prospects. Second baseman Eric Charles and out-fielder Barrett Serrato bolstered the lineup.

The team's top pitching prospect, Brad Schreiber (no relation to the coach), missed the entire season after undergoing "Tommy John" elbow ligament replacement surgery. Three right-handers emerged to form the starting rotation: Joe Haase, Lance Breedlove, and Robert Ramer. The bullpen featured one of the Big Ten's best combos in the late innings: left-hander Blake Mascarello and Nick

Wittgren, a local product from Lafayette's McCutcheon High School.

The program had never seen such a collection of talent—and they lived up to expectations. By the time Big Ten play began, the Boilermakers were drawing national attention for their high-powered offense and stable, consistent pitching. On April 15, Purdue swept a doubleheader against Illinois to make Schreiber the program's all-time winningest coach.

On May 12, Breedlove allowed one hit over seven shutout innings, and the Boilermakers piled up 17 hits in a 14–3 victory over Michigan to clinch that long-elusive Big Ten championship. The Boilermakers backed up their top seed by sweeping through the Big Ten Tournament. Plawecki, the Big Ten Player of the Year, hit a crucial home run in a 6–5 victory over Indiana to seal the championship.

Purdue was awarded a No. 1 seed for their regional in the NCAA Tournament. However, it could not host the tournament in the traditional sense. Construction on the team's new stadium—named Alexander Field after the family of the former coach—could not be completed before the end of the season. Lambert Field was deemed inadequate to host, so the tournament was played at U.S. Steel Yard in Gary, Indiana.

The Boilermakers' dream run ended there. After opening with a victory over Valparaiso, they bowed out with losses to Kent State (which ultimately advanced to the College World Series) and Kentucky.

The New York Mets selected Plawecki in the first round of the 2012 Major League Baseball First-Year Player Draft. Six more Boilermakers were chosen over 40 rounds, including two who joined Plawecki in the big leagues in 2017—Perkins (Philadelphia Phillies) and Wittgren (Miami Marlins). Plawecki and Wittgren subsequently reunited as teammates with the Cleveland Indians in 2019.

In 2018, under second-year coach Mark Wasikowski, Purdue returned to the NCAA Tournament.

47 Len Dawson

Len Dawson picked Purdue—over the likes of Notre Dame and Ohio State—because the Boilermakers featured a passing offense, and he believed he would have the opportunity to play early in his career.

Boy, was he right.

As a sophomore in 1954, Dawson took over at quarterback in the first quarter of the season opener against Missouri at Ross-Ade Stadium and proceeded to throw four touchdown passes in a 31–0 victory. The following week, Dawson threw four more touchdowns as Purdue upset top-ranked Notre Dame 27–14 in South Bend.

The media dubbed Dawson the "Golden Boy" following those two performances and, soon after, the Purdue "All-American" Marching Band named its newly introduced baton twirler the "Golden Girl," a position that remains a treasured tradition.

Dawson went on to set school season records with 1,464 passing yards and an NCAA-best 15 passing touchdowns.

A jammed thumb prior to the start of the 1955 season deterred Dawson's progress, but he still managed to throw for 1,005 yards. He topped the Big Ten in total offense three consecutive seasons and left Purdue as the school career record-holder in passing yards (3,325) and touchdown passes (29).

"I was fortunate that I was a passing quarterback in high school," said Dawson, who matriculated to West Lafayette from

Alliance, Ohio. "Purdue was one of the few schools in the country that threw the football."

The Pittsburgh Steelers selected Dawson with the fifth overall pick of the 1957 NFL Draft. He was a seldom-used backup for five seasons with the Steelers (1957–59) and Cleveland Browns (1960–61), passing for merely 204 yards and two touchdowns in 28 games, before getting a career-changing break.

The Dallas Texans of the upstart American Football League signed Dawson prior to the 1962 season. The Texans were coached by Hank Stram, an assistant at Purdue when Dawson played there, and the pair had a sterling relationship. Dawson promptly led the league with 29 touchdown passes and was named player of the year while guiding the Texans to the AFL championship with a 20–17 double-overtime victory over the two-time defending champion Houston Oilers.

The Texans became the Kansas City Chiefs in 1963, and Dawson led the Chiefs to Super Bowls I and IV. In Super Bowl IV on January 11, 1970, Dawson completed 12 of 17 passes for 142 yards and a touchdown en route to a 23–7 win over the Minnesota Vikings. He was named the game's Most Valuable Player.

Six times, the pinpoint accurate Dawson topped the AFL in completion percentage, and his 182 touchdown passes from 1962 to 1969 were more than any other pro quarterback. He was selected to six AFL All-Star games and the 1972 NFL Pro Bowl and was honored as the NFL Man of the Year in 1973.

Dawson owned the Chiefs' season record with 30 touchdown passes from 1964 to 2018, when Patrick Mahomes broke it.

Dawson retired following the 1975 season, finishing his career with 28,711 passing yards and 239 touchdown passes. He was inducted into the Pro Football Hall of Fame in 1987 and the Purdue Intercollegiate Athletics Hall of Fame in 1996.

As a player, Dawson also worked as a television announcer in Kansas City and would go on to gain fame as the host of *Inside the*

NFL on HBO from 1977 to 2001. He also served as radio analyst for Chiefs games from 1985 to 2017. Dawson received the Pete Rozelle Radio-Television Award for his longtime contributions as a sports broadcaster in 2012.

48 Big Draw in the Big Apple

In modern times, the biggest basketball games are played in the biggest arenas. Converted football stadiums host the latter rounds of the NCAA Tournament. The 2019 national championship game between Texas Tech and Virginia drew 72,062 fans to Minneapolis' U.S. Bank Stadium.

Early in the 20th century, however, they had not yet conceived of such venues for basketball. When Purdue visited Madison Square Garden on December 28, 1935, the game against New York University drew what at the time was the largest crowd ever to witness a basketball game of any kind: 18,000.

NYU had won 14 straight games dating to the previous season. Ward "Piggy" Lambert's Boilermakers grabbed the upper hand early, darting to a 24–16 halftime lead. With only four minutes remaining, the Violets had built a 42–31 advantage.

All-American forward Bob Kessler sparked a rally, with help from Jewell Young, orchestrating a 10–0 run. Young had a chance at the go-ahead basket with about 10 seconds remaining, but his shot—described in a special report to the Lafayette *Journal & Courier* as a "comparative setup," or easy shot—rolled off the rim and into the arms of an NYU defender.

Purdue lost two days later at Temple to fall to 5–3. Then it lost only once more all season while compiling an 11–1 Big Ten record.

The Boilermakers shared the conference championship with Indiana—their third consecutive season with at least a partial title and seventh in 11 years.

49 Elmer Oliphant

On the list of Purdue's greatest athletes, Elmer Oliphant sits at the top. He very well could hold the same spot among all college athletes.

From 1910 to 1914, Oliphant became the first Boilermaker to letter in four major sports: seven total in football, basketball, baseball, and track & field. Then, at the U.S. Military Academy from 1915 to 1918, he duplicated the achievement—becoming the first Cadet to letter in four major sports—while also earning monograms in boxing and hockey.

It was football at which Oliphant truly excelled. A halfback and kicker, he still holds the Purdue record with 43 points (five touchdowns and 13 extra points) in a 91–0 win over Rose Polytechnic Institute on November 17, 1912. His five touchdowns are tied for the most in school history (accomplished only twice since). Oliphant was named first-team All-Big Ten in 1912 and 1913, and he went on to become a two-time All-American at Army while establishing academy records for points in a game (45) and season (125).

All told, the 5'7", 175-pound Oliphant is credited with scoring 424 points, 135 at Purdue and 289 at Army. He was selected to the Early All-Time Football Team (1869–1919) and by the legendary Knute Rockne to his All-Time America Team.

From 1910 to 1914, Elmer Oliphant became the first Boilermaker to letter in four major sports: seven total in football, basketball, baseball, and track & field.

"There was not any aspect of football in which Ollie did not excel: running, passing, blocking, kicking field goals, punting and defense," it was written in the September 1976 issue of *Assembly*, the United States Military Academy Association of Graduates magazine. "He was unquestionably one of the greatest ever in all-around play."

Oliphant was born in Bloomfield, Indiana. His family moved to Washington, Indiana, when he was 8 years old and to Linton, Indiana, in his junior year of high school. Oliphant scored 60 points for Linton in a 128–0 win over rival Sullivan.

In order to pay his tuition to Purdue, Oliphant spent his summers working as a coal miner. He was a two-time All-American in basketball and earned a bachelor's degree in mechanical engineering.

Oliphant played two seasons in the fledging National Football League, with the Rochester Jeffersons in 1920 and the Buffalo All-Americans in 1921.

During his time in military service, Oliphant created the collegiate intramural sports system for students to compete in recreational athletics. He was appointed track instructor at West Point by Douglas MacArthur, who was the superintendent after returning from World War I. Oliphant subsequently served as athletics director at Union College from 1922 to 1924 before embarking on a 33-year career with the Metropolitan Life Insurance Company. He died in 1975 in New Canaan, Connecticut.

Oliphant was inducted into the College Football Hall of Fame in 1955, Indiana Football Hall of Fame in 1975, Purdue Intercollegiate Athletics Hall of Fame in 1997, and Army Sports Hall of Fame in 2004.

50 John Wooden Jersey

Among the memorabilia showcased on the Mackey Arena concourse, one glass display contains a basketball jersey. It bears the word Purdue in yellow letters on the front and the No. 13—but no name—on the back.

The yellowing shade of the white wool indicates the relic's age. But the journey this basketball treasure took to arrive at Purdue—from the man who originally wore it to its longtime caretakers to its current owner—deserves a chapter unto itself.

John Neff grew up attending Purdue basketball and football games with his grandfather, Frank. Years later as an adult, Neff received an old Purdue jersey from his late grandmother as a Christmas gift. Neff's aunt told him the jersey had once belonged to his grandfather, and his grandmother believed he would have wanted Neff to own it.

"I was totally surprised, and I was crying and emotional," Neff said in 2018. "It meant so much to me, the memories of him and I."

Neff believed the jersey to be old, based on its color, smaller size (compared to modern players), and heavy material. However, he never displayed it or had it examined by a professional. It sat untouched in a box in a closet at his parents' Clinton County home for years. Eventually he asked his mother to ship it to him at his home in California, and she obliged simply by using the United States Postal Service.

All along, Neff knew his grandfather has talked about befriending Purdue's star guard John Wooden when both were enrolled in the School of Education there in the early 1930s. Later, they stayed in touch as they began their teaching careers in northern Indiana.

Eventually, curiosity got the best of Neff. While watching a documentary on Wooden, discussion turned to what number Wooden had worn at Purdue. All photos from that era showed him only from the front, where no numbers were displayed. The interviewee said Wooden himself told him he had worn the number 13.

Neff went to his closet, opened the box, unfolded the jersey, and looked down at the No. 13.

It took Neff some time and work to find an expert who would examine the jersey. Once they did, however, excitement quickly built in the memorabilia community. The relic featured several distinguishing marks from the era, including labels of a manufacturer and a Louisville sporting goods store known to make and sell such jerseys in the 1930s.

With authentication from trusted memorabilia experts at MEARS, the item went up for auction with an expected bid of at least $30,000. As the online auction entered its final days, the sale price shot past that estimation.

After a small bidding war between the last couple of bidders, the final sale price stunned Neff: $220,000, with a $44,000 commission bringing the total to $264,000.

At the time, the buyer wished to remain anonymous, even to Neff. This, however, is where the story truly takes its turn into Purdue sports lore.

On May 29, 2018, Purdue coaches and fans gathered in Jeffersonville, Indiana, for the latest stop on the "Boilermakers on the Road" summer tour. Those in attendance expected nothing more than a meal, an autograph or two, and the chance to maybe ask a question of one of the coaches about the upcoming season.

If poor weather hadn't intervened, they would have walked away with a much bigger story than that. Drew Brees, the Purdue legend and at the time quarterback of the New Orleans Saints, had planned to surprise the attendees with an appearance, at which time it would be revealed that he, a longtime admirer of Wooden, was the winning bidder in the jersey auction.

Due to poor weather, Brees could not fly out of Peoria, Illinois. So he settled for a video presentation, in which he announced he would loan the jersey to Purdue, and that it "will reside in the halls of Mackey Arena forever."

Brees was assisted in the auction by Orlando Itin, the proprietor of West Lafayette establishment Bruno's and a noted memorabilia collector himself.

"The first words out of my mouth to him upon finding out the John Wooden jersey would be made available to the public was, 'We have to get this for Purdue University. This jersey belongs in Mackey Arena back at Purdue,'" Brees said.

When Itin's $100,000 bid on Brees' behalf was surpassed during the auction's final hours, he checked in with the Super Bowl-winning quarterback.

"He said, 'Big O, do whatever you've got to do,'" said Itin, who did just that.

"I can't think of a more exciting thing to have at Purdue than John Wooden's jersey," Itin said. "It may be the rarest of college basketball memorabilia."

Complementing the jersey is a Wooden letter sweater, donated by his family in 2010, and the two marquee pieces are flanked by jerseys and trophies of Purdue's two other basketball National Players of the Year—Glenn Robinson (1994) and Stephanie White (1999).

Neff planned to use the auction proceeds to start a college fund for his daughter. But the item had sentimental value, as well, which helped him cherish the auction results even more.

"I thought it was fantastic," said Neff, who only learned of Brees' identity when he watched a live stream of the announcement. "I'm thankful that it was a Purdue alum and that it's going to stay right where it belongs."

51 Katie Douglas

Katie Douglas combined her on-court talent with an engaging personality to become one of the most popular players in Purdue women's basketball history. She also was one of the toughest, on and off the court.

A Boilermaker from 1997 to 2001, Douglas is the only two-time first-team All-American and Big Ten Player of the Year in program history, earning both honors along with being selected Purdue Female Athlete of the Year her junior and senior seasons. She also was the Big Ten Female Athlete of the Year as a senior.

As a sophomore, Douglas was a key contributor to the 1999 national championship team that finished with a 34–1 record, including 16–0 in the Big Ten. She flung the basketball into the air as time expired in the Boilermakers' 62–45 victory over Duke.

"It was an awesome feeling," Douglas said. "All the hard work, sacrifice, everything we'd been through was all worth it."

Douglas was co-captain of the national runner-up squad two years later. The Boilermakers were Big Ten champions in 1999 and 2001 and conference tournament winners in 1998, 1999, and 2000. Purdue accumulated a 111–26 record (.810 winning percentage) with Douglas on the roster.

Douglas concluded her career as the only Purdue player in the top 10 in career points, rebounds, assists, steals, and blocked shots. Through the 2019–20 season, she ranked second with 327 steals, third with 526 assists, and fifth with 1,965 points. She made and attempted the second-most free throws of all-time (550 of 689, 79.8 percent). The 6'1" left-hander compiled all those lofty numbers while playing point guard, shooting guard, small forward, and power forward.

"Her versatility is what makes Katie special," Purdue head coach Kristy Curry said. "She can take it inside or outside. Katie can do just about anything a team needs. Good things are going to happen for us whenever Katie has the ball."

Katie Douglas is the only two-time first-team All-American and Big Ten Player of the Year in Purdue women's basketball program history. She was also the Big Ten Female Athlete of the Year as a senior. (Tom Campbell)

As a junior, Douglas averaged 20.4 points per game, the fourth-most in school annals. She topped the team in steals in three seasons, points and assists twice, and rebounds once.

Douglas played hard all the time and described herself as a soldier. "I get thoroughly involved in the game," she said. "I prepare myself for a battle as I would for a fight." But the battles she endured on the court paled in comparison to her off-the-court challenges. Her father, Ken, died of pancreatic cancer in 1997 and her mother, Karen, succumbed to breast cancer less than three years later. In addition, teammate Tiffany Young was killed by a drunk driver four months after the Boilermakers claimed their national championship. Through it all, basketball provided an escape.

"It's my refuge," Douglas said her senior year, when she sported a sweatband on her right elbow with her parents' initials and Young's No. 23 adorned on it. "There have been some hard days, and without basketball I would have been devastated."

Douglas was the inaugural recipient of The V Foundation Comeback of the Year Award in 2001.

"The perseverance and strength that Katie has displayed is an inspiration to all of us," said Nick Valvano, CEO of The V Foundation. "She is the perfect choice to receive this first-time honor. Like other terrible diseases, cancer impacts individuals and families. Katie has risen above all these challenges and typifies what Jim Valvano meant when he said 'Don't give up. Don't ever give up!'"

The well-spoken and quick-witted Douglas aptly majored in communication. She was recognized as a first-team Academic All-American as a senior, when she won the Varsity Walk Award for bringing national attention to Purdue.

The Orlando Miracle selected Douglas with the 10th overall pick in the 2001 WNBA Draft, where she was reunited with Carolyn Peck, who was Purdue's head coach her first two seasons. Douglas played in the WNBA for 14 seasons with Orlando (2001–02), the

Connecticut Sun (2003–07, 2014), and the Indiana Fever (2008–13). The Indianapolis native was named Most Valuable Player of the 2006 All-Star Game and helped her hometown Fever win the WNBA championship in 2012. She was a five-time All-Star and retired as the league's eighth-leading scorer. Douglas also enjoyed a successful career in European leagues.

Douglas was inducted into the Purdue Intercollegiate Athletics Hall of Fame in 2015.

52 Stuart Schweigert

Next to Drew Brees, it is fair to say that the most popular Purdue football player of the Joe Tiller era was Stuart Schweigert.

Fans roared "Stu-u-u-u-u" whenever the free safety made a big play from 2000 to 2003, which was often. Schweigert set the school career record with 17 interceptions and was the Boilermakers' leading tackler during two seasons.

His engaging personality was icing on the cake, not to mention his charming smile and wavy brown hair. He was the ultimate Big Man on Campus.

"He's got the whole package," Purdue quarterback Kyle Orton said. "He's a hard worker, a big-effort guy. He's a smart guy, and he also has the physical talent. You put all that stuff together, and he's just a great player."

A highly touted recruit out of Saginaw, Michigan, Schweigert chose the Boilermakers over Michigan State. The 6'3", 4.4-second speedster was a high school quarterback and safety but immediately found a home on defense in college.

On the Boilermakers' Big Ten championship and Rose Bowl team in 2000 Schweigert was named a Freshman All-American and the Big Ten Freshman of the Year. His team-leading five interceptions were the most by a true freshman in school history, and he also topped the team with 85 tackles, the first freshman to do so since Kevin Motts in 1976.

"Stu had an instant impact when he came to Purdue," Tiller said. "One of the things that changed was the elimination of long runs by our opponents. He's an exceptional open-field tackler."

Each of the next three seasons, Schweigert was a semifinalist for the Thorpe Award, which is presented to the nation's outstanding defensive back. He was a preseason Playboy All-American in 2003 and a first-team All-Big Ten performer as a sophomore and senior.

Schweigert was hampered by myriad nagging injuries his junior year, but on September 14, 2002, against Western Michigan at Ross-Ade Stadium, he picked off his 12th career interception to set the school record. It came in merely his 27th game and broke a seven-way tie for the record, a group that included the legendary Rod Woodson.

"It's great to be on top of a list of such great athletes you admire, including an All-Pro NFL player," Schweigert said. "I have so much respect for him."

What is it like when an interception is imminent?

"You know as soon as the ball leaves the quarterback's hand," Schweigert said. "You lock in, and nothing else around you matters. It's just you and the ball. Everything goes silent; I don't hear anything, and I don't see anything around me. It's like I'm out there playing catch with someone."

Schweigert finished his career with 360 tackles, a total that ranks second among defense backs in Purdue history (to Woodson with 445) and ninth overall entering the 2020 season.

Three times, Schweigert preserved Boilermaker victories—with interceptions in the end zone at both Cincinnati and Minnesota in

2001 and with a tackle for loss in the red zone at Wake Forest in 2003.

The Oakland Raiders selected Schweigert in the third round (No. 67 overall) of the 2004 NFL Draft. He was one of four Boilermakers taken in the third round that year and one of nine in all coming off a successful 9–4 season.

Schweigert played in Oakland for four seasons, recording four interceptions, before concluding his NFL career in 2008 with the Detroit Lions. He subsequently played for the Omaha (Nebraska) Nighthawks of the United Football League from 2010 to 2012, earning defensive player of the year honors in 2011.

Also in 2011, Schweigert and two others purchased his home-town Saginaw Sting of the Continental Indoor Football League, and a year later the trio bought the entire league. Saginaw went undefeated in 2012 and won the CIFL Championship Game, and Schweigert subsequently took over as head coach in 2015 after the franchise had joined American Indoor Football. The Sting suspended operations a year later.

Schweigert and his family have lived in West Lafayette since 2017.

53 Brees to Morales

On the heels of three consecutive victories—over Michigan, Northwestern, and Wisconsin—the Boilermakers were in the driver's seat for the Big Ten championship and Rose Bowl berth when 12th-ranked Ohio State visited Ross-Ade Stadium on October 28, 2000.

"Coming into the game, the team obviously was on a high," wide receiver Seth Morales said. "There was a lot of hype on campus. It was kind of a crazy fall, having that many high-profile games and winning them one after another."

After a scoreless first quarter, the Buckeyes kicked a field goal for a 3–0 lead and, from there, the game became a back-and-forth affair. Purdue held a 7–3 halftime advantage, Ohio State went up 20–10 after three quarters, and the Boilermakers led 24–20 with just under six minutes to play.

The rest of the game may go down as the most-pulsating roller-coaster ride in Boilermaker lore.

On third-and-6 from the Purdue 30-yard line, Drew Brees threw his fourth interception of the game, and Ohio State safety Mike Doss returned it to the 2. Three plays later, the Buckeyes scored to forge ahead 27–24 with 2:16 remaining.

"It was a back-and-forth game," Morales said. "After the interception, I remember feeling really deflated. But you have to emotionally prepare yourself to go back into the two-minute huddle and know that someone is going to have to make a play. There were a few guys on the sideline who looked at each other, and we knew we had worked in practice on situations like the one we were facing, and it was time to apply it in a game. I was thankful we had Drew in our back pocket, but it was nerve-wracking, as well. I've never been around another player who so many guys had confidence could get the job done at the end of the game."

On the sideline, Brees received some time-tested advice from reserve defensive end Warren "Ike" Moore. "He told me, 'What did your mom always say? If you break it, you fix it.'"

And fix it, he did.

Chris Clopton returned the ensuing kickoff 31 yards to the Purdue 36-yard line and, after an incomplete pass, Brees found a wide-open Morales for a 64-yard touchdown strike that put the Boilermakers back in front 31–27 with 1:55 left.

"Twins Right, 74X-Z Pole was the call," Morales said. "Drew's first two options were Vinny Sutherland running a stop route and John Standeford running a fade. Ohio State was in a two-man coverage designed to stop those guys. The next read was A.T. Simpson, running a crossing route that Doss bit on.

"I think I was on the field because I always gave 110 percent, and fortunately I ran my route as hard as I could with the little bit of gas that was left in my legs. The line did a fantastic job giving Drew time to sit back in the pocket and, being such a disciplined quarterback, he went through his progression. It was one of those things where the ball hung up in the air forever and you tell yourself, 'Don't drop the ball. Don't drop the ball.' Everything was quiet and, all of a sudden, I made the catch and the crowd erupted. It was one of those once-in-a-lifetime opportunities, a gift from heaven."

Ohio State still had an opportunity, but the Buckeyes fumbled on their second play from scrimmage. Landon Johnson recovered for the Boilermakers, who proceeded to run out of the clock and send the capacity-plus crowd of 68,666 into a Saturday night frenzy.

Morales may have been Brees' fourth option on the play, but the transfer from Butler University—who made the Boilermakers as a walk-on in 1999 and earned a scholarship a year later—had been a factor all game. He finished with what would prove to be career highs of seven receptions for 115 yards.

"I always tell people I was in the right place at the right time," Morales said. "It's an honor to have been involved in a play of that magnitude. It was special. I'm flattered, and I'm thankful."

Morales teamed with Sutherland (142 yards) and Tim Stratton (100 yards) to give Purdue just the second trio of 100-yard receivers in school history.

54 Places to Go on Campus

Every Big Ten town boasts its share of timeless restaurants. These gathering spots bridge generations as both contemporary hangouts and nostalgic destinations for fans and alumni on return trips.

West Lafayette is no exception. Here are a handful of places any diehard Purdue fan must set foot in as part of their out-of-town experience.

Bruno's
212 Brown Street
From the Swiss chalet-style exterior of this West Lafayette staple, you would not expect that Bruno's is synonymous with the Purdue Athletics experience.

Yet, you won't find a bigger or better-curated collection of Purdue sports memorabilia than in Big O's Sports Room. Named for co-owner Orlando Itin, the spacious dining area is chock-full of uniforms, framed autographed photographs, and other mementos of Boilermaker greats.

Bruno Itin Sr., who immigrated to Indiana from Switzerland, and his wife, Evelyn, opened the restaurant in 1955 and moved it to its current location in 1998. Orlando and siblings Bruno Jr. and Tina now run the business.

Besides the Boilermakers ambiance, Bruno's is best known for two things, its pizza and Bruno Dough—the fried delicacies fans have enjoyed before and after Purdue games for decades.

Harry's Chocolate Shop
329 West State Street

The most well-known of the Purdue-adjacent watering holes opened in 1919 as a soda fountain before eventually adding beer and other spirits. According to legend, it served as a speakeasy during prohibition.

Ever since, this bar at the corners of State and Pierce streets has welcomed generations of Boilermakers with its famous motto, "Go ugly early." Some of them wrote their names and other messages on the walls, tables, and even ceiling, and alums are known to come back and locate the work they left behind.

Pizza, burgers, and other sandwiches cater to the lunch and dinner crowds. But Harry's draws big weekend crowds in search of authentic college revelry.

Neon Cactus
360 Brown Street

Many football weekends officially kick off on Thursday nights, when this nightclub becomes the most popular destination in town. Any shortlist of Purdue rites of passage must include obtaining a Cactus Cup, used for drink specials each weekend.

The 22,000-square-foot dance floor alone would draw crowds. However, the Cactus may be just as famous for the time-honored tradition that takes place in the Rusty Bucket piano bar. Bruce "Piano Man" Barker holds court over the area's longest-running live act. He takes requests from the audience, with customers bidding against each other for the right to hear their songs. What results is a raucous, ribald and remarkable evening.

Triple XXX Family Restaurant
2 North Salisbury Street

This campus favorite opened in 1929 in Chauncey Village as one in a network of Triple-X "Thirst Station" root beer stands. It remains one of two still standing nationwide. That location on the incline of State Street gives the eatery its catchphrase, "On the hill, but on the level."

For years, Triple-XXX provided an all-night grub hub for students and a go-to breakfast spot for alums and locals. Greg and Carrie Ehresman are the second generation of Ehresmans to own the restaurant, taking over from Greg's parents, Jack and Ruth, in 1999. It has been featured on Food Network's *Diners, Drive-ins and Dives* and Big Ten Network's *Campus Eats*.

When fans take a stool at the counter and open a menu, they take a journey back through Purdue sports history.

The Duane Purvis burger may be the most famous item on the menu. Named for the two-way football All-American and track & field star of the early 1930s, the quarter-pound burger features a dollop of creamy peanut butter. It is an acquired taste people seem to love or hate.

The Drew Brees First Choice remains among the most popular breakfast items, loading patrons up with a big breakfast quarter-backed by either chicken fried steak or ground sirloin.

All-American end Bernie Flowers also has a personalized chopped steak burger. Olympic diver David Boudia, running back Leroy Keyes, and softball standout Ashley Burkhardt are other athletes with namesake menu items.

55 Ray Ewry

Ask a contemporary sports fan about the greatest athlete in Purdue history and names such as Glenn Robinson, Drew Brees, or perhaps David Boudia will come to mind.

Go back a generation and you will hear votes for Rick Mount, Bob Griese, and other basketball and football stars. Others will remind you of John Wooden's brilliant playing career with the Boilermakers before he headed to UCLA for coaching immortality.

Many fans, however, likely aren't familiar with Ray Ewry, if they have heard of him at all. That's because he was a turn-of-the-20th-century track & field star. Nicknamed "The Human Frog," he ranks as the greatest Olympic Games athlete ever to come out of Purdue.

According to USA Track & Field, Ewry's athletic career was a marvel of sorts before he even reached the Olympics. He overcame polio as a child in Lafayette to captain the track & field team and play football for the Boilermakers.

In 1900, Ewry traveled to Paris for his first Olympics and immediately established himself as one of the top jumpers in the world. He won gold in all three standing jumping events—high jump, long jump, and triple jump—then went back four years later and repeated his gold-medal efforts in all three events in St. Louis.

The standing triple jump then was removed from Olympic competition. Ewry repeated his gold performances in the other two events at both the 1906 Intercalated Games—a competition in Athens, Greece, organized by the International Olympic Committee—and the 1908 Olympics in London.

Ewry's eight Olympic golds (the 1906 medals are not recognized by the IOC) stood as the record for over a century before

Michael Phelps eventually accumulated 13. Ewry's world record in the standing long jump—11 feet, 5 inches—stood until the event was discontinued in the 1930s.

Ewry worked as a hydraulics engineer and competed into his late thirties while winning 15 national championships. He was inducted into the U.S. Olympic Hall of Fame in 1983 and was an inaugural member of the Purdue Intercollegiate Athletics Hall of Fame in 1994.

Ewry's jumping prowess began a Purdue Olympic tradition that held strong over the next 100-plus years. Other notables include swimmer Keith Carter's silver medal in the 200 meter breaststroke in 1948, swimmer Joan Rosazza's silver with the 400 freestyle relay team in 1956, Chris Huffins' bronze in the decathlon in 2000, former Purdue pole vaulter Douglas Sharp's bronze with the U.S. bobsled team in 2002, soccer player Lauren Sesselmann's bronze with Canada in 2012, and rower Amanda Elmore's gold in 2016.

David Boudia won four medals in diving over the 2012 and 2016 Games, including gold in 10-meter platform in 2012. He teamed with fellow Boilermaker Steele Johnson to win silver in 10-meter synchronized diving in 2016.

Two Purdue basketball players won gold medals with Team USA—Howie Williams in 1952 and Terry Dischinger in 1960.

56 Bang the "World's Largest Drum" with the "All-American" Marching Band

The Purdue "All-American" Marching Band is synonymous with Saturday afternoons at Ross-Ade Stadium. However, the band was actually established in 1886—one year before the creation of the first football team on campus.

The World's Largest Drum is one of many tradition-rich elements boasted by the Purdue "All-American" Marching Band.

Over the following century, the band was credited with establishing a number of firsts among fellow bands. In 1907, Purdue was the first to break military ranks to create a formation. That day, the band created a "Block P"—a tradition nearly every other school copied and incorporated into its halftime shows.

In 1920, Purdue became the first band to play an opponent's fight song. In 1935, they were the first to perform a halftime show with lights on their uniforms and instruments—a scene that prompted a television announcer to give them the "All-American" moniker.

The band's pregame routine is narrated by John Hultman, the "voice" of the Purdue "All-American" Marching Band. His signature moment is reciting "I Am An American," a tradition that began under longtime "voice" Roy Johnson.

I am an American. That's the way most of us put it, just matter of factly. They are plain words, those four: you could write them on your thumbnail, or sweep them across this bright autumn sky. But remember too, that they are more than just words. They are a way of life. So whenever you speak them, speak them firmly, speak them proudly, speak them gratefully. I am an American.

Among the other firsts credited to the band was the inception of the oversized bass drum, a gimmick that has been copied by numerous other schools. However, while the self-proclaimed title of "World's Largest Drum" may have been accurate at one time, it eventually became more tradition than truth.

While Purdue in recent years did its best to keep the drum's dimensions a secret, the Lafayette *Journal & Courier* archives from August 6, 1921, proclaimed the Big Bass Drum to measure "seven feet three inches in diameter and three feet nine inches wide."

Per tradition, the drum has a central place in the grand finale of every Saturday. To conclude the postgame concert on Slayter Hill, the drum majors release each section of instruments individually. Finally, the Big Bass Drum is pushed speeding toward the director, only to stop within inches of a collision.

57 Morgan Burke

Morgan Burke left an indelible mark on Purdue as athletics director from 1993 to 2016, while making his name as one of the visionary leaders in intercollegiate athletics.

Burke put his heart and soul into what he truly viewed as a labor of love. He worked vigorously to ensure every student-athlete had a positive experience at Purdue, his alma mater. No one wanted to see the Boilermakers succeed more than Burke did, and few expended more energy cheering them on to victory.

At the time of his retirement, Burke boasted the fourth-longest tenure among athletics directors at Football Bowl Subdivision institutions.

"For longer than any athletics director in Purdue history, Morgan has contributed to Purdue's reputation as a highly competitive program marked by integrity and fiscal soundness," Purdue president Mitch Daniels said when Burke announced his retirement. "He has worked to create an environment that fosters both academic and athletic success among our student-athletes."

When Burke succeeded George King, he pledged to build on the foundation already in place. Working with coaches and staff, aggressive goals were set. The department's mission outlined its goals for "Developing Champions/Developing Scholars/Developing Citizens."

On the athletics side, Burke's expectation was to improve the position of Purdue teams in the Big Ten and nationally. Significant strides were made on both fronts. In 2009–10, 14 teams finished in the upper half of the Big Ten, the high-water mark in Burke's time at Purdue. On the national scene, 14 squads earned NCAA postseason opportunities in 2011–12, the most in school history.

Two teams won NCAA championships, women's basketball in 1999 and women's golf in 2010, while eight student-athletes captured a combined 14 individual national crowns. The football team embarked on a run of 10 bowl games in 12 years from 1997 to 2008, and the men's basketball team achieved an unprecedented string of back-to-back-to-back Big Ten championships in 1994, 1995, and 1996. All told, Burke oversaw 20 regular season conference championships and 13 tournament titles.

Similar excellence was expected in the classroom, and student-athletes regularly performed equal to or better than the student body. The cumulative grade-point average for all Purdue student-athletes was above 3.0 for 15 consecutive semesters when Burke retired.

Five coaching hires stand out from Burke's tenure: Joe Tiller for football in 1996, Devon Brouse for golf in 1998, Dave Shondell for volleyball in 2003, Matt Painter for men's basketball in 2004, and Sharon Versyp for women's basketball in 2006.

Recognizing the need for contemporary facilities, Burke and his staff identified and addressed construction and renovation projects benefiting every program—making an investment of more than a quarter of a billion dollars—with major makeovers to Ross-Ade Stadium and Mackey Arena.

A 1973 Purdue graduate in industrial management and captain of the swimming team his senior year, Burke was a member of Phi Beta Kappa scholastic honorary. He earned a master's degree in industrial relations from Purdue in 1975 and a law degree from John Marshall Law School in Chicago in 1980. Burke pursued a successful career with Inland Steel Co. after law school, moving through 13 positions in an 18-year span. He was vice president when he departed to return to Purdue.

In May 2017, the Purdue Board of Trustees renamed the Boilermaker Aquatic Center in honor of Burke, who died June 15, 2020, at age 68.

58 Purdue in the Super Bowl

Purdue's history in the Super Bowl is as deep as the game itself. Quarterback Len Dawson and the Kansas City Chiefs played in the inaugural event—called the AFL-NFL World Championship Game—losing to the Green Bay Packers 35–10 on January 15, 1967, at the Los Angeles Memorial Coliseum. Dawson threw the second touchdown pass in the game, a seven-yarder in the second quarter.

Dawson and the Chiefs returned to the championship game three years later and won 23–7 over the Minnesota Vikings. Dawson was named Most Valuable Player after completing 12 of 17 passes for 142 yards and one touchdown.

Both of those Chiefs teams were coached by a Boilermaker—Hank Stram, a running back at Purdue in 1942, 1946, and 1947 and subsequently an assistant coach from 1948 to 1955.

The Miami Dolphins played in three consecutive Super Bowls in the early 1970s (VI, VII, and VIII) and had a standout Boilermaker on both sides of the ball, quarterback Bob Griese and defensive back Tim Foley. Their 14–7 win over the Washington Redskins in Super Bowl VII capped the only perfect season in NFL history (17–0). Griese's 28-yard touchdown pass in the first quarter gave Miami a lead it would not relinquish. The Dolphins made it back-to-back championships the following season.

Boilermakers played in five of the first eight Super Bowls.

Between the 1974 and 1980 seasons, running back Otis Armstrong was the only Boilermaker to play in a Super Bowl. He was a member of the Denver Broncos in Super Bowl XII.

However, over the next nine seasons (1981 to 1989), four Purdue players were on teams in eight Super Bowls, led by linebacker Keena Turner of the San Francisco 49ers and his four winning appearances: XVI, XIX (over Boilermakers linebacker Mark Brown of the Dolphins), XXIII, and XXIV.

Defensive lineman Dave Butz of the Washington Redskins played in three Super Bowls in seven seasons, winning XVII and XXII.

Wide receiver Mark Jackson of the Broncos also played in three Super Bowls in a span of four seasons, but lost all three, including two to other Boilermakers—Butz in XXII and Turner in XXIV.

Purdue was represented in one Super Bowl between the 1990 and 1998 seasons. In Super Bowl XXX, linebacker Jim Schwantz and the Dallas Cowboys defeated defensive back Rod Woodson and the Pittsburgh Steelers 27–17.

From 2000 to 2020, at least one Boilermaker was a part of 21 consecutive Super Bowls, the longest streak by any school in the country, including players on the active roster, practice squad, or injured reserve. Nebraska had owned the longest streak at 26 straight before it came to an end in 2020.

The streak began when defensive tackle Jeff Zgonina and the St. Louis Rams beat cornerback Steve Jackson and the Tennessee Titans 23–16 in Super Bowl XXXIV.

Woodson played in his second of three Super Bowls the following year with the Baltimore Ravens, recording six tackles in a 34–7 victory over the New York Giants.

The New England Patriots won three Super Bowls in a four-year span from 2002 to 2005 (XXXVI, XXXVIII, and XXXIX), and they had multiple Boilermakers on each roster. Offensive tackle Matt Light was on all three, while fellow offensive linemen Brandon Gorin and Gene Mruczkowski and linebacker Rosevelt Colvin were on two apiece.

Amidst that string, fullback Mike Alstott and the Tampa Bay Buccaneers won Super Bowl XXXVII 48–21 over Woodson and the Oakland Raiders. Alstott scored the first touchdown by a Boilermaker on a two-yard plunge in the second quarter.

Quarterback Drew Brees was named MVP of Super Bowl XLIV after his New Orleans Saints defeated the Indianapolis Colts 31–17. Brees completed 32 of 39 passes for 288 yards and two touchdowns. With Dawson, Griese, and Brees, Purdue is one of just two schools that can claim three Super Bowl champion quarterbacks (also Alabama).

A trio of Boilermakers played for the Patriots in Super Bowl XLVI: Light and linebackers Niko Koutouvides and Rob Ninkovich.

The eight most recent Super Bowls have featured a combined 10 Boilermakers. Seattle Seahawks defensive end Cliff Avril played in back-to-back games (XLVIII—a win over linebacker Shaun Phillips and the Broncos—and XLIX—a loss to Ninkovich and the Patriots). In the 43–8 victory over Denver, Avril recorded a first-quarter safety and helped pressure Broncos' quarterback Peyton Manning into throwing a pair of first-half interceptions, both of which resulted in Seattle touchdowns.

Running back Raheem Mostert, who was cut by six organizations in 2015 and 2016, led the 49ers to Super Bowl LIV after a record-setting performance in the NFC Championship Game against Green Bay: 220 rushing yards—the second-most in NFL postseason history—and four touchdowns. In the process, Mostert became the first player with 200 or more rushing yards and four rushing touchdowns in a playoff game. He subsequently scored the second Super Bowl touchdown by a Purdue player, a one-yard tote in the third quarter, but the 49ers lost to Kansas City 31–20.

All told, 39 different Boilermakers have been on Super Bowl teams combining for 66 appearances. Twenty-three have been on winning squads, amassing 36 titles.

Boilermakers in the Super Bowl

Super Bowl	Player(s)
I	Len Dawson, Kansas City Chiefs
IV	Len Dawson, Kansas City Chiefs* (MVP)
VI	Tim Foley, Miami Dolphins; Bob Griese, Miami Dolphins
VII	Tim Foley, Miami Dolphins*; Bob Griese, Miami Dolphins*
VIII	Tim Foley, Miami Dolphins*; Bob Griese, Miami Dolphins*
XII	Otis Armstrong, Denver Broncos
XVI	Keena Turner, San Francisco 49ers*
XVII	Dave Butz, Washington Redskins*
XVIII	Dave Butz, Washington Redskins
XIX	Mark Brown, Miami Dolphins; Keena Turner, San Francisco 49ers*
XXI	Mark Jackson, Denver Broncos
XXII	Dave Butz, Washington Redskins*; Mark Jackson, Denver Broncos
XXIII	Keena Turner, San Francisco 49ers*
XXIV	Mark Jackson, Denver Broncos; Keena Turner, San Francisco 49ers*
XXX	Jim Schwantz, Dallas Cowboys*; Rod Woodson, Pittsburgh Steelers
XXXIV	Steve Jackson, Tennessee Titans; Jeff Zgonina, St. Louis Rams*
XXXV	Rod Woodson, Baltimore Ravens*
XXXVI	Matt Light, New England Patriots*; David Nugent, New England Patriots*; Jeff Zgonina, St. Louis Rams
XXXVII	Mike Alstott, Tampa Bay Buccaneers*; Rod Woodson, Oakland Raiders

XXXVIII	Rosevelt Colvin, New England Patriots*; Brandon Gorin, New England Patriots*; Matt Light, New England Patriots*; Gene Mruczkowski, New England Patriots*
XXXIX	Ian Allen, Philadelphia Eagles; Rosevelt Colvin, New England Patriots*; Brandon Gorin, New England Patriots*; Matt Light, New England Patriots*; Gene Mruczkowski, New England Patriots*
XL	Niko Koutouvides, Seattle Seahawks; Chukky Okobi, Pittsburgh Steelers*; Craig Terrill, Seattle Seahawks
XLI	Gilbert Gardner, Indianapolis Colts*; Kyle Orton, Chicago Bears; John Standeford, Indianapolis Colts*
XLII	Rosevelt Colvin, New England Patriots; Matt Light, New England Patriots
XLIII	Chike Okeafor, Arizona Cardinals
XLIV	Drew Brees, New Orleans Saints* (MVP), Curtis Painter, Indianapolis Colts
XLV	Mike Neal, Green Bay Packers*
XLVI	Niko Koutouvides, New England Patriots; Matt Light, New England Patriots; Rob Ninkovich, New England Patriots
XLVII	Bernard Pollard, Baltimore Ravens*
XLVIII	Cliff Avril, Seattle Seahawks*; Shaun Phillips, Denver Broncos
XLIX	Cliff Avril, Seattle Seahawks; Rob Ninkovich, New England Patriots*
50	Kawann Short, Carolina Panthers
LI	Ricardo Allen, Atlanta Falcons; Rob Ninkovich, New England Patriots*
LII	Jason King, New England Patriots
LIII	Ja'Whaun Bentley, New England Patriots*
LIV	Raheem Mostert, San Francisco 49ers; Jacob Thieneman, San Francisco 49ers

denotes Super Bowl champion

59 Twirl with the Golden Girl

Al G. Wright wasted no time making his mark as director of the Purdue "All-American" Marching Band.

In 1954, his first year upon replacing legendary first director Paul Spotts Emrick, Wright introduced a baton twirler to perform with the band. Her name was Juanita Carpenter, and she came to Purdue from Colorado. Carpenter was charismatic and wore a gold-sequined costume with a high neck and a skirt. Fable has it that when she marched into Ross-Ade Stadium with the band for a football game, roses were thrown at her.

Meanwhile, sophomore quarterback Len Dawson was creating a buzz with his play, earning him the nickname the "Golden Boy." So, Wright's wife, Gladys, suggested that Carpenter be christened the "Golden Girl."

And so began a tradition that has remained treasured to this day. Katie Schleis of Oshkosh, Wisconsin, is the most recent Golden Girl, having performed in 2018 and 2019 as the 30th in band history.

The Golden Girl made headlines on October 25, 1958, when Wright suggested that Addie Darling perform on top of a bass drum on the field at halftime of the Boilermakers' game at Notre Dame.

Through the years, the Golden Girl had almost always had blonde hair, but three brunettes have been selected, including Schleis. Dazzling gold costumes have changed through the years with fashion trends but always have been a staple.

In addition to appearing with the band at all home football games and occasional road contests, the Golden Girl has regularly been in the spotlight at the Indianapolis 500 Festival Parade each

May. In January 1989, Dawn Beck, Golden Girl No. 15, and the band performed at the inaugural parade of President George H.W. Bush.

"The Golden Girl at Purdue is truly the 'queen of the nation's baton twirlers' because she is treated like royalty wherever she goes," said Sally Batina, Purdue's 12th Golden Girl in 1982 and 1983. "She is not only the top twirler for the Purdue Band, but an ambassador for the university."

The Golden Girl was joined by the Silver Twins (actual twins or look-a-likes) in 1960 and the Girl-in-Black in 1962. The accompanying twirlers have remained part of the band pageantry ever since.

Renowned for being a showman, Wright served as director until his retirement in 1981. Other highlights of his tenure included the introduction of the "I am an American" patriotic read prior to the playing of the national anthem at football games.

A native of London, Wright celebrated his 100th birthday on June 23, 2016. He and his wife continue to make their home in West Lafayette.

60 Cannon Trophy

The 1943 football meeting between Purdue and Illinois took on extra significance for both squads due to the ongoing World War II effort.

As outlined in the Purdue Athletics documentary *Perfect Warriors*, Purdue had been chosen as a training site for the V12 Navy College Training Program. That meant students already enrolled in the Naval reserves could study there while receiving their training ahead of active duty. More than 1,200 Marines and sailors enrolled at Purdue prior to the 1943 session—and by chance several of them happened to be among the best football players in the country.

A dozen former Illinois football players moved over to play for the Boilermakers, including All-American guard Alex Agase and fullback Tony Butkovich.

Prior to the 1943 season, the decision was made to signify the series between the nearby rivals with a traveling trophy.

Per Purdue lore, a group of students had taken a small cannon to a game at Illinois in 1905, intending to fire it to celebrate their expected victory. Instead, Illinois fans discovered the cannon and absconded with it before the Boilermakers could formally celebrate their 29–0 win.

One of the Fighting Illini backers, Quincy A. Hall, allegedly kept the cannon in his farmhouse near Milford, Illinois—about an hour northwest of the Illinois campus. The two schools had not played for 11 years prior to the resumption of the series in 1943. So Hall came forward with the cannon and suggested it serve as the traveling trophy going forward.

Purdue won that 1943 meeting 40–21, part of a perfect 9–0 season for a Boilermaker team loaded with Marine and Navy talent. Butkovich rushed for 207 yards and four touchdowns on 12 carries against his former team. Agase and Butkovich both earned All-American honors that season, with Butkovich setting a team record with 16 rushing touchdowns he still shares to this day.

Purdue won 11 of 15 meetings against Illinois between 2003 and 2019 to take a 36–30–2 advantage in the Cannon Trophy series.

The cannon is no longer functional, having last been fired after Illinois' home victory November 4, 2001. Care of the trophy is handled by either Purdue's Tomahawk Service and Leadership

Honor Society or Illinois' Illini Pride, depending on which school currently holds it.

Among the notable games:

October 25, 1947: Unranked Purdue beat No. 5 Illinois 14–7 at Ross-Ade Stadium, knocking the Illini off a potential conference or national championship trajectory.

October 25, 1952: A 40–12 victory in Champaign helped Purdue compile a 4–1–1 Big Ten record and claim a share of the Big Ten title behind Dale Samuels and Bernie Flowers.

October 29, 1966: The Boilermakers were coming off a disheartening 41–20 loss to No. 2 Michigan State and needed a boost. They got one with a 25–21 Homecoming victory over the Illini—the first of four straight wins that propelled Purdue to the Rose Bowl.

October 21, 1978: Head coach Jim Young's eventual Peach Bowl championship squad posted its second of three shutouts of the season with a 13–0 victory at Memorial Stadium. Young went 4–1 in Cannon games, winning in each of his final four seasons with the Boilermakers.

November 3, 2001: For the only time in the history of the series, both teams were ranked in the Associated Press top 25. No. 20 Purdue jumped out to a 13–0 lead at Ross-Ade Stadium. Behind quarterback Kurt Kittner and two long interception returns for touchdowns, the No. 21 Illini scored 38 unanswered points in a 38–13 victory. Illinois went on to win the Big Ten title.

October 12, 2002: Purdue's five regulation losses that season came by a total of 19 points, plus a 38–31 overtime heartbreaker at Illinois. Purdue rallied from a 24–0 deficit to take the lead in the fourth quarter. Illinois running back Antoineo Harris scored on fourth-and-goal from the 1-yard line with three seconds left to tie the game. John Standeford caught Kyle Orton's "Hail Mary" heave as regulation ended, but he was ruled down at the 1. Illinois got the ball first in overtime and scored a touchdown, then stopped Purdue.

October 8, 2016: Freshman J.D. Dellinger's 28-yard field goal in overtime lifted Purdue to a 34–31 victory at Memorial Stadium. A game-winning 41-yard field goal try by Illinois' Chase McLaughlin had bounced off the upright as regulation time expired. Two of the three Big Ten victories of Darrell Hazell's head coaching tenure came at Illinois.

61 The Three Amigos

Before becoming as close as any senior class in Purdue basketball history, Troy Lewis, Todd Mitchell, and Everette Stephens converged from different corners of the Midwest.

Lewis came to the Boilermakers with in-state bona fides. He grew up in the blue-collar town of Anderson, Indiana. The shooting guard set a state record with 76 points in a single state finals in 1983, leading the Indians to a runner-up finish.

Mitchell, a versatile 6'7" wing, hailed from Toledo, Ohio. Stephens, a 6'2" point guard, came from Evanston, Illinois.

What followed for the three men known then and now as the "Three Amigos" was an unprecedented run of Big Ten success and a connection that endures to this day.

"It's a special bond," Lewis said. "There's nothing like it. Everette and Todd and myself, we're brothers. We're so connected with one another. We see each other, and it's like we never missed a beat.

"It doesn't matter if we talk a week from now or a year from now, it just doesn't change. It's a great feeling to have two guys who no matter what happens will always have your back."

The group earned its nickname from longtime Purdue radio play-by-play broadcaster Larry Clisby, who played off the title of the 1986 comedy film starring Steve Martin, Chevy Chase, and Martin Short.

Not only were the players a complementary force on the court, they were seldom seen apart off it. The trio formed the nucleus of Purdue's 1987 and 1988 repeat Big Ten championship squads.

Lewis scored 2,038 career points, good for fifth place in school history. Head coach Gene Keady out-recruited Kansas to land Lewis, who went on to lead the Boilermakers in scoring for three straight seasons.

"He was the best shooter I played with," Stephens said. "But he was just as smart, with a good basketball body. He worked hard. He knew what he needed to do on the floor. He was one of those players who took care of business."

Mitchell, a third-team All-American as a senior, ranks 13th in Purdue history with 1,699 points. He averaged 15 or better in three straight seasons and earned first-team All-Big Ten honors as a junior and senior.

"He had the will to win," Lewis said. "He had the will to want to get better. He was unselfish, and he knew how to play the game.

"What we always said was, we all three knew how to play the game and we wanted to win. We could see things on floor coach didn't have to tell us."

Stephens' 481 career assists are tied with teammate Tony Jones for third among all Boilermakers. Yet he also made 44.7 percent of his career 3-point attempts—a hair behind Lewis for third in team history—and could bring Mackey Arena to a roar with his high-flying dunks.

"He led our team in blocked shots from the point guard position for three years," Mitchell said. "He was the best defender we had. He did things at the point guard with his athleticism and arm length you just didn't see. He was super athletic."

With those three leading the way, Purdue became one of the best teams in the county. The trio won 116 games over the course of their careers, including 16 in a row as seniors. That record stood until 2017–18, until another senior-led Purdue team won 19 in a row.

Yet for all of their successes, the Three Amigos ultimately ended on a sour note.

Purdue held the No. 1 seed in the Midwest Regional for the 1988 NCAA Tournament. After victories over Fairleigh Dickinson and Memphis in South Bend, the Boilermakers moved on to the Sweet 16 in Detroit.

There they encountered a familiar opponent. Purdue had waxed Kansas State at Mackey Arena, fouling emerging star Mitch Richmond out of the game early. The Lon Kruger–coached Wildcats, however, continued to improve. Kansas State used gimmick defenses to limit the Three Amigos, and the 73–70 loss ended their careers and Purdue's season.

"I remember coming back in the locker room and seeing Coach sitting on a bench in the shower," Mitchell said. "At that point, I knew, and he knew, it had been his best shot to get to a Final Four. We couldn't get it done, so that's something I will always remember."

Fittingly, all three players and Keady were inducted into the Purdue Intercollegiate Athletics Hall of Fame together in 2010.

62. No. 1 in the Country

No. 1 is not a title many teams will earn in a given season, or perhaps throughout their history. Purdue men's basketball has never reached No. 1, despite a rich tradition including All-Americans, Big Ten champions, No. 1 NCAA Tournament seeds, and Final Four teams.

The Boilermakers football team, however, reached the top of the mountain in 1968. To tell that story, we first step back one season.

The 1967 Boilermakers almost reached that pinnacle, too. At the time, only 10 teams were ranked. Purdue began the season unranked despite finishing the 1966 season No. 5 after its Rose Bowl victory over USC.

Considering what the Boilermakers had lost from that team, it made sense. Heisman Trophy runner-up Bob Griese had left to begin an illustrious NFL career with the Miami Dolphins. Other reliable performers—such as defensive backs John Charles and George Catavolos and receiver Jim Finley—were gone, as well.

However, the Boilermakers returned many other key contributors, not the least of which was a cornerback who had been sprinkled in on offense the previous season. Leroy Keyes announced himself as one of the top running backs in college football in 1967, totaling 1,744 offensive yards and 19 touchdowns from scrimmage.

Along with the emergence of sophomore quarterback Mike Phipps, Purdue quickly showed that 1967 would not be a rebuilding year. After a season-opening 24–20 victory over Texas A&M at the Cotton Bowl, the Boilermakers jumped to No. 10 in the Associated Press poll. A week later, they snapped No. 1 Notre Dame's 11-game winning streak 28–21 and vaulted to No. 4. After a home victory over Northwestern, Purdue moved up to No. 2, then defended that ranking with a 41–6 thrashing of Ohio State in Columbus.

It was as high as the 1967 team would climb. Oregon State came into Ross-Ade Stadium and ruined the Boilermakers' Homecoming—and probably any chance at the No. 1 spot—with a 22–14 upset. (It was the start of quite a month for the Beavers, who also tied No. 1 UCLA 16–16 and beat No. 1 USC 3–0 over the next three weeks.)

Purdue outscored its next four opponents 185–50 before falling at Indiana 19–14 in the game that sent the Hoosiers to their only Rose Bowl. But the stage had been set for the Boilermakers to enter 1968 as one of the top teams in the country.

Keyes, moved around from flanker to tailback to wherever else Purdue needed his elite talents, was a consensus first-team All-American. Phipps' 1,800 passing yards led the Big Ten.

In the AP preseason poll for 1968, Purdue received 14 first-place votes, USC received 10, and a handful of teams shared the others. The Boilermakers opened the season ranked No. 1.

Virginia put up little resistance as Purdue opened with a 44–6 victory at Ross-Ade. However, the Boilermakers' claim to college football's top spot was not absolute. Notre Dame held the No. 1 spot in the United Press International rankings and also received 19 first-place votes in the AP poll, compared to Purdue's 25.

A September 28 game in South Bend would decide the issue. It wasn't especially close. Keyes ran for two touchdowns and threw for another in a 37–22 victory. The Boilermakers received 42 first-place votes the following week as the clear No. 1 team in the AP poll.

After crushing Northwestern 43–6, it appeared Purdue might be able to string together a long run at the top spot. The biggest test to that staying power came up next: a trip to an Ohio State team that was about to embark on a three-year run of Big Ten excellence.

As chronicled in *Boilermakers: A History of Purdue Football* by Bob Collins, Keyes went into the game nursing injuries to his hip, ankle, and back. Used "mostly as a flanker decoy," he gained only 36 yards from scrimmage.

Collins also wrote that Phipps was "rapped on the head and didn't know where he was for a while." In modern football, concussion protocols might have caught that development. Purdue's coaches didn't realize Phipps' compromised condition until he had thrown two interceptions. One was returned for an Ohio State touchdown, and the other set one up.

The Buckeyes shut down the mighty Purdue offense in a 13–0 blanking. The Boilermakers dropped to No. 5, lost only once more all season, but settled for a No. 10 ranking in the final poll.

That Ohio State team? It went undefeated and finished No. 1 in the poll, giving the program its third AP national championship.

Keyes became Purdue's first 1,000-yard rusher in 1968, finishing second to USC's O.J. Simpson in the Heisman Trophy balloting.

The 1979 team opened the season at No. 6 and moved up one spot after the first week, but could climb no higher. The 2004 Boilermakers, led by quarterback Kyle Orton, won their first five games and reached No. 5 in the AP poll. But a 20–17 Homecoming loss to No. 10 Wisconsin started a four-game losing streak that ruined any chances of a lofty finish in the polls.

63 Ward "Piggy" Lambert

It's appropriate that Ward "Piggy" Lambert was a professor in the physical education department while also leading the men's basketball program at Purdue.

That's because Lambert viewed himself a basketball teacher more so than a basketball coach.

While educating the Boilermakers for 28½ seasons (1916–17 and 1918–46), Lambert's teams consistently earned good grades. His personal report card showed a 371–152 overall record (.709 winning percentage), including a 228–105 mark in Big Ten games (.685), with 11 conference championships.

Lambert was Purdue's winningest coach until Gene Keady passed him in 1997, and through the 2019–20 season, Lambert still ranked fourth in Big Ten history in conference victories and fifth in overall wins. He mentored 11 All-Americans, including three-time honorees Charles "Stretch" Murphy and John Wooden.

In an era when teams ran methodical offenses, Lambert pioneered an up-tempo style of play. "There was nothing mechanical about the play of his quintets, which had a tendency to confound a set defense," longtime Purdue sports information director Robert C. Woodworth said.

In the book *Boilermaker Basketball: Great Purdue Teams and Players*, Alan Karpick wrote, "Lambert's coaching philosophy did more than generate wins and stars. Lambert launched basketball into the modern era with his exciting, fast-breaking style. No team in the Big Ten—or anywhere else—approached Purdue's record during his tenure."

The diminutive Lambert, who stood 5'6", was as animated and fiery on the sideline as his teams were on the court. Game officials were often the target of his sharp tongue and quick wit.

Born in Deadwood, South Dakota, Lambert moved to Crawfordsville, Indiana, as a youngster and went on to attend Wabash College, where he played basketball, baseball, and football. According to his sister, Eleanor, Lambert received the nickname "Piggy" because he liked to hog the basketball in his formative years. During his lifetime, he saw the game evolve from a seven-man to a five-man sport.

Lambert graduated from Wabash in 1911 and after a brief stint as a graduate student at the University of Minnesota, he began his venture into teaching and coaching at Lebanon (Indiana) High School. Four years later, Purdue hired him at age 27.

The Boilermakers went 11–3 during the 1916–17 season, and then Lambert enlisted in the U.S. Army, serving as a lieutenant during World War I for a year, before returning to Purdue.

In 15 seasons from 1926 to 1940, the Boilermakers won nine Big Ten championships, including a three-peat in 1934, 1935, and 1936. They finished second on three occasions.

The 1931–32 team, led by Wooden, was recognized as the national champion by the Helms Foundation after fashioning a 17–1 record. In 1940, Lambert declined the conference-winning Boilermakers' automatic bid to the NCAA Tournament that was to be played at Madison Square Garden in New York because he did not want his players around gamblers he knew would be there.

Lambert authored a textbook, *Practical Basketball*, which was published in 1932 and recognized as one of the early basketball coaching bibles. Throughout his career, he conducted clinics across the country. In 1945, Lambert was selected as the country's outstanding basketball coach in a nationwide poll by *Esquire* magazine. He served two years as the inaugural chairman of the rules committee of the National Basketball Coaches Association and spent two years on the board of directors, as well.

About the recurrent changes to the game that he observed, Lambert always said, "Well, they still have a basket at each end of the floor, don't they?"

Lambert's teams won 25 of their first 30 games against intra-state rival Indiana en route to a 31–13 overall record versus the Hoosiers.

On January 22, 1946, Lambert retired, citing the "nervous strain and mental punishment that accompanies a head coachship." He had desired to step down for several years but carried on while the athletics department was short-handed during World War II. Lambert subsequently served from 1946 to 1949 as commissioner of the Professional Basketball League, a precursor to the NBA. He then returned to Purdue as freshman baseball and basketball coach.

Lambert also fulfilled three stints as head baseball coach for the Boilermakers (1917, 1919–35, and 1945–46), compiling a 163–158–7 record.

Lambert, who died in 1958, was inducted into the Naismith Basketball Hall of Fame in 1960, Indiana Basketball Hall of Fame in 1962, and National Collegiate Basketball Hall of Fame in 2006. He was an inaugural member of the Purdue Intercollegiate Athletics inaugural class in 1994.

Lambert Fieldhouse, built in 1937 and home of the Boilermakers for 30 years, was named in Lambert's honor in 1971. Similarly, the baseball program played at Lambert Field from 1965 to 2012.

64 The House That "Piggy" Built

As the winter of 1937 approached, Purdue men's basketball was considered one of the best programs in the country. The Boilermakers had won seven Big Ten championships in the previous 12 seasons, including the John Wooden–led 1932 team which would retroactively be declared the national champion.

That year, the Boilermakers opened a new venue fit for one of the country's elite teams. Purdue Fieldhouse, as it was first known, sat at the corner of Stadium and Northwestern Avenues, providing an imposing new athletic centerpiece adjacent to the football stadium at the heart of campus. Sunlight shining in from the windows on one end spread out beneath the building's arched roof.

On December 11, 1937, Purdue christened its new 8,500-seat facility with a 61–18 thrashing of Indiana State. Tickets went for 75 cents that day, including tax.

Purdue's head coach was Ward "Piggy" Lambert. The building later was renamed for the man who coached the Boilermakers to 371 victories over three decades from 1916 to 1946. He coached baseball for many years, as well, and the school's former baseball field also was named for Lambert.

Lambert Fieldhouse served as Purdue basketball's home until the opening of Mackey Arena in 1967. Boilermakers legends such as Dave Schellhase and Terry Dischinger spent their careers there. On February 24, 1947, a collapse of the bleachers during halftime of a game against Wisconsin claimed the lives of three students and injured dozens more.

Lambert Fieldhouse also hosted swimming & diving until 2001. It remains home to indoor track & field and the wrestling program's Blake Training Center.

65 1999 NCAA Women's Basketball Champions

The ceiling was sky-high for Purdue women's basketball leading up the 1998–99 season.

Two of the greatest players in school history, senior guards Stephanie White and Ukari Figgs, headlined a roster that also featured burgeoning sophomore stars Katie Douglas and Camille Cooper to go with a deep and talented supporting cast. All 13 players returned from the team that had won the 1998 Big Ten Tournament and advanced to the NCAA Tournament Elite Eight.

Everyone, inside and outside the program, talked about reaching the Final Four and winning the national championship. Heady stuff, to be sure, but equally legitimate.

Then came a midsummer bombshell that could have cast a cloud over everything. Head coach Carolyn Peck, set to enter her second season after taking over for Nell Fortner, agreed to become head coach and general manager of the expansion Orlando Miracle of the WNBA.

White and Figgs, betrayed and frustrated at the prospect of playing for their fourth head coach in as many seasons, urged—perhaps challenged—Peck to stay. And because the Miracle was not going to begin play until the subsequent summer, it was resolved that Peck would remain at Purdue for the highly anticipated campaign.

"I came back because when I called Stephanie and told her that I had the opportunity to go to the pros, her response was, 'How dare you. We have everything we need to win a national championship,'" Peck recalled as the team celebrated its 20th anniversary in 2019. "She and Ukari both believed that, and when you have that kind of confidence from your two seniors, you don't want anyone else coaching that team."

What transpired ranks as one of the paramount seasons in Purdue Athletics history.

For starters, the Boilermakers hosted three-time defending national champion Tennessee on November 15 and put the country on notice with a 78–68 victory that snapped the Lady Vols' 46-game winning streak. The following week, Purdue was ranked No. 1 in the Associated Press national poll for the first time ever.

The 1998–99 Purdue women's basketball team captured the NCAA Championship with a 62–45 victory over Duke in San Jose, California. The Boilermakers finished with a 34–1 record. (Tom Campbell)

After a 73–72 setback at Stanford on November 22, the Boilermakers did not lose the remainder of the regular season. The 23 straight victories included a perfect 16–0 conference record, as Purdue became just the second team to go undefeated in Big Ten play en route to capturing its fifth championship in nine years (also 1991, 1994, 1995, and 1997). Two wins were particularly notable, a 76–74 overtime thriller at 15th-ranked Penn State on February 12—which Figgs traveled to on gameday after attending her grandmother's funeral—and an 88–58 crushing of Ohio State two days later before the first-ever capacity crowd of 14,123 at Mackey Arena.

The Boilermakers defended their Big Ten Tournament title and earned the No. 1 seed in the NCAA Tournament Midwest Regional. They advanced to the Final Four by beating Oral Roberts, Kansas, North Carolina, and Rutgers by an average of 17.5 points and then exacted revenge on Louisiana Tech, which knocked out Purdue the previous year, with a 77–63 victory in the national semifinals.

Awaiting the Boilermakers in the championship game in San Jose, California, on March 28 was Duke, which was led by Nicole Erickson and Michele VanGorp. The duo transferred from Purdue three years earlier on the heels of the ouster of head coach Lin Dunn. Furthermore, the Blue Devils were coached by Gail Goestenkors, a former Purdue assistant under Dunn.

Facing a 22–17 halftime deficit, the Boilermakers stormed out of the locker room and ultimately took a 32–30 lead on a driving layup by Figgs with 12:53 remaining. Purdue led 47–42 with 4:01 to go when White left the game with a severely sprained ankle and did not return. Sparked by Figgs, the Boilermakers scored 11 straight points to take control and steam to a 62–45 victory. Figgs scored a game-high 18 points, all in the second half, to earn most outstanding player honors for the Final Four.

"I know I let my team down in the first half," Figgs said. "I had 20 minutes to be a winner or a loser, and I wanted to go out a winner.

"Steph got hurt and everybody just rallied around. And that's just the way our team flows. Somebody goes down, we rally around them."

The Boilermakers wound up with a 34–1 record, recording what was then the fifth-most wins in NCAA history, and finished the season on a Big Ten-record 32-game winning streak. They became the first Big Ten women's basketball team to win a national championship. President Bill Clinton honored the Boilermakers at a White House ceremony the following fall.

White, who averaged 20.2 points, 5.4 rebounds, and 4.6 assists, earned first-team All-America honors and was named Big Ten Player of the Year and Female Athlete of the Year. She also received the Wade Trophy as the nation's most outstanding senior player based on athletics, academics, leadership, community service, and sportsmanship.

Peck, meanwhile, reaped national and Big Ten Coach of the Year recognition. The title marked the first ever for an African American women's basketball coach.

"At the end of the championship game, I still remember looking at my team and having this awesome feeling that they had committed from start to finish," Peck said. "I'm a lame-duck coach, they know I'm not coming back, but they committed to each other."

Tragedy struck the Boilermakers on July 31, 1999, when rising senior guard Tiffany Young was killed by a drunk driver in Gary, Indiana.

Postscript to the championship season: Purdue hired Kristy Curry as head coach on April 2, 1999, and the winning streak reached 36 games before being snapped, ironically at Tennessee. Curry led the Boilermakers to the 2001 Final Four, losing to Notre Dame in the championship game. The Boilermakers advanced to the Elite Eight in 2003 and the Sweet 16 twice, while winning the 2001 and 2002 Big Ten championships and the conference tournament three times in seven seasons under Curry.

66 Brian Cardinal and the 2000 Elite Eight Boilermakers

On January 8, 2000, the Purdue men's basketball team faced something of a crossroads.

Head coach Gene Keady's team began the season in the top 25 and carried Big Ten championship aspirations. A senior-led squad knocked off eventual national runner-up Florida in its second game and began to climb the national rankings.

But on January 8, after a double-overtime loss at home to an unranked Michigan team, the Boilermakers had lost three of their last six games and dropped to 9–5 overall. Some wondered if the program's seven-year streak of NCAA Tournament appearances might come to an end.

"The Michigan loss was devastating," center John Allison said later that season. "We were questioning ourselves. Where were we headed?

"The coaches talked about how it was something we could recover from."

Four days later, the Boilermakers went to Champaign and knocked off No. 22 Illinois 69–66. Purdue did not lose again at Mackey Arena, barely fell short of another Big Ten championship, and eventually came within a game of ending the program's 20-year Final Four drought.

Keady's last great Purdue team won 24 games with a balanced mix of chemistry and grit. Jaraan Cornell, a guard from

South Bend, averaged 12.5 points per game. Fellow senior Mike Robinson, a McDonald's All-American wing from Peoria, Illinois, averaged a team-high 6.2 rebounds along with 11.8 points. Junior point guard Carson Cunningham, a Hoosier native who would later become a college professor and Division I head coach, averaged 4.1 assists and 11 points.

Tying it all together was the man they called "The Custodian"—a player whose grit and willingness to do the dirty work would help define the essence of Purdue basketball for future generations.

Brian Cardinal grew up in the Big Ten footprint in Tolono, Illinois, not far from the University of Illinois. His father, Rod, was the athletic trainer for the Fighting Illini men's basketball program. But Illinois did not recruit the local star, so he headed across Interstate 74 to join Keady's program, where he established himself as one of the best—and most respected—players in Boilermaker history.

Through the 2019–20 season, Cardinal remains one of only five players in school annals to amass 1,000 points, 500 rebounds, and 250 assists. Yet it was everything from his knee pads to his scrappy style to his demonstrative on-court behavior that made him the kind of player opposing fans loved to hate.

"I liked it when people hated me, because if they were worried about me, they weren't thinking about the other four guys," said Cardinal, who led the 1999–2000 Boilermakers with 13.9 points, 6.3 rebounds, and two steals per game—along with hustle plays and floor burns. "You've got to play the tough-guy card. You've got to play the villain card at times."

Folks developed a particular grudging respect for Cardinal in his native central Illinois. Going into that January 2000 game, Purdue had won eight straight against the Illini, and seven with Cardinal and fellow Land of Lincoln native Robinson on the roster.

Cardinal scored a team-high 21 points that night, and Robinson posted 12 points and 12 rebounds (nine offensive) in the Boilermakers' sixth straight victory in the venue then known as Assembly Hall.

That victory sparked a four-game winning streak and 12 wins in the next 14 contests. Purdue took an eight-game winning streak into the regular season finale at the other Assembly Hall—the one in Bloomington. The Boilermakers had beaten Indiana back in January, and if they could solve the Hoosiers and a hostile sellout crowd of over 17,000, they would share the Big Ten regular season championship with Michigan.

But Indiana jumped out to a 17–2 lead, setting the stage for a 79–65 victory. Purdue settled for a second-place finish and prepared for the Big Ten Tournament.

"We didn't match their intensity at the beginning of the game," Cardinal said. "We just went through a Senior Night and knew how emotional it was going to be, but we didn't match their toughness."

More disappointment followed in the Big Ten Tournament in Chicago—and once again, a slow start contributed. Purdue had split the season series with Wisconsin, with both teams winning on their home turf. The Badgers grabbed a 14–4 lead and sent the Boilermakers home after one game 78–66. On the cusp of the NCAA Tournament, Purdue was suddenly reeling and talking openly about its inability to match opponents' intensity in the opening minutes.

Despite its considerable success in conference play, Purdue received only a No. 6 seed in the NCAA Tournament. The Boilermakers headed for Tuscon, Arizona, to play a team based only three hours from West Lafayette—the Dayton Flyers.

While Dayton came into the game with a reputation for perimeter shooting, the Flyers made only 2 of 17 from behind the arc. Yet that didn't prevent them from pushing the Boilermakers to the brink of a first-round upset. Dayton led 58–55 as the clock wound down to the two-minute mark.

Cornell, whose scoring had lagged behind his junior-year production all season, hit a big 3-pointer with 2:05 to play. Then Cardinal, who totaled 18 points and eight rebounds, added another 3 with 1:20 left to break the tie. Purdue held on for a 61–60 victory, living up to the tournament's "survive and advance" motto.

The Boilermakers earned a second-round matchup with No. 3 seed Oklahoma, which had ended the season ranked No. 12 in the country. With 66 seconds to play, the teams were tied at 60. The game, and the season, fittingly turned on Cardinal making a play on a loose ball. He deflected it to Cunningham, who passed to Cornell, who was fouled while attempting a 3-pointer. He made all three resulting free throws, and two more from Rodney Smith with 23.6 seconds to play sent Purdue to its third straight Sweet 16.

In the West Region semifinals in Albuquerque, New Mexico, the Boilermakers faced Gonzaga, still building its basketball reputation. The Bulldogs were the No. 10 seed, and that day they could not solve Purdue's defense. The Boilermakers built a 16-point lead with under 12 minutes to play and went on to a 75–66 victory.

With one more victory, Purdue would send Keady to the Final Four for the first time as a Boilermaker and end a national semifinal drought that stood since 1980. A familiar name, however, stood in the way.

Wisconsin was making its own Cinderella run in the tournament as the West's No. 8 seed. After opening with a win over Fresno State, the Badgers shocked top-seeded Arizona and stifled No. 4 seed LSU to reach the Elite Eight.

Cardinal didn't score in the first half, and the Boilermakers were fortunate to trail only 31–28 at halftime. He responded with 13 points in the second half, and his last basket in a Purdue uniform gave his team a 50–49 lead. But the Badgers' Jon Bryant couldn't have picked a better day to light it up from 3-point range. He hit five shots behind the arc, including one with 5:47 reamining that gave Wisconsin a 52–50 lead.

The Badgers led the rest of the way en route to a 64–60 victory. Purdue and its stellar senior class fell one game short of that coveted Final Four trip.

"It was one of those things where they played just a little bit better, and we could never get over the hump," Keady said.

Wisconsin then faced another Big Ten rival, Michigan State, in the national semifinals. The Spartans ended the Badgers' over-achieving run, then defeated Florida 89–76 for, what remains as of 2020, the conference's last men's basketball national championship.

The blue-collar Cardinal started 125 games for Purdue, third-most in school history. He ranks second with 259 steals, ninth with 749 rebounds, and 20th with 1,584 points. Cardinal was chosen in the second round of the 2000 NBA Draft and played only 28 games over his first three seasons for the Detroit Pistons and Washington Bullets. But he developed into a valuable reserve and played 12 seasons for six franchises. In 2011, he helped the Dallas Mavericks win the NBA championship.

Cardinal since returned to Purdue to work in external relations for the athletics department. Yet to many fans, he will always be "The Custodian."

67 Mark Herrmann

Over the course of his career, Mark Herrmann became the most prolific passer in NCAA history, establishing nine records, including passing yards and completions.

Herrmann's lifetime numbers—all Big Ten records at the time—included 1,309 passing attempts, 772 completions, .590 completion percentage, 9,946 passing yards, 71 passing touchdowns, and 9,134 yards of total offense. The NCAA did not include bowl games in its statistics until 2002, meaning his national record numbers were 1,128 passing attempts, 717 completions, 9,188 passing yards, and 8,444 yards of total offense. He became the first quarterback in NCAA history to throw for 8,000 yards and subsequently the first to throw for 9,000 yards.

Senior Joe Metallic started the 1977 season opener at quarterback for the Boilermakers but gave way to Herrmann in the first half. Herrmann went on to start 45 of the next 46 games, missing only the opener of the 1980 season at Notre Dame with an injured right thumb.

As a senior, Herrmann was named the Big Ten Most Valuable Player and a unanimous All-American while finishing fourth in Heisman Trophy balloting. He set school season records for passing attempts (368), completions (242), completion percentage (.658), yards (3,212), touchdowns (23), and total offense (3,026). The last three figures also established Big Ten marks.

In a 36–25 win over Michigan State at Ross-Ade Stadium on October 25, 1980, Herrmann became the NCAA career passing yards leader, topping the record of 7,818 yards thrown by Jack Thompson of Washington State from 1975 to 1978. Herrmann broke the record with a 14-yard completion to senior split end Bart

Burrell—"an act of God," according to center Pete Quinn, because the duo had been playing together since the seventh grade.

Herrmann was the MVP of three straight bowl games: 1978 Peach, 1979 Bluebonnet, and 1980 Liberty.

"I had a fantastic college experience," Herrmann said. "Those four years at Purdue shaped my life, and the ongoing interaction with Purdue continues to be a focal point for me and my family. Without Purdue's offer of a football scholarship, nothing that came after college for me would have happened. I have a degree from a great institution that has continued to support me and my family year after year."

Selected by the Denver Broncos in the fourth round of the 1981 NFL Draft, Herrmann had a 12-year professional career with the Broncos (1981–82), Baltimore Colts (1983), Indianapolis Colts (1984 and 1990–92), San Diego Chargers (1985–87), and Los Angeles Rams (1988–89).

Herrmann, a Cincinnati native who grew up in Carmel, Indiana, and now makes his home in Indianapolis, was inducted into the Purdue Intercollegiate Athletics Hall of Fame in 1997 and the College Football Hall of Fame in 2010. Following his NFL career, he served as a radio color commentator for the Colts from 1994 to 2004 and as the associate director of Education Programs for the NCAA from 2002 to 2009. He joined the Purdue Athletics staff in April 2020 as director of leadership and alumni engagement for the John Purdue Club.

68 Take a Photo in Front of the John Wooden Statue

Growing up only 12 miles from Martinsville, Indiana, a young Jim Hicks knew plenty about basketball legend John Wooden.

Hicks learned more when he arrived at Purdue in 1957 to pursue a degree in agriculture economics. Many on campus still talked about the exploits of the player who earned All-American honors as a Boilermaker each season from 1930 to 1932.

By the time Hicks moved to California in the late 1960s, Wooden had begun his streak of seven consecutive national championships as the head coach at UCLA. Hicks used to make the 40-mile drive to watch Bruins teams he admired for their discipline and fundamentals.

"He had a lot of class and a lot of integrity and was kind of a role model for me," Hicks said. "I've often said to myself, 'What would Johnny Wooden do if he were in these circumstances?' If I figured out what he would say, I always thought I had the right answer."

Yet Hicks worried that not enough people, not even at Purdue, knew the extent of Wooden's history as a Boilermaker. When Hicks' own professional success allowed him to make an impact, he wanted to do his part to secure his role model's legacy.

Hicks commissioned the seven-foot-tall bronze statue of Wooden that has stood on the north side of Mackey Arena since 2016. Fittingly located just off John R. Wooden Drive in the Sally & Bob Weist Plaza, the statue depicts Wooden as a Boilermaker player.

The statue comprised $250,000 of a $2 million donation to create the Jim and Neta Hicks Endowment for Leadership in

Agriculture in 2014. That gift primarily supports the College of Agriculture Transformational Experiences (CATE) program.

The statue may be the most visible sign of Hicks' generosity to Purdue, but it is only part of his story and the legacy he has created for himself.

"This whole project came together from one donor's vision and passion for student success at Purdue," said Kyle Bymaster, chief development officer for the College of Agriculture, who served as the liaison between donor and artist.

In the infancy of the project, Bymaster showed Hicks the John Purdue statue near University Hall. Hicks liked it enough that he suggested using the same artist for the Wooden statue.

Hicks later learned that the artist, Julia Rotblatt-Amrany, and her husband, Omri Amrany, were already known for recreating iconic basketball figures. The statue of a dunking Michael Jordan that stands outside Chicago's United Center is their work. So is the statue of Kareem Abdul-Jabbar, in mid-hook shot, erected outside of Los Angeles' Staples Center.

Statues of Wooden in Indianapolis and Los Angeles depict him as he's most known—as a coach. Hicks wanted a statue of a young Wooden, honoring the player old-timers still talked about during Hicks' college days.

The months-long process of creating the statue began with a well-known photo of Wooden posing with a basketball from 1932. Rotblatt-Armany needed more than one dimension, however, so she sought out clips from YouTube and other sources, then made still photos of other angles. The original photo was enlarged to the statue's eventual height of seven feet, and Omri Armany constructed a steel armature to support the sculpture.

The statue sculpture began as a clay mold before eventually taking on its current form—a quarter-inch thick bronze, welded together from several separate pieces.

Wooden's No. 13 Purdue jersey is tucked into black shorts fastened with a belt. Athletic socks extend out of his black Chuck Taylors. Even the size of the basketball, larger than that used by college players today, met historical specifications.

Yet Rotblatt-Amrany wanted to capture Wooden's youth, which she accomplished by detailing "the intensity of the face and communication of the eyes."

"You want to make that inanimate object look like it's alive," Rotblatt-Armany said. "That's the objective, that when the viewer stands and looks at the piece, they feel something or it activates something in them. It's a focus, I guess. He had a certain softness to him, as well."

Hicks had one other requirement. He wanted the statue to celebrate Wooden as a teacher and emphasize his Pyramid of Success. The 15 elements—industriousness, friendship, loyalty, cooperation, and enthusiasm on the bottom level; self-control, alertness, initiative, and intentness on the second; condition, skill, and team spirit in the middle; poise and confidence on the fourth level, and competitive greatness at the top—form the backdrop to the statute. Those tenets are illuminated at night.

"All of a sudden, it makes it all relevant," said Cathy Wright-Eger, longtime leadership advisor for the Purdue athletics department who created the Wooden Leadership Academy for student-athletes. "John Wooden, the Pyramid of Success, Purdue—they all start going together. That's what I love about it the most."

Hicks had never before commissioned a statue. He wanted a permanent tribute to a man who had inspired his own success.

Yet Hicks had already established a lasting legacy, not just of Wooden's principles, but his own.

Hicks graduated from Purdue in 1961. Eight years later, he and his wife, Neta, moved to California when Hicks began working for Chevron Corporation. In 1982, he left that job to cofound his own business before launching a wholesale fertilizer distribution company, Jim Hicks and Co.

That business grew into one of the largest fertilizer distributorships on the West Coast. Hanging on the wall at his office is what Hicks called "one of my lifelong treasures." It is a copy of Wooden's Pyramid of Success, autographed by the author, FROM ONE HOOSIER FROM MORGAN COUNTY TO ANOTHER.

"I think the greatest contribution he's left to society is his Pyramid of Success," Hicks said. "I think it has contributed certainly to our company's success and to a lot of other people's success.

"We've tried to practice some of the same principles that Johnny Wooden had. We have a small company, and we tried to instill in our staff the things he tried to instill in the players."

Hicks wanted to give back from his own success to his alma mater. He initially funded one scholarship for agriculture economics students based on two criteria he chose—academics and leadership. The first recipient, 2011 graduate Emily (Hirsch) Cooper, wrote Hicks a thank-you letter.

Hicks was so touched by the letter, he decided to give more. Since 2008, the Hickses have created two undergraduate endowments and one graduate endowment for agriculture economics scholarships. According to Bymaster, the gifts have benefited more than 150 undergraduates and 10 graduate students with over $560,000 in scholarships and nearly $54,000 in graduate student support. In addition to this generous scholarship support, the Hickses also established the Jim and Neta Hicks Leadership Endowment, supporting the College of Agriculture Transformational Experiences program. This endowment provides nearly $90,000 in annual support for programs focused on student leadership development and communication skills, interpersonal skills, personal well-being, and ways of thinking as students prepare for life after Purdue.

Hicks called Wooden "an inspiration." He hopes the students who walk by the statue for decades to come take some piece of that inspiration for themselves.

"It has exceeded my wildest expectations," Hicks said. "It came out perfect."

69 Matt Light

Matt Light could have been a productive tight end. But he wound up as an All-American offensive tackle, a Big Ten champion, and a three-time Super Bowl winner.

Light played in seven games as a true freshman tight end in 1996, catching one pass for 16 yards for head coach Jim Colletto. When Joe Tiller replaced Colletto after the season, he suggested to Light that his future would be better suited as an offensive lineman.

"I was upset, but I just decided to give it a shot," Light recalled in 2000.

Tiller was highly regarded for putting his players in position to succeed, and Light is arguably his greatest testament. After redshirting in 1997 and pushing his weight from 255 to 277 pounds, Light became a fixture at left tackle, starting all 37 games over the next three seasons and providing the foundation for perhaps the greatest offensive line in Purdue history.

While quarterback Drew Brees was running Tiller's pass-oriented offense in record-setting fashion, Light and his linemates were skillfully protecting him. From 1998 to 2000, the Boilermakers allowed merely 41 sacks out of 1,690 passing attempts, one out of every 41.2, far and away the fewest in the Big Ten.

In 2000, Light and Co. surrendered just 10 sacks as the Boilermakers won the Big Ten championship and played in the Rose Bowl. Light earned All-America honors.

Light, who came to Purdue from Greenville, Ohio, was more than a pass blocker. While most teams are "right-handed" with their running game, the Boilermakers favored the left side because of Light's run-blocking ability.

"We primarily passed at Purdue, but when we ran the ball, we were very effective," Light said. "That's a statistic people kind of leave out because we had Drew passing for 3,000 yards."

Although Light and his fellow linemen were all business on the field, they had plenty of fun off it. At the Boilermakers' media and photo day prior to the 2000 season, Light, Brandon Gorin, Gene Mruczkowski, Chukky Okobi, and Rod Turner showed up wearing shoulder pads and Speedos, dubbing themselves "The Lifeguards."

"We figured, as offensive linemen, if we don't do something a little bit out there, we're not going to get recognized," Light said. "We figured this ought to do it."

Even before the days of social media, the image almost instantly became one of the most memorable in Purdue lore. Four of the five Lifeguards went on to win Super Bowl championships.

Light was selected in the second round (No. 48 overall) of the 2001 NFL Draft by the New England Patriots. As a rookie, he started 15 regular season and playoff games for the Super Bowl XXXVI champions. Light became a fixture at left tackle—protecting quarterback Tom Brady—for the next decade. Light played in four more Super Bowls, winning two, and New England boasted a 15–5 record in playoff games when he was in the lineup. He was a three-time Pro Bowl selection (2006, 2007, and 2010).

Through all the success, Light overcame 13 surgeries and an ongoing battle with Crohn's disease.

Inducted into the Purdue Intercollegiate Athletics Hall of Fame in 2013, Light was named to the Patriots' All-2000s team and 50th Anniversary team and enshrined in the storied franchise's Hall of Fame.

As an NFL rookie, Light started the Light Foundation to provide opportunities for underprivileged youth to lead healthy lives through outdoor experiences. He also runs leadership camps for kids.

70 Visit the Hidden Gems of Purdue Golf

Relative to its peers, one can argue that no Purdue Athletics programs have better playing and training venues than the men's and women's golf teams.

The Birck Boilermaker Golf Complex features two 18-hole championship courses designed by renowned golf course designer Pete Dye.

Kampen, the links-style course, is considered one of the most difficult golf courses in Indiana and has hosted both women's (2003) and men's (2008) NCAA Championships. Parkland-style Ackerman-Allen sits across the street, adjacent to Ross-Ade Stadium.

It is a complex befitting a championship program, which Purdue is. Half of the Boilermakers' national championships have come in golf.

The men's golf program kept knocking on the door of a championship in the middle of the 20th century. Purdue finished second in 1949, 1950, and 1956. The Boilermakers were runners-up to Houston in both 1959 (by 10 strokes) and 1960 (by four strokes).

The Cougars, who with that last championship ran their streak of consecutive titles to five, were led by two-time medalist Dick

Crawford of Houston. He returned for the 1961 event, as well. However, this time Purdue had an advantage: it hosted the tournament on its home course.

Led by Mark Darnell's second-place effort and Jerry Jackson's top-10 performance, Purdue held off Arizona State by 11 strokes to win the national championship. Darnell fell one stroke short of medalist honors to another Big Ten golfer who went on to greater fame after college: Ohio State's Jack Nicklaus.

At the 2008 NCAA Championships in Wilmington, North Carolina, the Purdue women's golf team set a school record for lowest 72-hole score. But that wasn't enough for the Boilermakers to easily claim the crown. The tournament came down to the final grouping.

Purdue led by two strokes on the final hole when Maude-Aimee LeBlanc settled for bogey on the par–5 No. 18. Southern California's Jennifer Song could have forced a playoff, but missed a 10-foot putt, and the Boilermakers became the first Big Ten women's golf team to win a national championship.

Numa Gulyanamitta paced Purdue with a ninth-place individual finish.

"I think it's a tribute to our players and how hard they worked to prepare for this championship," Purdue head coach Devon Brouse said. "It's also a reflection of the level of support our golf program and the entire athletics department receives.

"I'm a Purdue graduate and my wife's a Purdue graduate, and I've always felt like Purdue is a special school. I'm proud and happy to be able to contribute. It's been a great honor to work with this group of young ladies."

71 Joe Barry Carroll

The story is a common one not only throughout Purdue basketball history but in all of college sports.

A coach goes on a recruiting trip to see one player and ends up chasing after someone different.

When Purdue assistant coach George Faerber went on a scouting trip to Denver in the mid-1970s, he wasn't there to scout Joe Barry Carroll. The 7'1" phenom was hard to miss, however, and his arrival eventually changed Boilermaker history.

"It was a great time," Carroll said, "and I'm grateful for it."

In 1976–77, Carroll made an immediate impact as a first-year reserve behind Tom Scheffler, setting the school freshman record for blocked shots (82) that has withstood recent challenges from A.J. Hammons and Matt Haarms. He helped the Boilermakers secure their second NCAA Tournament invitation.

Elevated to full-time starter as a sophomore, Carroll blossomed. He averaged 15.6 points, 10.7 rebounds, and 3.8 blocks. In an 80–78 victory at Arizona on December 10, 1977, Carroll became the first and still only Purdue player to achieve a triple-double with 16 points, 16 rebounds, and a school-record 11 blocks.

Yet even with Carroll playing alongside another first-time starter headed for stardom, Jerry Sichting, those Boilermakers won only 16 games. After the season, Fred Schaus departed and Lee Rose arrived.

What followed were perhaps the two greatest big man seasons in the history of a program with a reputation for producing them.

Carroll's 22.8 points per game led the Big Ten. His 352 rebounds set a Purdue season record that stood until Caleb Swanigan came along. With Carroll dominating inside, the Boilermakers rose to as high as No. 13 in the nation. His career high of 42 points came in the NIT semifinals, leading to an 87–68 victory over Alabama and setting up a championship matchup with intrastate rival Indiana. The Hoosiers effectively limited Carroll to 14 points in their 53–52 victory.

Both Carroll and Purdue rode the momentum of that season to even greater heights in 1979–80. Carroll averaged 22.3 points and 9.2 rebounds as the focal point of every opponent's scouting report.

After stumbling to an 11–7 record in the tough Big Ten, the Boilermakers surged at the right moment. They reached the NCAA Tournament regional in Lexington, Kentucky, where Purdue exacted its revenge on Indiana in the semifinals and beat Duke in the final to earn a Final Four trip.

UCLA knocked the Boilermakers out of championship contention with a 67–62 semifinal victory. Carroll responded with 35 points in the consolation victory over another Big Ten rival, Iowa, to close his career with 2,175 points.

Only Rick Mount has scored more points at Purdue than Carroll, and no one has more total rebounds (1,148, with Terry Dischinger's 958 a distant second) or blocked shots (349). His 53 double-doubles stand one behind Dischinger's career record.

The Golden State Warriors selected Carroll first overall in the 1980 NBA Draft. He went on to average 17.7 points and 7.7 rebounds over 11 seasons with five teams, earning All-Star recognition in 1986–87.

Carroll's stellar career also included an at-times difficult relationship with fans and media. His unemotional approach to the game earned derisive nicknames such as "Joe Barely Cares" and "Just Barely Carroll." Three decades later, Carroll returned to Purdue and saw a similar storyline playing out with Hammons—another 7-footer who faced questions about his commitment.

"I hope they're kinder to him than they were to me," Carroll said.

Carroll's achievements continued after retiring from basketball in the early 1990s. Now living in Atlanta, he works as a wealth advisor and an artist and author.

"We all have something inside of us," said Carroll, who was inducted into the Purdue Intercollegiate Athletics Hall of Fame in 1995. "We usually stop at the first good thing we do, the first thing we're good at, or the first thing that pays well. But there's all these other things we don't get a chance to explore."

72 Lamar Lundy

Lamar Lundy made history at Purdue—twice.

When Lundy came to West Lafayette from Richmond, Indiana, in 1953, he became the Boilermakers' first African American scholarship football player.

Lundy also played basketball for the Boilermakers, and as a senior was named team Most Valuable Player in both sports—the only Purdue athlete to accomplish that feat.

At 6'6" and 225 pounds, Lundy excelled as a tight end and defensive end in football and as a forward in basketball. His senior year he led the football team with 15 receptions for 248 yards and four touchdowns and was the basketball squad's second-leading scorer at 13.4 points per game and top rebounder at 9.3 boards per game. He earned All-Big Ten honors in both sports.

Lundy was inducted into the Indiana Football Hall of Fame in 1975, Indiana Basketball Hall of Fame in 1990, and Purdue Intercollegiate Athletics Hall of Fame in 1995.

"Lamar was a terrific athlete," Purdue quarterback Len Dawson said in a 1994 interview with *Gold & Black Illustrated.* "He was very big man, and at that time most receivers didn't go higher than probably 6'1" or 6'2". The defensive backs averaged around 5'9" to 5'10", so besides having tremendous skills, his height was a great advantage. I never had trouble finding him downfield."

As a minority, Lundy endured his share of critics at Purdue.

"There just weren't a lot of African Americans in college, and very few were playing college basketball or football," Lundy said. "A lot of people had set thoughts on what every minority was like, so they would ignore you, continually look away and try not to speak to you."

The situation improved by Lundy's senior year after his wife gave birth to their son, Lamar III.

Lamar Lundy was the first African American scholarship football player at Purdue and went on to be named team Most Valuable Player in football and basketball—the only Boilermaker to accomplish that feat.

"The atmosphere changed once everybody got to understand each other and exchange thoughts and ideas," Lundy said. "It went from what I was talking about to a wonderful situation. That was all part of the educational process, not only for me but for the people of Lafayette and West Lafayette."

In 1957, Lundy was drafted by the Los Angeles Rams of the National Football League (fourth round) and faced a decision whether to pursue football or basketball professionally. Lundy picked football because he always dreamed of living in California.

"It was so exciting for this country boy," Lundy told the Richmond *Palladium-Item* in 1999. "I had never seen orange trees, palm trees, or the making of movies. That made it easy for me to decide."

He chose wisely.

Lundy played 13 seasons with the Rams. After three years as a tight end and slot back on offense, he moved to defense in 1960 and became a member of the Fearsome Foursome with Rosey Grier, Deacon Jones, and Merlin Olsen that is widely regarded as one of the most dominant defensive lines in football history. Lundy was selected to the 1959 Pro Bowl.

Following his playing days, Lundy immediately got into coaching with the San Diego Chargers. But in 1971, he was diagnosed with myasthenia gravis, a disorder that weakens the muscles. He was bedridden for nearly a year.

Doctors feared for Lundy's life, but his condition went into remission. He eventually returned to his hometown of Richmond and worked with the city's youth while also broadcasting high school football games. A diabetic who continued to battle health issues, including prostate cancer, Lundy died in 2007.

One of Lundy's grandchildren, Damon Lewis, was an offensive lineman for Purdue from 1993 to 1995.

73 Football Tragedies

Tragedy has struck the Purdue football program twice in its history.

On Halloween in 1903, Purdue was scheduled to play Indiana at Washington Park in Indianapolis in a highly anticipated game of the budding rivalry. Two special trains had been chartered from the Big Four Railroad to transport the Boilermakers, band, students, faculty, and fans from Lafayette.

About 9:55 AM, the first train, consisting of 14 cars, crashed into a 10-car section of coal cars being backed down the track near 18th Street, about three miles away from Union Station. A clerk up the line had failed to inform a yardmaster of the approaching train.

The first car of the train—the place of honor—carrying the players, coaches, and staff was completely demolished, one end thrown about 50 feet to the right of the track and the remainder torn to bits and either jammed against the end of the coal car train or flung to either side of the track.

Sixteen Boilermakers died: assistant coach Edward Robertson; athletic trainer Patrick McClaire; and players Thomas Bailey, Joseph Coates, Gabriel Drollinger, Charles Furr, Charles Grube, Jay Hamilton, Walter Hamilton, Roswell Powell, Wilbert Price, Walter Roush, George Shaw, Samuel Squibb, Samuel Truitt, and Harry Wright. Lafayette businessman Newton Howard, who was with the team as a special honor for his fan interest and favors extended, was also killed. Some 30 additional passengers were injured or maimed for life.

The tragedy was summed up succinctly in the November 11 Purdue *Exponent*: "Within a second the flower of the University student body had been almost annihilated...A more pathetic incident cannot be imagined or one of more lasting impression."

Among those injured were head coach Oliver Cutts and player-manager Harry Leslie, who later served as governor of Indiana from 1929 to 1933. Band members, riding in the second car, miraculously escaped serious harm when the car left the track and plunged down an embankment.

The balance of the 1903 season was canceled. With the help of the Big Four Railroad, money was raised, and in 1909 Memorial Gymnasium was dedicated on the Purdue campus to those killed in the wreck. The building now is known as Felix Haas Hall, serving the Department of Computer Science.

On September 12, 1936, a water heater exploded in a shower room at the Boilermakers' training facility at Ross Camp, about 10 miles west of campus, severely burning six players and ultimately killing two.

In those days, gasoline was used to remove adhesive tape from players' bodies, and some of the gasoline, upon being rinsed off in the showers, came in contact with the heater, causing a sea of fire along the floor.

Those injured were guard Carl Dahlback, fullback Lowell Decker, fullback John Drake, halfback Pat Malaska, guard Jim Maloney, and halfback Tom McGannon. Dahlback died the following morning and McGannon four days later.

In his report to Purdue president Edward Elliott, head coach Noble Kizer concluded: "Although the use of inflammable fluids, such as gasoline, naphtha, and benzene, as tape softeners, have been common practice, we have definitely determined to ban their use at Purdue."

74 Purdue Grand Prix

Sixty-five miles north of "The Greatest Spectacle in Racing" resides "The Greatest Spectacle in College Racing."

The Purdue Grand Prix is a 50-mile, 160-lap go-kart race that runs on a Saturday every April. All 33 participating karts—mirroring the 33 cars that race in the Indianapolis 500—are created from scratch by seven-person student teams with a Yamaha KT-100 engine and driven by students. The average cost is $5,000, and the money is funded in part by a sponsor. Karts can reach top speeds upward of 50 mph.

The race dates to 1958, when a group of students brainstormed ideas for engineering majors to "exercise their skills, knowledge, and enthusiasm." The inaugural race consisted of karts built with lawnmower engines and was run on a field and adjacent parking lot. James Moneyhun was the winner with an average speed of 22.6 mph.

From 1969 to 2008, the Purdue Grand Prix was run on a track located northeast of Ross-Ade Stadium at the corner of Northwestern Avenue and Cherry Lane. As part of the Mackey Arena Complex project, a new track was built in 2009 at what is now the corner of Cherry Lane and U.S. Highway 231—in the vicinity of Alexander Field, Bittinger Stadium, Folk Field, and the Schwartz Tennis Center, an area often referred to as the Northwest Athletics Complex. The current track, which cost $1 million to build, features an advanced computer scoring system that provides up-to-date race-day information for crews and spectators.

Jimmy Simpson, a 2016 graduate in organizational leadership, is the only four-time winner of the Purdue Grand Prix (2013, 2014, 2015, and 2016). The Indianapolis native has made a career out of racing. There has been a pair of three-time champions, Ian Smith (1993, 1994, and 1995) and Timothy O'Brien (2002, 2003, and 2005). Liz Lehmann was the first female winner, in 2007. The victor celebrates by chugging milk à la the Indy 500.

Originally sponsored by the Purdue Auto Club, the Purdue Grand Prix has been sanctioned by the Purdue Grand Prix Foundation since 1965. The nonprofit organization aims to raise $10,000 annually for scholarships based on its motto of "students helping students." Recipients are awarded $750 apiece based on campus and community involvement, academic achievement, and need.

Each Purdue Grand Prix has a grand marshal, and among those who have held that title is Purdue alum Neil Armstrong, the first man to walk on the moon.

An alumni race takes place every five years.

75 24 Big Ten Men's Basketball Championships (and Counting)

Purdue proudly boasts itself as the leader in Big Ten men's basketball championships.

Since the league originally known as the Western Conference first sponsored men's basketball in 1905–06, the Boilermakers have won 24 regular season titles: 1911 (co), 1912 (co), 1921 (tri), 1922, 1926 (four-way), 1928 (co), 1930, 1932, 1934, 1935 (tri), 1936 (co), 1938, 1940, 1969, 1979 (tri), 1984 (co), 1987 (co), 1988, 1994, 1995, 1996, 2010 (tri), 2017, and 2019 (co).

By head coaches, Ward "Piggy" Lambert patrolled the sidelines for 11 championships, followed by Gene Keady with six. Current coach Matt Painter has won three crowns, while Ralph Jones won two and George King and Lee Rose both captured one.

Fittingly, Purdue had to beat intrastate rival Indiana in the season finale to win its inaugural championship in 1911. The Boilermakers, who had won their first seven conference games before enduring a four-game losing streak, defeated the Hoosiers 21–16 at Memorial Gymnasium on March 4 to share the title with Minnesota.

In 1912, the Boilermakers won their first of two unde-feated championships with a 10–0 conference record (tied with Wisconsin at 12–0, and obviously the schools did not play that season). Purdue duplicated such perfection in 1930, led by Charles "Stretch" Murphy and John Wooden.

Purdue and Indiana have wound up tied for first place in the Big Ten four times: 1926 (8–4), 1928 (10–2), 1936 (11–1), and 1987 (15–3). Joining the Boilermakers and the Hoosiers atop the standings in 1926 were Iowa and Michigan, resulting in a four-way shared championship. Purdue and Indiana did not face one another in 1936, during a time when the Big Ten played a rotating schedule (each team faced an opponent for two seasons and then did not play that foe for one year).

In 15 seasons from 1926 to 1940, the Boilermakers won nine championships, all under Lambert, including the program's first three-peat in 1934, 1935, and 1936.

Lambert retired on January 22, 1946, after 28½ seasons as head coach, and his 228 Big Ten wins still ranked fourth in conference history through the 2019–20 season behind Bob Knight, Tom Izzo, and Keady.

Post-Lambert, Purdue did not win a Big Ten championship until 1969, when King engineered the Boilermakers to an outright title by four games over Illinois and Ohio State, the largest margin in school history. That team went all the way to the NCAA Final Four before losing to UCLA in the national championship game.

Ten years later, the Rose-coached Boilermakers were conference tri-champs en route to a runner-up finish in the NIT.

Keady arrived in West Lafayette from Western Kentucky University on April 11, 1980, and in his fourth season won his first Big Ten championship after Purdue was picked to finish ninth. The Boilermakers followed with back-to-back titles in 1987 and 1988, and they then won three in a row (all outright) for the second time in school history in 1994, 1995, and 1996. They were the first Big Ten team to accomplish the feat since Ohio State from 1960 to 1962.

The Boilermakers' all-time wins leader with 512 overall and 265 in Big Ten games, Keady was succeeded by one of his former players, Painter, following the 2004–05 season. Two of Painter's three Big Ten crowns to date (2017 and 2019) came in a three-year span, and in the other season the Boilermakers finished tied for second by one game. All told, Purdue has wound up as conference runner-up on 18 occasions, with Lambert, Keady, and Painter's squads each doing so four times.

Painter piloted Purdue to its only Big Ten Tournament title in 2009.

The Boilermakers have finished last in the Big Ten merely nine times. Four of those came in a five-year span from 1950 to 1954.

Through the 2019–20 season, Indiana owned the second-most Big Ten championships with 22, while Ohio State had 20.

Purdue also is the all-time leader with 977 Big Ten wins. Illinois (947) and Indiana (941) rank second and third.

76 Bob DeMoss

Bob DeMoss is the patriarch of the Cradle of Quarterbacks.

DeMoss initially gained fame as a freshman at Purdue in 1945. He helped the Boilermakers win their first four games and move into the national rankings at No. 9. Their next opponent was fourth-ranked Ohio State on October 20 in Columbus. Purdue raced to a 28–0 lead and went on to an improbable 35–13 victory before 73,585 fans, the most ever to watch the Boilermakers at that time.

DeMoss went on to be Purdue's primary quarterback through 1948, passing for 2,759 yards and 23 touchdowns during his career, and then played professionally with the New York Bulldogs in 1949.

DeMoss subsequently embarked on a 42-year tenure at Purdue as an assistant coach (1950–69), head coach (1970–72), and assistant athletics director (1973–92). Along the way, he recruited and developed many members of the Cradle—Dale Samuels, Len Dawson, Bob Griese, Mike Phipps, and Gary Danielson—earning fame as a "quarterback architect."

Twice as an assistant, DeMoss served as acting head coach for Jack Mollenkopf.

Prior to Purdue's game at Michigan on October 21, 1961, Mollenkopf was sidelined with an intestinal ailment. DeMoss filled in for two games, including a 9–0 victory over fifth-ranked Iowa on October 28 at Ross-Ade Stadium. The Hawkeyes were held scoreless for the first time in 79 games, dating to 1952, and DeMoss was honored as coach of the week by United Press International.

Mollenkopf missed the final four games of the 1968 season with acute infectious hepatitis. DeMoss again assumed control of the team, and the Boilermakers won three games to finish 8–2 overall and tie for third in the Big Ten at 5–2.

Two days after Mollenkopf announced his retirement on January 7, 1970, DeMoss was named his successor, becoming the third and most recent Purdue alum to serve as head coach.

In DeMoss' three seasons as head coach, the Boilermakers posted a 13–18 record, including an 11–12 Big Ten mark. On October 3, 1970, Purdue upset third-ranked Stanford 26–14 on the road, earning DeMoss coach of the week laurels by UPI.

In 1972, DeMoss decided to instill the wishbone offense, which was growing in popularity around the country. But after the Boilermakers lost their first three games, he opted to bring back their conventional Power-I formation. Purdue rebounded to finish 6–5 overall and 6–2 in the Big Ten, good for third place behind co-champions Michigan and Ohio State (7–1).

The Boilermakers had a chance to at least share the title before losing to the third-ranked Wolverines 9–6 on November 18 in Ann Arbor. On a third-down play in the first quarter, halfback Otis Armstrong appeared headed for a first down or perhaps a touchdown before slipping on the slick Michigan Stadium turf at the 8-yard line. Purdue was forced to settle for a 25-yard field goal by Frank Conner, and the Wolverines won the game on a 30-yard field goal by Mike Lantry with one minute remaining.

DeMoss resigned as coach on December 3, 1972. Wrote Bob Collins in his book *Boilermakers: A History of Purdue Football*: "The gangly, timid youngster from Dayton, Kentucky, had completed the cycle...Purdue's first great quarterback...the developer of All-Americans and right-hand man of Mollenkopf...and, finally, the head coach. Few men have contributed as much, in so many ways, to a school's football program."

On three occasions, DeMoss was an assistant coach in postseason All-Star games: 1960 Blue-Gray Game, 1967 Hula Bowl, and

1968 All-American Bowl. He previously played in the inaugural North-South Shrine Game in 1948 and the 1949 Hula Bowl.

As assistant athletics director, DeMoss oversaw the baseball, men's cross country, men's golf, men's swimming & diving, men's tennis, men's track & field, and wrestling programs. Following his retirement in 1992, DeMoss maintained his residence in West Lafayette and was a fixture at Boilermaker games and other events. He was inducted into the Purdue Intercollegiate Athletics Hall of Fame in 1999.

DeMoss, who earned a bachelor's degree in forestry, died in 2017, at age 90.

77 Jim Young

His tenure lasted but five seasons, but Jim Young still ranks as one of the most successful football coaches in Purdue history.

Under Young from 1977 to 1981, the Boilermakers compiled a 38–19–1 overall record (.664 winning percentage), including a 26–14–1 Big Ten mark (.646). They played in and won three bowl games: 1978 Peach (41–21 over Georgia Tech), 1979 Bluebonnet (27–22 over Tennessee), and 1980 Liberty (28–25 over Missouri).

Young came to Purdue from the University of Arizona, where in four seasons he posted a 31–13 record, with two nine-win seasons and a Western Athletic Conference co-championship. Beforehand, Young was an assistant under legendary coach Bo Schembechler at Miami (Ohio) (1964–68) and Michigan (1969–72) and filled in as the Wolverines' head coach in the 1970 Rose Bowl after Schembechler suffered a heart attack prior to the game. A native of Van Wert, Ohio, Young attended Ohio State for one year—playing on the Buckeyes' 1954 national championship team—before transferring to Bowling Green University.

In an introductory conference call with members of the media, Young declared, "We'll throw more than most teams in the Midwest," and later said, "Purdue fans will enjoy our style because the school has had success passing before." He made good on his word.

Young and the Boilermakers proceeded to beat out Notre Dame for highly touted quarterback Mark Herrmann from Carmel, Indiana. Over the next four seasons, Herrmann completely rewrote the Purdue and Big Ten record book for passing, setting nine NCAA records along the way.

Regarded as a visionary, Young brought a new dimension to the run-dominated Big Ten.

"Coach Young felt like with our personnel and what my abilities were that we needed to open things up a little bit and not be that traditional 'three yards and a cloud of dust' that certainly Ohio State and Michigan were at that time and many of the others in the Big Ten," Herrmann said. "We really felt we had an advantage with the passing game. We did a lot of motion and some three wide receiver sets, which you didn't see much back in those days, and spread things out. Ultimately, he decided to put me back in the shotgun to give me a little more time to throw the ball. There is no question that Coach Young was kind of ahead of the game."

The 1977 Boilermakers started 2–4, won three games in a row, and then dropped their last two to finish 5–6—the program's fifth straight losing season and seventh in eight years. But what followed was arguably the most successful three-year run ever at Purdue: 9–2–1 in 1978, 10–2 in 1979 (the only 10-win campaign in school history), and 9–3 in 1980. With 28 victories during that stretch, the Boilermakers won more games than Ohio State (27) and Notre Dame (25) and matched Michigan. In Big Ten games, Purdue was 20–3–1, just behind the Wolverines and Buckeyes at 21–3.

Young was named Big Ten Coach of the Year in 1978 on the heels of a third-place conference finish highlighted by a 27–16 victory over No. 16 Ohio State at Ross-Ade Stadium on October 14, Purdue's first over the Buckeyes since 1967 and the 400th win in school history. The Boilermakers tied for second in the Big Ten in 1979 and 1980, their best showing since capturing the championship in 1967.

Three days prior to the 1981 season finale, Young announced he was resigning as coach. He said he wanted to devote all his time to the associate athletics director position he had accepted in August after Fred Schaus left to become athletics director at West Virginia University.

"This is a career change," Young told his players. "After 26 years of coaching, my family and I have decided to concentrate on athletic administration here at Purdue."

Athletics director George King marveled at the run Young made at conference giants Michigan and Ohio State. "Naturally, I hate to see Jim give up the reins," King said. "He changed the philosophy of the Big Ten when it was the 'Big Two' and the 'Little Eight' at a time when I thought even hiring Bo Schembechler or Woody Hayes wouldn't make a difference. I didn't think one man could change it, but Jim proved me wrong."

Young also reinvigorated what had become an apathetic Purdue fan base. The Boilermakers' three highest season attendance averages came under Young, including the high-water mark of 69,892 in 1981. The largest crowd ever at Ross-Ade—71,629—saw the Boilermakers rally to defeat Indiana 24–23 on November 22, 1980. Purdue boasted a 24–6 home record under Young, including a 12-game winning streak in 1978 and 1979.

Young remained at Purdue just one more year before resuming his coaching career at Army from 1983 to 1990, posting a 51–39–1 record and leading the Black Knights to the three bowl games.

"I've always done what I felt was right at the particular time," Young said. "I enjoyed coaching at Purdue very much. At the time I got out, I had spent a lot of time on the program and put a lot into it. I thought I should explore other possibilities, perhaps going the athletics director route. I certainly wasn't unhappy at Purdue. Pursuing an athletics directorship didn't excite me as much as I thought it might. When the West Point job opened, it appealed to me."

With a career record of 120–71–2, Young was inducted into the College Football Hall of Fame in 1999. He was a member of the Purdue Intercollegiate Athletics Hall of Fame class of 2004.

78 1929 Big Ten Football Champions

An experienced team, led by three senior standouts—quarterback Glen Harmeson, tackle Elmer Sleight, and halfback Ralph "Pest" Welch—with the addition of sophomores Charles Miller at center and Alex Yunevich at fullback, led to lofty expectations for the 1929 Boilermakers.

They did not disappoint.

The season would be defined in the fourth quarter of the second game, the first contest against Michigan since 1900. The visiting Wolverines led 16–6 after three quarters on October 12 before Purdue erupted for four touchdowns to win 30–16 before 25,000 fans. Yunevich scored three times while rushing for 127 yards on 21 carries in his first Big Ten game. Harmeson, who had been shifted from quarterback to halfback, gained 126 yards rushing.

After allowing 30 points in its first two games, the Purdue defense stiffened and surrendered merely two touchdowns the rest of the season. The offense scored at least 26 points in five of the first six games, and the Boilermakers were unblemished at 6–0 when Iowa came to town as the Homecoming opponent for what the Purdue *Exponent* called "the most crucial game ever played by a Boilermaker football team" on a gloomy November 16 afternoon. The Hawkeyes had knocked off previously unbeaten Minnesota 9–7 in their last game. Harmeson connected with end Bill Woerner on a 17-yard passing play in the second quarter for what proved to be the game's only score, and Harmeson intercepted a pass by Oran Pape to thwart Iowa's final possession. The 7–0 victory before 26,000 fans—the largest crowd ever assembled at Ross-Ade Stadium to that point—guaranteed Purdue its first, and to date only, outright conference championship.

Wrote Gordon Graham, sports editor of the Lafayette *Journal & Courier*, on November 18: "It has been a long, hard climb, but after more than thirty years of waiting, a Purdue football team is finally perched on the Big Ten gridiron throne, lording it over nine other inferior elevens who for weeks have been fighting to attain the same exalted position now held by Jimmy Phelan's courageous group of warriors."

Now, Indiana was all that stood between Purdue and perfection, and the Boilermakers put an exclamation point on their season with a 32–0 victory in Bloomington. Fittingly, Harmeson passed to Welch for a 52-yard touchdown, Welch passed to Harmeson for a 55-yard score and Sleight recovered a Welch fumble in the end zone for the final touchdown.

The Boilermakers finished 8–0 (5–0 Big Ten), and Sleight and Welch were named the first All-Americans in school history. They were consensus choices, being picked by the American Football Coaches Association, Associated Press, *Collier's Weekly*, International News Service, and Walter Camp Football Foundation.

Not only did the Boilermakers lose key senior players from their championship squad, they also lost Phelan, who left to become head coach at the University of Washington in the spring of 1930. Welch accompanied him as an assistant, and the Huskies went to the Rose Bowl in 1937. Phelan stayed at Washington through 1941 and was succeeded by Welch. Phelan went on to coach professionally and later served three terms as county commissioner of Sacramento County in California. He was inducted into the College Football Hall of Fame in 1973.

For its next head coach, Purdue picked Noble Kizer, an assistant who trained the linemen under Phelan and a fellow Notre Dame alum. That's where the similarities ended. According to Howard Kissell, a halfback who played for both coaches, Phelan was high-strung and had a "crisp tongue," while Kizer was more laid back and "never cursed his players." Kizer, from Plymouth, Indiana, was an offensive guard for the Fighting Irish under coach Knute Rockne from 1922 to 1924 and a member of the 1924 national championship team that featured the fabled Four Horsemen.

79 Darryl Stingley

The story of Darryl Stingley is tragic and enriching. On August 12, 1978, the former Purdue halfback and split end saw his football career come to an end in an NFL exhibition game.

In his fifth season with the New England Patriots, Stingley was paralyzed from the neck down as the result of a vicious hit leveled by Oakland Raiders' defensive back Jack Tatum. On the play, which was pronounced controversial but not illegal, Tatum lowered his shoulder and laid his forearm and helmet into Stingley's face mask as the receiver leapt for an overthrown pass from quarterback Steve Grogan.

Stingley's neck was broken and his spine fractured, and he was left a quadriplegic at age 26. He eventually regained limited movement in his right arm and was able to operate his electric wheelchair.

"I have relived that moment over and over again," Stingley said in a 1988 interview with the Associated Press. "I remember thinking, 'What's going to happen to me? If I live, what am I going to be like?' And then there were all those whys, whys, whys?

"It was only after I stopped asking why, that I was able to regroup and go on with my life."

Stingley accomplished his greatest goal post-injury on May 9, 1992, when he received his bachelor's degree in physical education from Purdue. He was 24 hours short of graduating when he left after the 1972 season to pursue an NFL career. Stingley completed the work by taking courses via cable television offered by the Citywide College of Chicago. He took part in commencement ceremonies in the Elliott Hall of Music at Purdue and was given a standing ovation by the crowd of some 6,000.

"There's a sense of accomplishment that equals anything I've ever done in my life," Stingley said. "Graduating completes the dream, and it's proof that despite whatever setback you have in life, any kind of adversity can be overcome."

Bob DeMoss, who was Stingley's coach at Purdue, helped his former player get on track to finish his education.

"I'm proud of Darryl's effort and his dedication," DeMoss told *Gold & Black Illustrated*. "This was a tough thing for him to do, and he did it. He was the same way as a player—dedicated and unselfish. He's a good example for other people."

Although Stingley was given the position of executive director of player personnel for the Patriots in 1979, it was little more than a title, and he channeled his remaining life's work on humanitarian efforts. Among them, he started a nonprofit foundation to help inner-city youth in Chicago, where he was born and raised. Stingley also visited paralyzed patients in hospitals and counseled them.

"When I'm gone, I'd like to be remembered not as the football player who had an accident, but as a man who made a great contribution to his fellow man," said Stingley, who co-authored his autobiography *Happy to be Alive*.

At Purdue, Stingley earned honorable mention All-America honors as a junior in 1971, when he had 36 receptions for 734 yards, an average of 20.4 yards per catch. The Patriots selected him with the 19th pick in the 1973 NFL Draft, the third Purdue player selected in the first round that year. Stingley went on to be named to the NFL All-Rookie team.

Stingley was inducted into the Purdue Intercollegiate Athletics Hall of Fame in 2004.

Meanwhile, Stingley and Tatum never reconciled. They were scheduled to meet in 1996, but Stingley canceled after learning that the meeting was to promote Tatum's book. Stingley died in 2007 at age 55, and Tatum died three years later.

Stingley's grandson, Derek Stingley Jr., played cornerback for 2019 national champion LSU.

Lin Dunn

Lin Dunn built the Purdue women's basketball program into one of the finest in the country.

In nine years, Dunn guided the Boilermakers to eight 20-win seasons; seven NCAA Tournament berths, including the 1994 Final Four; and three Big Ten championships. She coached a trio of first-team All-Americans: Joy Holmes, MaChelle Joseph, and Stacey Lovelace.

When Dunn was hired on July 18, 1987, after stints at Austin Peay State, Mississippi, and Miami, the Boilermakers had never won 20 games in a season or played in the postseason and had finished higher than fifth place in the Big Ten only once.

Dunn made her presence felt immediately, leading the 1987–88 Boilermakers to their first-ever 20-win season at 21–10 and their inaugural national postseason tournament, in which they finished as runner-up in the eight-team National Women's Invitational Tournament.

The following season, Purdue played in the NCAA Tournament for the first time and a year later advanced to the Sweet 16.

When Dunn took the reins at Purdue, she promised a Big Ten championship within four years, and she proved to be right on target. In 1990–91, the Boilermakers captured the Big Ten title with a 17–1 record in conference play. They went 26–3 overall and received a first-round bye and No. 2 seed in the NCAA Tournament.

Meanwhile, interest in the Boilermakers soared. Dunn, a native of Dresden, Tennessee, became a fan favorite with her Southern twang and fun-loving personality, traits that also were key to her success as a recruiter.

The 1993–94 Boilermakers had no seniors on their roster and were picked to finish fifth in the Big Ten, but they wound up going 29–5 overall and sharing the conference championship en route to reaching the Final Four. They defeated a No. 1–ranked team for the first time in school history (57–54 over Penn State on February 11 at Mackey Arena) and took down Stanford 82–65 in the West Regional final on the Cardinal's home court.

As an extra means of incentive, Dunn had offered to get a tattoo if the Boilermakers made the Final Four, and seven months

Head coach Lin Dunn led the Purdue women's basketball program to eight 20-win seasons; seven NCAA Tournament berths, including the 1994 Final Four; and three Big Ten championships.

after they did, she got the word FINAL and the number 4 emblazoned above her right chest.

"I was kidding, and they were not," Dunn said. "It came back to haunt me the minute we beat Stanford because the chant was not 'Final Four, Final Four' but 'tattoo, tattoo.'"

Purdue repeated as co–Big Ten champions in 1995 and advanced to the NCAA Tournament Elite Eight.

Dunn was famous for her "Thought for the Day," shared with her players before every practice. Her favorite: "The three most important bones—the wishbone: you've got to have a dream; the funny bone: laughter is a tranquilizer with no side effect; and the backbone: if you don't stand for something, you will fall for anything!"

After a disheartening first-round exit from the NCAA Tournament in 1996, Dunn did not have her contract renewed on March 23. She left Purdue as the winningest women's basketball coach in school history with a 206–68 record (a crackling .752 winning percentage), but since has been passed by one of her former players, Sharon Versyp.

Incredibly, Dunn's Purdue teams were a perfect 18–0 against intrastate rival Indiana. They were 28–1 against all schools from the Hoosier State, losing only to Notre Dame in Dunn's final game with the Boilermakers.

Dunn was honored as Big Ten Coach of the Year in 1989 and 1991.

Her accomplishments did not go unnoticed when it came to selecting coaches for United States women's basketball teams in international competition. Dunn was an assistant for the bronze medal–winning 1992 Olympic team in Spain and the gold medal–winning 1990 World Championships squad in Malaysia. She served as head coach for the 1995 R. William Jones Cup Team that won bronze in Taiwan.

Dunn and Purdue went through a bumpy breakup that finally came to an end when she returned to Mackey to coach in an alumnae game on February 22, 2004. She was inducted into the Purdue Intercollegiate Athletics Hall of Fame in 2012.

"I've always said this...99.9 percent of every experience I had here was wonderful," Dunn said during her homecoming. "I want to send the message that the past is the past, and I'm happy to be included in the Purdue family."

Post-Purdue, Dunn enjoyed success as a professional coach, first with the Portland Power of the American Basketball League and later with the Seattle Storm and Indiana Fever of the WNBA. She piloted the Fever to the league championship in 2012.

In 38 years as a head coach (25 collegiately and 13 professionally), Dunn, a true pioneer in women's athletics history, won 683 games. She was a member of the Women's Basketball Hall of Fame class of 2014 and two years later received the Jostens-Berenson Lifetime Achievement Award in recognition of her lifelong commitment of service to women's basketball.

Since 2016, Dunn has been an assistant at the University of Kentucky. She is founder of the consulting firm Coaches for Coaches, which helps train head coaches in all aspects of leading successful programs.

81 NFL Draft Streak

On April 30, 2016, a lifetime of dreaming and waiting culminated a stressful, anxious day for Purdue defensive back Anthony Brown.

Finally, when the call came, Brown heard Dallas Cowboys owner Jerry Jones' voice on the other end. One of the league's storied franchises would select Brown in the sixth round with the 189th overall pick of the NFL Draft.

"I don't wish it on anybody," Brown said of the agonizing wait. Then, of the life-changing call: "Just unreal—it was finally happening."

Jones' call also brought relief to Purdue fans who wondered if the program's streak of having at least one player selected in every NFL Draft since 1998 would remain alive. A pair of fifth-round selections the following two seasons—wide receiver DeAngelo Yancey to the Green Bay Packers in 2017 and linebacker Ja'Whaun Bentley to the New England Patriots in 2018—extended that streak to 21 consecutive years.

Purdue's streak ended with the 2019 draft after 22 seasons. A total of 48 players were selected in that span, including three who went in the first round: linebacker Anthony Spencer to Dallas in 2007, tight end Dustin Keller to the New York Jets in 2008, and linebacker Ryan Kerrigan to the Washington Redskins in 2011.

The streak also encompassed the NFL entrances of some of Purdue's biggest stars, including quarterback Drew Brees (second round to the San Diego Chargers in 2001) and defensive tackle Kawann Short (second round to the Carolina Panthers in 2013).

While the Boilermakers' consistency is impressive, Michigan and USC have both had a player chosen in every draft since 1939. Michigan State (78 years), Nebraska (56), Iowa (41), and Wisconsin (40) were the only Big Ten programs with longer streaks than Purdue through 2019.

Two Boilermakers were subsequently drafted in 2020—tight end Brycen Hopkins by the Los Angeles Rams in the fourth round and linebacker Markus Bailey by the Cincinnati Bengals in the seventh round.

82 Charles "Stretch" Murphy

At 6'6", Charles Murphy stood out in a crowd. Even more so on a basketball court, where "Stretch" became the game's first bona fide big man and the Boilermakers' first three-time All-American.

Murphy came to Purdue in the fall of 1926, a few months after leading Marion (Indiana) High School to the state championship and earning all-state honors. He spent a season on the freshman team before moving up to the varsity and embarking on a record-setting career. His first start was on January 2, 1928, and Murphy scored 16 points in a 40–32 win at Wabash.

In those days—when the average height of a basketball player was 6'2"—after each made basket a jump ball ensued. Murphy won practically every one, giving the Boilermakers a substantial advantage.

"That was naturally down my alley," Murphy said in a 1990 interview with *Gold & Black Illustrated.* "I could get the tipoff 99 percent of the time against anybody they put in at center. The tipoff was a quite a thing then. We had plays from it."

By the 1928–29 season (Murphy's junior year), interest in Purdue basketball was on the rise, so much so that the Boilermakers moved four home games from Memorial Gymnasium on campus across the Wabash River to the new Lafayette Jefferson High School gymnasium, which had twice the spectator capacity. In the first game on January 14, 1929, the Boilermakers set a conference scoring record in a 64–16 win over the University of Chicago. Murphy scored 26 points, then the most ever by a Big Ten player. For the season, he totaled 143 points to establish another high-water mark.

The 6'6" Charles "Stretch" Murphy became the game of basketball's first bona fide big man and the Boilermakers' first three-time All-American from 1928 to 1930.

After sharing the Big Ten championship with Indiana in 1928, the Boilermakers finished third in 1929. With the addition of eventual All-America guard John Wooden in 1930, Purdue returned to the top, going 10–0 in conference play. Along the way, Murphy topped his game scoring record with 28 points against Ohio State on February 2. For the season, he averaged a record 13.7 points per game.

In addition to his scoring exploits, Murphy was a dominant rebounder and defender around the basket.

The Boilermakers, under legendary head coach Ward "Piggy" Lambert, posted a 41–8 record during Murphy's three seasons.

In a 1991 interview with the *Tampa Tribune*, Wooden said, "Today, only the real basketball buffs who lived in the Midwest are aware of just how great Stretch Murphy was. In my opinion, he was one of the all-time great players."

Murphy accomplished so much despite having to cram his size 15 feet in size 12 shoes, the largest made in his era.

After graduating from Purdue, Murphy continued to play briefly as a professional—making $25 per game, $50 tops—before becoming a coach and director of physical education at Edinburgh (Indiana) High School for several years. He then earned his master's degree at Columbia University and embarked on a distinguished career with the Boys Clubs of America, first in Bristol,

Boilermakers in the Naismith Basketball Hall of Fame

Player	Played at Purdue	Inducted
Charles "Stretch" Murphy, C	1927–30	1960
John Wooden, G	1929–32	1960

Coach	Coached at Purdue	Inducted
Ward "Piggy" Lambert	1916–17, 1918–46	2006

Connecticut, and then in Tampa, Florida. He ultimately retired in Tampa and died in 1992.

Murphy was inducted into the Naismith Basketball Hall of Fame in 1960, Purdue Intercollegiate Athletics Hall of Fame in 1995, and National Collegiate Basketball Hall of Fame in 2006.

83 Remember the 1998 Alamo Bowl

After a program-shifting 1997 season, capped by an Alamo Bowl victory, Lafayette *Journal & Courier* sports editor Jim Lefko questioned, "How does the most popular man in Greater Lafayette—head coach Joe Tiller—take the momentum from a 9–3 season and use it to springboard into 1998?"

The answer: Drew Brees. A member of Tiller's first recruiting class—one that was ranked 10th in the Big Ten by guru Tom Lemming—Brees arrived at Purdue as a little-known quarterback from Austin, Texas. Even Tiller and his staff weren't completely confident in Brees, and they signed junior college signal-caller David Edgerton.

Following a 3–4 start, the Boilermakers won their last five regular season games, outscoring the opposition 211 to 75, capped by a 52–7 victory over Indiana at Ross-Ade Stadium on November 21 for the 500th win in school history.

Purdue returned to the Alamo Bowl for a December 29 date with fourth-ranked Kansas State in San Antonio, Texas. The Wildcats were 11–1, having only lost to Texas A&M 36–33 in double-overtime in the Big 12 Championship Game. Despite its flashy record, that lone setback kept Kansas State from competing for the national championship in the inaugural Bowl Championship Series, and the Wildcats were also passed over on invitations to the Cotton Bowl and the Holiday Bowl (the Big 12's top bowl destinations).

Kansas State, which led the nation in scoring at 46.9 points per game, no doubt felt slighted and fair to say looked disinterested in playing in the Alamo Bowl.

After a scoreless first quarter, the Boilermakers built a 17–7 halftime advantage thanks to two Brees touchdown passes (five yards to Chris Daniels and 30 to Isaac Jones) and a 25-yard field goal by Travis Dorsch.

When Dorsch kicked a 26-yard field goal late in the third quarter, Purdue appeared primed for the upset with a 27–13 advantage. But the Wildcats, behind Heisman Trophy runner-up quarterback Michael Bishop, awakened and scored three fourth-quarter touchdowns to take their first lead at 34–30 with 1:24 remaining.

Then Brees went to work, manufacturing a six-play, 80-yard drive that culminated with a 24-yard touchdown pass to Jones with 30 seconds to play. Brees completed three passes for 45 yards on the drive and ran 11 yards for a first down.

Brees finished the game with pedestrian numbers through the air: 25 of 53 for 230 yards and three touchdowns with three interceptions. And Purdue mustered merely five rushing yards to finish with a season-low 235 yards of total offense in the memorable 37–34 victory.

Defense was the story for the Boilermakers, who kept Bishop bottled up to the tune of 9 of 24 passing for 182 yards. They came up with four interceptions (two by safety Billy Gustin) and five sacks (3½ by end Chike Okeafor). End Rosevelt Colvin had one-and-a-half sacks, forced and recovered a fumble, and blocked a field goal.

"Of all my games at Purdue, this is the best," Colvin said. "I think our defensive success was a combination of good coverage and rushing the passer."

David Nugent recovered a fumble in the end zone for a touchdown, one of seven total turnovers by the Wildcats, who were whistled for 125 penalty yards. Two botched Purdue punt snaps resulted in a pair of Kansas State touchdowns.

"Right now, I'm thinking, how did we win that game?" Brees said. "All I can say is that offense wins games and defensive truly wins championships."

Brees and Colvin were tabbed the game's most valuable players.

Years later, Tiller remembered the Alamo thusly: "Kansas State had been ranked No. 1 in the country until losing the Big 12 Championship Game. I think we were like the rest of the football world, and that is surprised that they wound up in the Alamo Bowl. They had a great football team. What I remember most is how well we played defensively. That might have been the best game we have played on defense against a quality offense. Our two ends, Colvin and Okeafor, really dominated their offensive tackles. Obviously, I remember the final throw. But earlier on that drive, Drew pulled the ball down and ran for a critical first down."

Purdue finished the season with a 9–4 record and ranked 23rd in the final Associated Press poll.

84 Other Memorable Bowl Games

Through the 2019 season, Purdue football has played in 19 bowl games, boasting a 10–9 record.

Joe Tiller took the Boilermakers to 10 bowl games in his 12 seasons as head coach from 1997 to 2008, while Jim Young engineered three consecutive bowl teams from 1978 to 1980 over the course of his five-year tenure. Current head coach Jeff Brohm revived the program with back-to-back bowl appearances in his first two seasons (2017 and 2018) after a four-year absence.

The Boilermakers' two trips to the Rose Bowl (a 14–13 win over USC in 1967 and a 34–24 loss to Washington in 2001) stand head and shoulders above the others, followed by the pulsating 37–34 victory over fourth-ranked Kansas State in the 1998 Alamo Bowl.

Among the other memorable bowl games:

1978 Peach Bowl (Atlanta)
Purdue scored three touchdowns, two by Wally Jones, in just over four-and-a-half minutes to race to a 21–0 first-quarter lead and went on to make easy work of Georgia Tech, winning 41–21 on Christmas Day. The 17th-ranked Boilermakers led 34–7 at halftime. Mark Herrmann passed for two touchdowns and rushed for another to earn most valuable player honors. Purdue's "Junk Defense," which employed myriad unusual formations, forced four turnovers (two fumbles and two interceptions).

1979 Bluebonnet Bowl (Houston)
A 17-yard touchdown pass from Herrmann to Dave Young with 1:30 remaining gave the Boilermakers a dramatic 27–22 victory

over Tennessee. Herrmann enjoyed another MVP performance with 303 passing yards and three touchdowns. Purdue built a 21–0 advantage in the third quarter but wound up falling behind 22–21, setting up the heroics by Herrmann and Young. With the victory, the 12th-ranked Boilermakers recorded the only 10-win season in school history.

1980 Liberty Bowl (Memphis, Tennessee)

Herrmann captured his third straight MVP award in a 28–25 Purdue win over Missouri. In his final game, Herrmann, who took over play-calling duties midway through the first quarter from flu-ridden head coach Jim Young, completed 22 of 28 passes for 289 yards and four touchdowns. Bart Burrell had a pair of touchdown receptions. The Boilermakers, who were up 28–12 in the third quarter, fended off a furious Missouri rally.

1997 Alamo Bowl (San Antonio, Texas)

The 17th-ranked Boilermakers, playing in their first bowl game in 13 years, scored three touchdowns in the third quarter on the way to a 33–20 win over No. 24 Oklahoma State. Billy Dicken passed for 325 yards, including a 69-yard touchdown pass to Chris Daniels to give the Boilermakers a 30–13 lead in the third quarter. Purdue amassed 454 total yards of offense while holding the Cowboys to 368 and forcing four turnovers.

2002 Sun Bowl (El Paso, Texas)

The Boilermakers overcame a 17–0 deficit in the first quarter (in which they were held without a first down and to minus-eight yards total offense) by scoring 34 uninterrupted points to beat Washington 34–24 in a rematch of the 2001 Rose Bowl. After Joey Harris put Purdue ahead 24–17 in the third quarter with a 10-yard touchdown run, Gilbert Gardner put the game away when he forced a fumble and returned it 19 yards for a touchdown. Kyle

Orton completed 25 of 37 passes for 283 yards with two touchdowns en route to being named the game's MVP.

2007 Motor City Bowl (Detroit)
Chris Summers drilled a 40-yard field goal as time expired to give Purdue an exhilarating 51–48 victory over Central Michigan. The Boilermakers rolled to a 34–13 halftime advantage before the Chippewas mounted a remarkable comeback that saw the game tied at 41 and 48. Curtis Painter put on an MVP display by setting school records with 546 passing yards and 540 yards of total offense. The teams combined for 1,022 yards of total offense (Purdue 587 and Central Michigan 435).

2011 Little Caesars Pizza Bowl (Detroit)
The Boilermakers put on a special teams display, recovering two onside kicks and returning a kickoff 99 yards for a touchdown en route to a 37–32 win over Western Michigan. Trailing 15–10 in the second quarter, Raheem Mostert took a Bronco kickoff to the end zone, and the Boilermakers led the rest of the way. Purdue surrendered 439 passing yards but limited Western Michigan to 46 rushing yards and forced six turnovers (four interceptions, two fumbles), including a game-sealing strip by Ryan Russell.

2017 Foster Farms Bowl (Santa Clara, California)
Elijah Sindelar threw a 38-yard touchdown pass to Anthony Mahoungou with 1:44 left in the game. Then, on Arizona's ensuing possession, Jacob Thieneman came up with an interception at the Purdue 36-yard line with 1:16 remaining to seal an exhilarating 38–35 win. Sindelar completed 33 of 53 passes for 396 yards and four touchdowns, all while playing with a torn anterior cruciate ligament in his left knee. Gregory Phillips hauled in a Purdue bowl-record 14 receptions.

85 Spend a Fiery Night at Holloway Gymnasium

One of the hottest tickets on campus during the fall doesn't involve spending a Saturday afternoon in Ross-Ade Stadium.

Increasingly, fans have found their way to Holloway Gymnasium on Friday and Saturday nights to watch Boilermaker volleyball take on the best teams in the best volleyball conference in the country. The fast-paced, hard-hitting action in the intimate confines has established its place in the fall sports landscape in West Lafayette.

Volleyball debuted as a Purdue varsity sport in 1975 and became the athletics department's first women's "revenue" sport four years later. In 1981, the Big Ten recognized volleyball and began awarding championships in the sport. But by then, the Boilermakers had already begun to earn national attention under the program's first head coach, Carol Dewey, who won a school-record 469 matches over 20 years. She coached five All-Americans and six Academic All-Americans.

Her 1982 squad went 33–1, winning the Big Ten championship and reaching the NCAA Tournament regional finals to earn a tie for fifth place. The Boilermakers won the 1985 Big Ten title, as well, going 34–4 overall.

Beginning with Dave Shondell's hiring as head coach in 2003, Purdue volleyball has enjoyed its most successful era. The Boilermakers made nine NCAA Tournament appearances in his first 11 seasons, including trips to the Elite Eight in 2010 and 2013.

Holloway has hosted the NCAA Tournament for first- and second-round competition on multiple occasions as well. The venue is named for Bob Holloway, a 1948 alumnus who donated $2 million.

86 "Defense Lives Here"

On one end of Mackey Arena, adjacent to the visiting team bench, the Paint Crew student section displays its most well-known mantra.

A gold sign with black letters proclaims, DEFENSE LIVES HERE. On the same sign, a "play hard" counter flips over each time a Boilermaker performs a hustle play or some other shutdown defensive maneuver.

That sign celebrates Purdue men's basketball's recent reputation as a blue-collar defensive-minded program under head coach Matt Painter. But the tradition of defensive excellence precedes this most recent era.

Seven Boilermakers have combined to win nine Big Ten Defensive Player of the Year awards, per vote of the conference coaches.

"It's the competitor in you," Rapheal Davis said during his award-winning season of 2014–15. "I love going out there guarding the best player, playing against the best player and competing, playing as hard as I can against their best guy. It's something that you live for to play basketball. If you shy away from it you're not a competitor."

Ricky Hall (1984)

The point guard from Fort Wayne grew into a double-digit scorer by his senior season. By then he already was established as one of the Big Ten's toughest matchups, and his 172 steals rank fifth in school history.

Porter Roberts (1996)

At 6'3", this point guard could use his big-for-the-position frame to boost Purdue's rebounding (he averaged 4.6 per game as a senior) and stifle opponents defensively. And his 464 assists rank fifth in team annals.

Kenneth Lowe (2003, 2004)

Purdue's first two-time winner of the award helped head coach Gene Keady reach the NCAA Tournament for the final time in 2003. Lowe later tutored other Boilermaker defenders when he returned to begin his coaching career as video coordinator.

Chris Kramer (2008, 2010)

Few Boilermakers are more synonymous with defensive intensity. He is the only Purdue player to average more than two steals per game for his career (2.06), and his 274 total steals are a school record.

JaJuan Johnson (2011)

The first Purdue big man to win the award, the 6'10" Johnson blocked 2.3 shots per game while also winning Big Ten Player of the Year honors as a senior.

Rapheal Davis (2015)

After admittedly arriving at Purdue with little defensive acumen, this Fort Wayne product made himself into one of the league's most tenacious perimeter defenders. His leadership is credited with helping restore the program's culture, transitioning from a last-place Big Ten finish in 2014 to a return to the NCAA Tournament the following season.

A.J. Hammons (2016)

Davis' chance to repeat as the league's top defender was thwarted by a fellow Boilermaker, who happened to also be a former summer roommate. Ironically, Hammons led the Big Ten in blocks for three straight seasons but did not do so as a senior while winning this award. His 343 career blocks rank only behind Joe Barry Carroll at Purdue.

The 2018–19 Boilermakers, who advanced to the NCAA Tournament Elite Eight, featured a pair of Big Ten All-Defensive selections in point guard Nojel Eastern and center Matt Haarms. Eastern was honored again the following season.

87 Sing and Dance Along to "Shout!"

Every Big Ten football game is marked by traditions and rituals that rile up the home crowd and provide a unique connection between fans and their team.

When you go to Iowa's Kinnick Stadium, for instance, you can participate in the "Iowa Wave"—an entire stadium waving to the patients watching from top floor of the Iowa Children's Hospital, which overlooks the stadium.

Wisconsin has "Jump Around," where 80,000 fans make Camp Randall Stadium shake by doing as the song suggests in unison. At Ohio State, most of the Ohio Stadium crowd keeps its seats at halftime to watch a sousaphone player dot the *i* when the "Best Damn Band in the Land" forms "Script Ohio."

Ross-Ade Stadium has its own tradition, held in the break between the third and fourth quarters. Since 2006, a Purdue-connected notable or other celebrity leads the crowd in Otis Day and the Knights' version of the song "Shout" from the movie *Animal House*.

Two-time All-American Leroy Keyes led the first rendition on October 21, 2006. Since then the song leaders have included Super Bowl champion quarterbacks Drew Brees and Bob Griese, legendary coaches Gene Keady and Joe Tiller, and astronauts Neil Armstrong and Gene Cernan.

If the Boilermakers have the lead heading into the fourth quarter, you may see some players dancing along from the sideline.

88 The Game That Would Not End

Today, fans are accustomed to college basketball teams working their offense within the strictures of a 30-second shot clock.

Until the introduction of the 45-second shot clock for the 1985–86 season, however, college teams operated much as high school teams in Indiana and many other states still do. Possessions ended only with a basket, a missed basket, a turnover, or a foul.

When you read about what happened when Purdue and Minnesota played on January 29, 1955, you might wonder what took the NCAA 30 more years to add that little clock above the scoreboard.

This game—featuring a then-NCAA record-tying six overtimes—is best remembered not for a particularly heroic individual performance or spectacular play.

This was the game of stalls.

It began before halftime, with Purdue leading 27–23. Boilermaker Denny Blind stood at half court and held the ball. No Minnesota players left their zone defense to engage him defensively. However, the Boilermakers could not re-start and get off a final shot in time and settled for that four-point halftime lead.

Purdue again tried this strategy at the end of regulation, tied at 47. Again, the plan did not wind up productive. Joe Sexson missed a long rushed shot, and Ted Dunn's tip-in attempt at the buzzer did not fall.

Standing only 6'5", Don Beck gave up six inches at center court to Minnesota's Bill Simonovich. But Beck won the overtime jump ball, and Purdue proceeded to hold on to it for the entire first overtime. Blind's long shot rimmed out, and the game continued.

Beck won the second overtime jump, as well, and again, the Boilermakers went into their now-familiar stall. Gordon Graham of the Lafayette *Journal & Courier* described the plan as Purdue's "best chance to make its strategy pay off." A couple of passes set Beck up for a short jumper, but he missed.

On to triple overtime. Beck ended up with the jump ball, and the Golden Gophers again stuck to their zone defense. Dan Thornburg's shot missed in the final seconds. The score remained 47 apiece.

On his fourth try in overtime, Simonovich finally won the jump. Minnesota decided to try its own stall—with even worse results than Purdue accomplished. The Golden Gophers called a timeout with 18 seconds left to set up a play. However, Thornburg deflected a pass to Sexson, whose long shot at the buzzer again was off the mark.

Action finally picked up in the fifth overtime. Sexson scored on a layup with 4:25 to play to break that 47–47 stalemate. Minnesota turned up the pressure, and Gerald Lindsley's steal-and-score tied the game again with 2:45 left.

Of course, Purdue responded by holding for one shot. Sexson took the final shot, and according to Graham's account, Simonovich reached up through the net and rim with the ball still coming down.

However, officials either waved off the shot or simply declined to call basket interference. The postgame accounts of observers differed as to whether or not Simonovich actually touched the ball.

Nevertheless, the marathon extended to a sixth overtime.

Beck again tipped the jump to Blind, who was fouled and made both free throws for a 51–49 Purdue advantage. More work at the line gave the Boilermakers a 54–51 lead with 3:26 to go. Again, the Gophers turned up the pressure, and again, the Boilermakers did not respond.

Purdue was again trying to stall when Sexson threw the ball out of bounds. Lindsley's second basket of the night, with 1:50 left, put Minnesota up 55–54, and it never trailed again in a 59–56 victory.

Purdue won the rebounding battle 41–32, led by an astonishing 29 from Beck. The Boilermakers committed fewer fouls and made more free throws. Yet Purdue could not overcome its shooting deficiencies, making only 31.7 percent of its field goals compared with 46.2 for Minnesota.

Of the 30 overtime minutes, Graham calculated 27:27 involved no action other than a player holding the ball. Purdue accounted for 22:37 of that time.

That game remained tied for the most overtime periods in an NCAA Division I contest until 1981, when Bradley and Cincinnati played seven extra periods.

89 1984 Upset of No. 2 Ohio State

Leon Burtnett's first two seasons as head football coach in 1982 and 1983 yielded a combined six victories. Heading into 1984, however, the Boilermakers had a new lease on life thanks to a strong-armed quarterback who had waited his turn to take over as the starter—Jim Everett.

Purdue opened that season with a 23–21 victory over No. 8 Notre Dame in the christening of the RCA Dome in Indianapolis. After four weeks, the Boilermakers stood 3–1, losing only to No. 5 Miami, when No. 2 Ohio State visited Ross-Ade Stadium. Trailing 17–14 in the second half, Purdue's defense stepped up big.

Don Anderson intercepted Ohio State quarterback Mike Tomczak at the Purdue 21-yard line late in the third quarter. Everett took over and orchestrated a 79-yard scoring drive, capped by his four-yard touchdown pass to Bruce King to give the Boilermakers a 21–17 lead.

The Buckeyes attempted to respond on the legs of running back Keith Byars, who rushed for 191 yards and two touchdowns that day. But eventually, Rod Woodson intercepted another Tomczak pass and returned it 55 yards for the game-clinching touchdown.

The victory temporarily gave Purdue control of first place in the Big Ten.

"I'm so, so happy for our players," Burtnett said after the game. "This team is not going to quit. We might get beat a couple times, but they're never going to quit."

Everett passed for 257 yards and three touchdowns in the statement victory. Later that season, he also beat Michigan, as the Boilermakers defeated the Wolverines, Ohio State, and Notre Dame in the same season for the first time.

Purdue, previously unranked, shot up to No. 14 in the Associated Press poll after the Ohio State upset. A week later, however, Iowa came to West Lafayette and won 40–3. The Boilermakers ended up sharing second place in the Big Ten, finishing 7–5 overall after losing to Virginia in the Peach Bowl.

90 One Win Shy of the Men's Basketball Final Four in 1994

On March 26, 1994, the course of Purdue basketball history may have shifted in a Knoxville, Tennessee, hotel room.

The Boilermakers—the Big Ten champions and top seed in the South Region—were scheduled to play No. 2 seed Duke that night in a game featuring two of the nation's elite players—Purdue's Glenn Robinson, on his way to being the No. 1 pick in the NBA Draft, and the Blue Devils' Grant Hill.

On the line: a trip to the Final Four and, perhaps, a shot at college basketball supremacy.

So the Boilermakers prepared for that challenge the only way they knew how. As multiple team members hung out in a hotel room, an impromptu wrestling match broke out. Triggered not by animosity or a disagreement, such skirmishes simply evolved from—and created—that team's tight-knit, ultra-competitive bond.

"I think it's what made us close as a team, because we did it all the time," said junior forward Cuonzo Martin, now the head coach at Missouri.

At some point in the tussle, Robinson's back slammed into a bed headboard. Perhaps affected by the roughhousing, Robinson struggled to make baskets in the season-ending 69–60 loss to Duke. At the time, the sore back was blamed on a collision with Kansas center Greg Ostertag in the regional semifinals.

Only years later did one of the other Boilermakers come clean with head coach Gene Keady as to the real culprit.

In some ways, that unfortunate end for one of Purdue's greatest teams remains a fitting testimony to its essence. Looking back more than 25 years, those Boilermakers say they fought so hard on the court because they fought so hard with the teammates they loved every day.

"We were a team," said sophomore guard Todd Foster, a future Purdue assistant coach who now serves the program in academic support services. "I'm not making excuses because we were having fun. Not, 'You two in your room, you two in your room.' We were together."

To understand what led Purdue to that clash with Duke, one must go back one year, to a brief NCAA Tournament stay in Winston-Salem, North Carolina. Robinson's brilliant freshman season led the Boilermakers to 18 victories. But they also lost four of their last seven regular season games, and No. 9 seed Rhode Island knocked out the No. 8 seed 74–68.

"That summer, coach Keady made us get up every morning at 6 o'clock and lift weights," said sophomore forward Brandon Brantley, now a Purdue assistant coach. "We really grew as a team, and everybody stayed here and we played ball all day and worked out. Everybody bought in, and it paid off for us."

The first word out of Keady's mouth when asked to explain the 1993–94 team's success is "chemistry." A group assembled from a variety of geographic and socioeconomic backgrounds jelled together in punishing practices and the resulting battles—sometimes literally—on the practice court.

Keady cultivated that competitive identity with practices designed to be tougher than games. The Boilermakers credited their cohesiveness in part to a willingness to accept roles, no matter how small. Yet they also said no one settled for that role without battling for a bigger one.

"If somebody goes down or somebody's not performing, coach Keady always gave you the belief you'd be the next one in," said Ian Stanback, a senior forward on the 1993–94 team. "We all had the mentality of, 'Maybe I'll go lift a little bit extra, maybe I'll shoot a little bit more than the next guy.' Somebody will see him shooting and think, 'Oh, I've got to go shoot some more, I've got to go run some more.'"

That intensity regularly surpassed rough play between the whistles. Martin said barely a week went by without two players trending toward fisticuffs, or occasionally crossing the line. Foster said he got in a fight with probably everyone else on the roster—except Robinson, "because he knew how to punch back."

"We would go into games with a reputation for being tough and playing hard, and physically we had to back that up, because teams expected us to be that way," Martin said.

Keady entered his 14th season as one of the most respected coaches in the Big Ten. He also went in with enough perspective not to assume anything about his team's potential.

He knew Martin was a respected leader among his teammates with a knack for getting off tough shots in any situation. He knew guards Matt Waddell and Porter Roberts, who combined to average nine assists that season, provided a stable backcourt. He knew players such as Brantley, Stanback, Justin Jennings, Herb Dove, and Linc Darner bought into their roles and provided quality depth.

And he knew Robinson, the sophomore from Gary, Indiana, they called "Big Dog" was as talented—and as competitive—as anyone he had ever coached.

Brantley was a distant cousin of Robinson's who first played against him as high school freshmen in Northwest Indiana. Stanback remembered going to the IHSAA semistate games at Mackey Arena when he was a Purdue freshman to watch Robinson lead Gary Roosevelt to two victories and a trip to the state finals.

Robinson averaged 30.3 points in 1993–94 and is the only Big Ten player to score more than 1,000 in a season. He averaged 10.1 rebounds and balanced that interior muscle with the skill to shoot 38 percent from 3-point range.

"Our best play was to give it to Glenn and get the hell out of his way and get in the corner, draw your man out," Foster said.

With expectations high for both Robinson and the team, Purdue opened the season ranked No. 21 in the Associated Press poll. Both the Boilermakers and their star spent the next five months exceeding those expectations.

After winning the Great Alaska Shootout, Purdue steadily rose in the polls during a season-opening 14-game winning streak. Robinson, however, saved some of his truly superlative performances for Big Ten play.

Playing at No. 3 and conference-leading Michigan on March 6, Robinson's jumper at the buzzer gave the No. 9 Boilermakers a 95–94 victory. Robinson poured in a career-high 49 points a week later as Purdue clinched the Big Ten championship with an 87–77 victory over Illinois. As a No. 1 seed, the Boilermakers entered the NCAA Tournament with designs on reaching the Final Four.

"When we've got the best player in America, with the way he could score the ball, of course we felt we could do it," Martin said.

Purdue unloaded on Central Florida 98–67 in the opening round in Lexington, Kentucky, then knocked off Alabama 83–73 to reach the Sweet 16.

First up in the regional was national power Kansas, a 27-win team led by Ostertag, Scot Pollard, and Jacque Vaughn. The Jayhawks had star power, experience, and their own renowned coach in Roy Williams.

They did not, however, have Robinson.

Robinson made 15 of 33 field goals that night, including 6 of 10 from 3-point range, and scored 44 points. Martin also rose to the occasion, hitting eight 3-pointers and scoring 29 points in an 83–78 victory.

Ostertag, however, did fall on Robinson during that game. So perhaps his back was already gimpy before the royal rumble in the hotel. Considering those wrestling matches usually involved multiple teammates, it is difficult to place the blame—if that word is even applicable—on any one person.

Keady said at least two years passed before anyone confessed as to what happened.

"I was sick," Keady said. "I was not happy about that. You're goofing around in a hotel room and hurt your best player's back? It was dumb."

Against Duke, Waddell scored 16 points, and Purdue went into the second half tied. Behind big games from Jeff Capel and Antonio Lang, however, Mike Krzyzewski's squad pulled away.

"I still haven't watched that tape to this day," Brantley said. "We didn't play our best game. Hats off to Duke for beating us."

Keady, as usual, blamed himself for the loss. A Final Four trip was the only missing achievement of a Hall of Fame career that included 550 victories, six Big Ten championships, and six national Coach of the Year awards.

He felt he let his players down. His players felt the opposite.

"That's who you play for, No. 1," Foster said. "Every time we lost a game, I felt bad, like I let my father down, which was coach Keady. And No. 2, we let the Purdue fans down. It hurt everybody on our team. We wanted to win."

Martin said the sense of loss stemmed from recognizing the rarity of such a collection of talent and dedication. Yet he also remembers a team that made a great run and a team that valued winning a Big Ten championship.

Today, that season is lumped in with those marred by Robbie Hummel's knee injury late in 2009–10 and Isaac Haas' broken elbow in the 2018 NCAA Tournament. It deserves its own status as one of the singularly great runs in Purdue history.

"They were a good group of young men totally locked into the team philosophy, and nobody was selfish," Keady said. "It was just one of those things that Duke beat us."

2009 Victory at the "Big House"

On October 15, 1966, Purdue traveled to Michigan with a Heisman Trophy contender at quarterback in Bob Griese.

The Boilermakers snuck out of Ann Arbor with a 22–21 victory that helped propel them to their first trip to the Rose Bowl.

More than four decades passed before Purdue's next win in the "Big House."

It took another quarterback from Evansville, Indiana, to get the job done.

Joey Elliott was a three-time Academic All-Big Ten selection who attempted only 49 passes over 10 games during his first three seasons. He took over as the starter in 2009 under first-year head coach Danny Hope. A former Purdue offensive line coach, Hope had served one year as coach-in-waiting under Joe Tiller in a succession plan similar to the one by which Matt Painter had followed Gene Keady.

Hope and Elliott opened with a 52–31 victory over Toledo. Then came five straight losses, the first four by a combined 18 points.

The losing skid ended with a stunning 26–18 upset of No. 7 Ohio State at Ross-Ade Stadium. But when a 37–0 loss at Wisconsin on October 31 dropped Purdue to 3–6, it did not seem like a team on the verge of breaking a 17-game losing streak at Michigan.

Purdue trailed 24–10 at halftime, and it seemed the despair in Ann Arbor would continue. However, another sort of gloom had descended around a Michigan team that had suffered a program-record nine losses a year earlier and would eventually miss a bowl game in consecutive seasons for the first time in 35 years.

The Boilermakers stormed back with 21 third-quarter points. The third one was set up by a surprise onside kick, followed one play later by Elliott's 54-yard touchdown pass to Cortez Smith.

"We had that play greased up all season long, but never used it," Hope said after the game. "You have to wait for the right moment."

Purdue recovered another onside kick, this one on Michigan's attempt with just over two minutes to play.

Elliott threw for 367 yards and two touchdowns and scored another on the ground. In his lone season as a starter, he passed for 3,026 yards and 22 touchdowns. Elliott went on to play five seasons in the Canadian Football League before beginning a career in NFL scouting.

92 1974 NIT Champions

There has been one time in Purdue men's basketball history that the Boilermakers walked off the court of a national tournament with a championship victory.

It came in 1974, after Rick Mount led the Boilermakers to the 1969 Final Four and before Joe Barry Carroll took them back in 1980.

Up to and including 1974, there was no shame in "missing" the NCAA Tournament. That was the final season in which only conference champions and independents were eligible for the tourney. Michigan represented the Big Ten in the 1974 tournament, losing in the regional finals to eventual national runner-up Marquette.

The NIT was once the most prominent of college basketball's postseason tournaments, though the NCAA Tournament slowly overtook it in terms of prestige. With only 25 teams playing in the NCAA tourney, however, winning the NIT still carried some cache.

The 1973–74 squad under head coach Fred Schaus thrived behind one of the Big Ten's best frontcourts. John Garrett, an Indiana Basketball Hall of Famer from Peru, Indiana, was a 6'11" center who averaged 21.6 points and 7.9 rebounds per game. Frank Kendrick, a 6'6" forward from Indianapolis, averaged 18.5 points and 10.1 rebounds. His 18 double-doubles that season were the most in school history until Caleb Swanigan came along.

Forwards Jerry Nichols and Bruce Rose and center Tom Schefter also contributed to the frontcourt depth.

Point guard Bruce Parkinson averaged 12 points, 6.1 assists, and 4.1 rebounds in the sophomore season of a career in which he would eventually set Purdue career records for assists (690) and assists per game (6.2).

That nucleus compiled a 21–9 record, though it easily could have been much better. Purdue lost three overtime games by a combined three points—to Clemson and Miami (Ohio) in a four-day span in December and a 112–111 triple-overtime setback at Iowa on February 11. The Boilermakers also suffered a two-point loss at Utah, an 86–81 defeat against eventual national champion N.C. State, and a one-point loss at 13th-ranked Indiana.

That's six losses by a total of 11 points. The one to the Hoosiers knocked Purdue into third place in the Big Ten, while Indiana shared the conference title with Michigan. Those teams played a third game to decide who would represent the Big Ten in the NCAA Tournament, and the Wolverines prevailed. The Hoosiers were invited to the Collegiate Commissioners Association Tournament, which invited eight second-place teams to a postseason tournament, and went on to win the championship.

So the third-place Boilermakers set their sights on reaching New York's Madison Square Garden to compete for an NIT title.

First, Purdue had to find a way past North Carolina. The Tar Heels brought the No. 8 team in the country to Mackey Arena, led by future pros Bobby Jones, Walter Davis, Mitch Kupchak, and Tipton, Indiana, native Darrell Elston.

Purdue won 82–71 to earn a shot at redemption in New York City. The NIT bracket afforded the opportunity to even the score for two of their losses from New Year's week.

Purdue had played Hawaii for the championship of the Rainbow Classic on December 29, losing 76–67. Two days later came that narrow loss at Utah 87–85 as the team made its way back home.

The Boilermakers avenged themselves against the Rainbow Warriors with an 85–72 quarterfinal victory. Four days later, they rolled over Jacksonville 78–63. Purdue held the Dolphins to only 20.8 percent field goal shooting in the second half. That turned out to be a precursor to the formula that would win a championship 24 hours later.

Utah won 22 games behind a trio of high-scoring guards— Luther Burden, Mike Sojourner, and Tyron Medley. Sojourner was also a talented rebounder, evidenced by the 19 he pulled down against Purdue in the title game.

With under four minutes to play and Purdue leading 76–74, Mike Steele missed the front end of a 1-and-1. Freshman forward Gerald Thomas, however, tipped the rebound back to Steele, who scored to make it a four-point game. Thomas then added a pair of free throws 17 seconds later to make it 80–74.

The Boilermakers subsequently strung together five consecutive defensive stops. While Utah won the rebounding battle 45–32, Purdue kept the possession war in balance by forcing 23 turnovers.

"We wanted to go inside more to Sojourner, starting the second half," Utah head coach Bill Foster said. "But Purdue's defense cut us off, and we had to go back to our outside game. We also got careless with the ball at crucial times, and you can blame their defense for some of that."

Kendrick and Garrett combined for 49 points, nearly matching the combined 50 points of Sojourner and Burden. Parkinson led the tourney with 30 total assists, including seven in the championship.

"I've been involved in several postseason tourneys, but this is the first time I've coached a team that won one, and I just can't say enough about this bunch of guys," Schaus said.

Five years later, under Lee Rose, Purdue returned to the NIT championship game but fell to Indiana 53–52. In 1982, Gene Keady took the Boilermakers to the NIT title game, but Bradley pulled out a 67–58 victory. Keady also took teams to the NIT in 1992, 2001, and 2004, though the event lost luster as the NCAA Tournament expanded to 64 teams.

Larry Burton

He was known as "the fastest man on earth."

Yet, Lawrence (Larry) Burton was a football player before becoming a track star. He came to Purdue from Melfa, Virginia, in 1970 on a football scholarship and enjoyed a productive career.

But upon being told by football teammate Carl Capria that he was "pretty fast," Burton went out for the track team and ran in his first competitive meet on January 28, 1972.

"I was worried about running track," said Burton, whose high school did not offer the sport. "Most of the guys I would be running with and against would be as many as eight or 10 years

Larry Burton, known as "the fastest man on earth," was an All-American in football and track & field. He finished fourth in the 200-meter at the 1972 Olympic Games in Munich.

ahead of me in experience, and a big concern was that I didn't want to go out there and make a fool of myself."

Hardly.

In his first eight months on the track, Burton tied the world record in the 60-yard indoor dash with a :05.9 clocking, won the NCAA 200-meter outdoor championship, and finished fourth in the 200 meters at the 1972 Olympic Games in Munich.

Burton was a two-time All-American and a four-time Big Ten champion, including back-to-back 60-yard indoor titles his junior and senior seasons. He still holds two school records—6.14 in the 55 meters (indoor) and 20.37 in the 200 meters (outdoor).

Meanwhile, Burton was catching passes as a blazing wide receiver for the football team. He led the Big Ten with 38 receptions and 702 receiving yards as a senior in 1974 en route to earning consensus All-America honors.

"He had a lot of raw talent but didn't know a lot about football," said coach Bob DeMoss, who recruited Burton to Purdue. "But he had great speed, a good body, and a willingness to learn, and he did that. He was very coachable and team-oriented."

Burton was named Most Valuable Player of the football team and co-MVP of the track & field squad as a senior, when he also earned the Big Ten Medal of Honor for demonstrating great proficiency in scholarship and athletics and the Varsity Walk Award for bringing national attention to Purdue. A sociology major, he earned Academic All-Big Ten honors.

Burton was inducted into the Purdue Intercollegiate Athletics Hall of Fame in 1996.

The New Orleans Saints selected Burton with the seventh overall pick of the 1975 NFL Draft. He played three seasons with the Saints and two with the San Diego Chargers, totaling 44 receptions, before beginning a second career.

During NFL training camp in 1980, Burton decided his calling was to help youth. He wound up working for Boys Town in Omaha, Nebraska, where the born-again Christian was dubbed a modern-day Father Flanagan, the legendary founder of the institution. Burton and his wife, Ida, later ran a Boys Town facility in Long Beach, California.

Burton had been an offseason motivational speaker for NFL Ministries.

"After a speech, kids would come up to me like I was a psychoanalyst, and they would pour their hearts out to me," Burton said in a 1994 interview with the *Indianapolis Star.* "They talked like they had no future. That was really sad. It began to dawn on me that indeed I was giving them a fleet moment of hope, but I wasn't staying around to bring about the healing.

"Not that football wasn't important. It enabled me to have a certain lifestyle that was good. But if you don't have a purpose in life, why live it?"

94 Visit the Tyler Trent Student Gate at Ross-Ade Stadium

On September 7, 2019, before the Purdue football team hosted Vanderbilt at Ross-Ade Stadium, the university unveiled and dedicated the Tyler Trent Student Gate.

The Tyler Trent Student Gate replaced Gate E on the east side of Ross-Ade. It features gold lettering and the moniker T2, the Boilermaker superfan's signature mark. Below, on Ross-Ade's brick facade, two plaques display Trent's image and chronicle his remarkable story.

Purdue Athletics never had a more devoted fan than Tyler Trent. On September 22, 2017, just hours after undergoing chemotherapy, he demonstrated his commitment by camping out at Ross-Ade Stadium before Purdue's football game against Michigan the following day. Outside this gate, Tyler met and immediately forged a bond with head coach Jeff Brohm that extended to the entire team, which named him an honorary captain. Over the next 15 months, while resolutely battling osteosarcoma, Tyler provided motivation to the Purdue community and beyond with his positive spirit and unwavering faith. Tyler appeared on national television repeatedly, including an October 20, 2018, profile on his strength of character. That day, Tyler predicted the stunning upset by the Boilermakers of No. 2–ranked Ohio State (49–20), as he cheered on his team at Ross-Ade. Tyler selflessly and enthusiastically used his adversity as a platform to increase awareness for pediatric cancer and to raise money for research. The embodiment of a true Boilermaker, Tyler received the 2018 Disney Spirit Award as college football's most inspirational figure. He will be forever our captain, and we always will be #TylerStrong.

Following the dedication ceremony, Tyler's parents, Tony and Kelly, and his brothers, Ethan and Blake, were the first to enter Ross-Ade through the gate. They were accompanied by Purdue students Josh Seals, who camped out with Trent prior to the Purdue-Michigan game in 2017, and Sean English, who in March 2019 was selected as the first recipient of the Tyler Trent Courage and Resilience Award, a memorial scholarship in Trent's name.

"Tyler showed the character and resiliency to which we all should aspire," Purdue president Mitch Daniels said. "His message of hope and positivity resonated far beyond our campus; it truly touched the entire nation. His story is now a big part of the Purdue history, and this gate and scholarship will serve to preserve it forever."

Trent, from Carmel, Indiana, was diagnosed with bone cancer at age 15 and died on January 1, 2019, at age 20. He founded Teens with a Cause, which recruits young people to perform service projects for families affected by cancer. At Purdue, Trent joined the Dance Marathon club, a student organization that raises funds and awareness for Riley Hospital for Children, where he received treatment. He also worked as a sportswriter for the *Exponent*, Purdue's student newspaper. He earned an associate degree in computer information technology.

As the first student member of the director's advancement board of the Purdue Center for Cancer Research, Trent helped raise cancer awareness with a younger audience. The Tyler Trent Cancer Research Endowment subsequently was created to fund cancer research at Purdue.

"My spiritual gift is the ability to serve others, and advocacy comes with that," Trent said in 2018. "Once you've been through cancer one, two, three times, you develop a passion to be an advocate.

"Our experiences shape who we are, and I wanted to turn my experience into something useful by being an advocate. You can get cancer and be someone who just goes through cancer, but then you're just another number. I want to be more than just a number. I want to get others involved."

Trent received the Sagamore of the Wabash—the highest honor for Indiana civilians—in November 2018. The Trent family received the Stuart Scott ENSPIRE Award at the 2019 Sports Humanitarian Awards.

Mike Carmin of the Lafayette *Journal & Courier*, who was the first to report about Trent when he discovered him camping out with Seals, regularly covered Trent's odyssey.

"Not many 20-year-olds are allowed to have a legacy," Carmin said. "They haven't lived long enough to create one, but Tyler is different. He put together his own legacy for his life and a blueprint for everyone to follow. How to live. How to die. How to fight. How to show courage in the face of adversity. His legacy spreads across generations, and his story will be one that is told over and over again and will live in the history of Purdue University. The world only knew him for a short period of time—15 months—but his impact continues to resonate, and we all carry his life lessons with us forever."

Trent wrote a book, *The Upset*, that has an afterword from legendary Purdue and National Football League quarterback Drew Brees.

Purdue board of trustees chair Mike Berghoff, founder and president of Lenex Steel in Indianapolis, donated fabrication and the installation of the gate and plaques.

"Just being around Tyler made you feel good about humanity," Berghoff said. "Instead of you uplifting him during a very difficult time in his life, he uplifted you. I'm just honored to have a way to say, 'Thank you.'"

The date of the gate dedication would have been Trent's 21st birthday.

95 Otis Armstrong

Otis Armstrong saved his best for last.

In his final collegiate game on November 25, 1972, against Indiana on a muddy Ross-Ade Stadium field, the elusive halfback rushed for a Purdue-record 276 yards on 32 carries and three touchdowns.

"For years to come when the talk turns to football's great running backs whether in front of a fireplace, on the golf course, or in a neighborhood watering hole, the conversation will eventually be about Otis' performance against the Hoosiers," wrote John Bansch of the *Indianapolis Star*.

Armstrong broke his own school record set just a month earlier (233 yards against Northwestern), which bettered the previous mark of 225 yards by Leroy Keyes at Illinois in 1967.

In the Boilermakers' 42–7 victory over the Hoosiers, Armstrong amassed 312 all-purpose yards (he had 36 yards on kickoff returns) to set another school record, one that stood for 46 seasons until Rondale Moore eclipsed it by a single yard against Northwestern in 2018.

"Man, I don't know anything about any records," Armstrong said after the climax. "They just give me the ball, and I run and run and run."

All told for 1972, Armstrong finished with school season records of 1,361 rushing yards and 1,868 all-purpose yards. Those totals still ranked second and fourth entering the 2020 campaign. In addition to leading the Big Ten in rushing, Armstrong was tops in total offense, the first time a player accomplished that feat without attempting a pass since 1945. He was feted as the Big Ten Most Valuable Player and a consensus All-American and finished sixth in Heisman Trophy voting. Furthermore, Armstrong earned the Swede Nelson Award, presented by the Greater Gridiron Club of Boston to "the player who by his conduct on and off the gridiron demonstrates a high esteem for the football code and exemplifies sportsmanship to an outstanding degree."

Armstrong left Purdue with a Big Ten record of 3,315 rushing yards, accomplished in just three seasons (since freshmen were not eligible to play in those days). The previous mark of 3,212 by Wisconsin Heisman-winning fullback Alan Ameche was logged in four seasons. Armstrong's total was the sixth-most in NCAA history at the time and has been surpassed by only two Boilermakers— Mike Alstott (3,635 yards) and Kory Sheets (3,341 yards).

The 5'11", 194-pounder was a workhorse, still owning the Purdue career record with 670 rushing attempts. Armstrong had a penchant for the dramatic, turning 19 plays into gains of over 30 yards while averaging 4.95 yards per rush and 6.2 yards every time he touched the football. He had 13 games of 100 or more rushing yards (out of 31 that he played), second-most to Alstott's 16 in the Boilermaker record book. Armstrong scored 24 touchdowns (17 rushing, five receiving, and two on kickoff returns).

"Otis had the ability to turn every play into a touchdown," Purdue head coach Bob DeMoss said. "In high school, he always ran outside, and I told him in college he couldn't outrun the defenders and had to run north and south. He said, 'Okay, coach.' He was a pleasure to coach and a joy to be around. He always had a grin on his face. He had an outstanding career."

Armstrong was inducted into the Purdue Intercollegiate Athletics Hall of Fame in 1997, the College Football Hall of Fame in 2012 and the Indiana Football Hall of Fame in 2017.

"O.T." prospered after growing up in a Chicago ghetto chock-full of obstacles.

"There was poverty, unemployment, dope, and gang wars in my neighborhood," Armstrong said. "The odds against my getting anywhere in the world were staggering. But I managed to make it because of football."

Additionally, Armstrong suffered from a congenital intestinal abnormality that created a blockage and limited him to eating finely chopped food his entire life until undergoing surgery during the spring of his junior year at Purdue. Only then could he efficaciously eat a pizza.

Armstrong relished the headlines he made at Purdue but not for self-adulation. "I hope the publicity I receive will help other Black kids go the right way," he said. "I'd like to set an example for them, so they will stay in school and have some future."

Armstrong enjoyed an eight-year National Football League career with the Denver Broncos after being selected with the ninth overall pick of the 1973 draft. He was one of nine Boilermakers drafted that year. Armstrong led the NFL with 1,407 rushing yards in 1974 (the only Purdue player ever to do so) and was a two-time Pro Bowl honoree. The Broncos won the 1977 AFC championship.

96 Billy Keller

What Billy Keller lacked in height, he more than made up for in heart, hustle and basketball intellect.

Listed at 5'10", Keller was a vital member of the 1968–69 Purdue men's basketball team that won the Big Ten championship and advanced to the championship game of the NCAA Tournament.

As the Boilermakers' point guard, Keller directed an offense that averaged a school-record 93 points per game en route to a 23–5 overall record, including 13–1 in the Big Ten. While Rick Mount did the lion's share of the scoring, Keller averaged 13.3 points to go with 4.6 rebounds per game. Assists had not yet become a recorded statistic. He scored a career-high 31 points against Indiana on March 6, 1969, on Senior Day, as the Boilermakers steamrolled the Hoosiers 120–76 at Mackey Arena.

"It was fun to play for [head coach] George King," Keller said. "I can't say that guys didn't care who scored the points, because they did, but somehow George convinced us that filling our roles would help us win big. I credit George for that. We had a lot of fun."

Keller concluded his Purdue career as the most accurate free throw shooter in school history at 85.9 percent (262 of 305), a mark that has been topped just twice in the 50-plus years since. He led the Big Ten both his junior and senior seasons.

When he scored his 1,000th career point, Keller became the eighth Boilermaker to do so, and he finished with 1,056 points in 75 games (14.1 average).

As a senior, Keller was the inaugural recipient of the Frances Pomeroy Naismith Award, which is given to the top collegiate player under 6'0".

"A guy my size has to be able to set up the offense and get the ball and the players moving," Keller said. "I have to be able to get the action started. This is the little guy's game."

Keller shared the Boilermakers' team most valuable player award his junior year with Herman Gilliam after averaging 16 points and 4.5 rebounds per game.

In the Kentucky-Indiana College All-Star Game following his senior season, Keller first played with the 3-point line and made 6 of 7 shots from beyond the arc. It was a sign of good things to come.

Keller was selected in the seventh round (No. 87 overall) of the 1969 NBA Draft by the Milwaukee Bucks, but instead played for his hometown Indiana Pacers of the ABA, who made him a sixth-round draft pick. He went on to lead the Pacers to three league championships (1970, 1972, and 1973) and two other finals appearances (1969 and 1975) as part of a seven-year career. Along the way, Keller drained 506 3-pointers, the second-most in ABA history, and twice he led the league in free throw percentage. Keller averaged 11.8 points, 3.6 assists, and 2.4 rebounds per game as a professional. He scored a career-high 39 points, including nine 3-pointers, in a 1974 playoff game against the San Antonio Spurs.

Born and raised in Indianapolis, Keller led George Washington High School to the state championship and was named Mr.

Basketball his senior year. He was the second of three consecutive Indiana Mr. Basketball winners who became Boilermakers (Denny Brady of Lafayette Jefferson in 1964 and Mount of Lebanon in 1966).

In 1979, Keller returned to Purdue as an assistant coach under Lee Rose, and the Boilermakers made it back to the Final Four that season. The following season, Keller embarked on a seven-year career as the head men's basketball coach at the University of Indianapolis. He was a candidate for the Purdue women's basketball head coaching job when Lin Dunn was hired in 1987.

Keller, who has enjoyed a successful career as a basketball camp owner and director, was inducted into the Indiana Basketball Hall of Fame in 1992 and the Purdue Intercollegiate Athletics Hall of Fame in 2007.

97 Listen to Purdue Games on the Radio

Purdue fans who listen to men's basketball and football games on the radio have been fortunate to be informed and entertained by some of the best in the business through the years.

From legends like John DeCamp, Joe Pate, and Joe McConnell to contemporaries Larry Clisby and Tim Newton, the play-by-play description has been accurate, crisp and professional.

Clisby has been behind the microphone for men's basketball since 1984, calling more than 1,100 games. The Indiana Sportscasters and Sportswriters Association Hall of Famer also did football play-by-play from 1989 to 1994 after several seasons as color analyst and sideline reporter. "Cliz" served as a sports anchor at WLFI-TV in West Lafayette, as well.

In June 2018, Clisby was diagnosed with Stage 4 metastatic brain cancer that had spread from his lungs. A previous two-time cancer survivor, he underwent 10 rounds of radiation and four doses of chemotherapy and was back ready to go for the 2018–19 season. To help offset medical costs, a GoFundMe.com webpage was established with the goal of raising $10,000. Purdue head coach Matt Painter immediately contributed that amount, and more than $70,000 wound up being collected in three months.

"You want people that are passionate about your school, and he's had that passion and he cares," Painter said. "When we lose, he hurts like he played in the game or coached in the game. I think that's pretty cool."

On November 16, 2019, Clisby announced on the air that because of his ongoing health issues, he and longtime color analyst Rob Blackman would swap roles for the balance of the 2019–20 season.

"The one thing I can say about Rob is he is an incredibly loyal person who has been terrific to me, and during my two years of really struggling he has stood right by me every step of the way," Clisby said. "I really care for him, and I am really tickled to death to leave this job to him."

Newton is a 1981 Purdue graduate who has been part of the football radio crew since 1995. The 2019 season marked his 10th in the play-by-play chair after 14 years as the pregame/halftime/postgame host and producer with McConnell.

"It's a humbling experience to stand in the shadow of some of the greatest talents and sports broadcasters in the field," Newton said. "In an industry that changes talent on a constant basis, Boilermakers fans have become accustomed to familiar voices bringing Purdue Athletics into their living rooms for decades. Two of them, John DeCamp and Joe McConnell, were both professional guides and personal mentors for me, and I owe a great deal of my career to them."

At the same time, the 2019–20 season was Newton's 30th doing play-by-play for Purdue women's basketball. He called his 900th game on January 26, 2020, against Penn State. That total includes the 1999 NCAA Tournament championship, all seven Big Ten regular season championships in program history and all nine conference tournament titles. Newton has had a handful of color analysts, most notably former Purdue player Jane (Calhoun) Schott.

Former Purdue football center Pete Quinn, who played for the Boilermakers from 1977 to 1980 and was part of three bowl championship teams, completed his 28th season as football color analyst in 2019, working with Clisby, McConnell, and Newton, who he described as "three consummate professionals."

"I credit Larry Clisby with teaching me the business," Quinn said. "My first year with him will always be a fond memory because that is when I learned how much broadcasting Purdue football meant to me. Larry wore his passion for Purdue on his sleeve. When you listened to Larry broadcast, you could always tell how the Boilermakers were doing just by listening to his voice.

"Then Joe McConnell came in, a broadcasting giant with that distinguished voice. I think I frustrated Joe at the beginning because I was such a homer. He didn't like it when I said 'we' or 'us' when referring to Purdue, but after a couple of seasons, Joe started doing the same thing. It was so appropriate that he finished his career broadcasting games from the John DeCamp radio booth because John was his mentor.

"When Joe retired, Tim Newton was the obvious choice to take over. Tim is extremely intelligent and knows the game better than anyone I know. He learned a lot about preparing for a broadcast from Joe and is one of the best in the country. Tim and I were students at Purdue at the same time and, like Larry and Joe, he is passionate about the Boilermakers."

As for Quinn, when he was approached about interviewing for the analyst position in 1992, "I thought it was a buddy playing a joke on me. I told my wife, Susan, that they would never offer me the job because I had no experience. But here I am, 28 years later, having been blessed with amazing talent sitting next to me every year."

DeCamp was the voice of Purdue football and basketball for 43 years from the 1940s to the 1980s. In 1996, he was enshrined in the Purdue Intercollegiate Athletics Hall of Fame and was a charter member of the Indiana Sportscasters and Sportswriters Association Hall of Fame. The Purdue radio booth at Ross-Ade Stadium was named in DeCamp's honor in 2003.

McConnell, the Indiana Sportscaster of the Year in 2000, has his name on the visiting team radio booth at Ross-Ade. He served as assistant sports information director at Purdue from 1965 to 1967 and then embarked on a distinguished broadcasting career that included stints in Major League Baseball, the NBA, and the NFL, in addition to the Boilermakers.

98 Jim Everett

Despite being a starter for only two seasons, Jim Everett ranks as one of the most prolific quarterbacks in Purdue history.

Everett compiled lofty statistics as a junior and senior in 1984 and 1985, enough to still find him seventh on the school career lists for passing yards (7,411), passing touchdowns (43), and total offense (7,284) despite starting only 25 games. Most impressive, however, is that he remains the Boilermakers' all-time best with a 132.7 passing efficiency mark.

Born in Emporia, Kansas, and raised in Albuquerque, New Mexico—where he led Eldorado High School to the state championship his senior year—the 6'5" Everett served as Scott Campbell's backup during his first three seasons with the Boilermakers (including a redshirt year). Everett came to Purdue in what wound up being head coach Jim Young's last season, and new head coach Leon Burtnett considered moving the young signal-caller to tight end.

When Everett finally got his chance to start in 1984, he made the most of it. En route to being named honorable mention All-Big Ten and team Most Valuable Player, Everett led the conference and ranked fifth in the country in total offense. He became the first Boilermaker to pass for more than 3,000 yards during a regular season schedule.

Everett engineered the Boilermakers to wins over eighth-ranked Notre Dame (23–21 in the dedication game of the Hoosier Dome in Indianapolis), second-ranked Ohio State (28–23), and Michigan (31–29)—the only time a Purdue team has pulled off that trifecta.

"I'm very proud of that," Everett said. "It's very rare. I don't think it was a fluke. You saw a talented team. It was a special season."

The Boilermakers finished tied for second in the Big Ten and played in the Peach Bowl, losing to Virginia 27–24 to wind up with a 7–5 record.

As a senior, despite battling a staph infection most of the year, Everett led the nation with an average of 326.3 yards of total offense per game. He set or tied school season records that would stand until Drew Brees came along in the late 1990s for passing attempts, completions, yards, touchdowns and total offense. His 3,651 passing yards were the sixth-most in NCAA history at the time.

"I think that Jim is the finest quarterback in the country," Burtnett said in 1985. "He's very intelligent, he's a great leader, and he's very unselfish. He wants to do whatever it takes to win. The way he has performed for us has been astounding."

Against Ohio State on October 19, 1985, in Columbus, Everett completed 35 of 55 passes for 497 yards. The yardage total was the second-most in Purdue annals then and still was good enough for eighth all-time entering the 2020 season.

Everett finished sixth in the Heisman Trophy race, earned third-team All-America honors, and was a second-team All-Big Ten performer. He was named team MVP and Purdue Male Athlete of the Year for the second straight year and received the Big Ten Medal of Honor for demonstrating great proficiency in scholarship and athletics.

The Houston Oilers selected Everett with the third pick of the 1986 NFL Draft, tying him with Leroy Keyes (Philadelphia Eagles in 1969) and Mike Phipps (Cleveland Browns in 1970) as the highest Boilermaker ever chosen.

But the Oilers did not need a quarterback and took Everett reportedly to prevent the Indianapolis Colts from doing so with the next pick. Everett subsequently was traded to the Los Angeles Rams, where he became one of the NFL's top quarterbacks. He passed for 3,000 yards in five consecutive seasons from 1988 to 1992 and seven total for his career. In 1989, while guiding the Rams to the NFC Championship Game, Everett became the 11th quarterback in NFL history to pass for 4,000 yards (4,310). He twice led the league in touchdown passes and was selected to the 1990 Pro Bowl.

Everett, who started 87 consecutive games from 1988 to 1993, was traded to the New Orleans Saints in 1994 and concluded his career with the San Diego Chargers in 1997. Upon his retirement, he ranked 12th in NFL history with 34,837 passing yards.

In April 1994, during a live appearance on the ESPN2 show *Take2*, Everett was called Chris Evert multiple times by host Jim Rome. The reference to the women's tennis legend was believed to be a slight at Everett's toughness. An agitated Everett eventually overturned a table and sent Rome to the floor. "I really don't condone my actions, but I was put in a position that I thought was going to be in a journalistic-type interview and, instead, I was put into what I felt was a taunting attack," Everett said shortly after the episode. "I don't regret what I did."

Everett was inducted into the Purdue Intercollegiate Athletics Hall of Fame in 1999.

An industrial management major at Purdue and two-time Academic All-Big Ten honoree, Everett earned an MBA from Pepperdine University and started a highly successful asset management company in Southern California that he ran for 14 years.

99 George Steinbrenner

George Steinbrenner, the legendary principal owner of the New York Yankees from 1973 to 2010, was an assistant football coach at Purdue.

Steinbrenner served as a volunteer coach with the Boilermakers during the 1956 season—Jack Mollenkopf's first year as head coach. Steinbrenner coached the ends and freshman team (with Al Parker) during his one fall on campus.

Steinbrenner, who also coached at Northwestern, left Purdue to help his father, George II, run the family business, the American Shipbuilding Company in his hometown of Cleveland.

Steinbrenner's connection with Purdue remained after he left campus. He provided numerous summer jobs to athletes prior to becoming owner of the Yankees. Under Mollenkopf and successors Bob DeMoss and Alex Agase, the Boilermakers found the Cleveland area fertile for cultivating talent, and Steinbrenner played a role in their success.

On January 3, 1973, a group formed by Steinbrenner purchased the Yankees from CBS for a net of $8.7 million. During the 36-plus years he owned the club, the Yankees boasted the best winning percentage in Major League Baseball at .566 (3,364–2,583 record), with 11 American League pennants and seven world championships (also the most in the majors).

In 1980, Steinbrenner, who was involved with the fledgling men's basketball program at the University of South Florida, helped lure Purdue head coach Lee Rose to Tampa by offering him a $10,000 bonus. In turn, Purdue replaced Rose with Gene Keady, who, ironically, is a longtime Yankees fan and became friends with Steinbrenner after they met at the 1991 Pan-American Games in Havana, Cuba. Steinbrenner was a member of the United States Olympic Committee and Keady was head coach of the bronze-medal winning men's basketball team.

"I had heard a lot about him and how demanding he was, which I enjoyed because I like demanding people," said Keady, whose Yankees fandom dates to his youth growing up in Larnard, Kansas. "He and I marched in together for the opening ceremonies, and he told me that he spent a season coaching football at Purdue before going home to run the shipping business for his daddy.

"I've been a lifelong Yankees fan. My eighth-grade teacher was the niece of Notre Dame football coach Frank Leahy, and she was a big sports advocate. If we read two or three books and wrote a book report, she would let us listen to the World Series games on the radio, and the Yankees beat the Brooklyn Dodgers that year [1949]. That's how I became a better reader and a big Yankees fan."

Steinbrenner was honored with the Gold Medal Award from the National Football Foundation and College Hall of Fame in 1982 for a lifetime of "outstanding commitment, dedication, and dynamic leadership in both his business and personal lives." It is the highest and most prestigious award bestowed by the College Football Foundation.

100 Seconds Away from the 2019 Final Four

A mere 5.7 seconds separated Purdue men's basketball from a celebration for which the program, and its fans, had waited a generation.

Yet the Boilermakers' final gathering in a locker room during the 2018–19 season carried a somber, funereal atmosphere.

Purdue and Virginia played arguably the greatest game of the 2019 NCAA Tournament with the South Regional championship on the line in Louisville, Kentucky. The Cavaliers ripped victory from the Boilermakers' hands in abrupt, almost sadistic fashion at the end of regulation and capitalized in the fleeting final seconds of overtime for an 80–75 victory.

One team was guaranteed to leave the arena with its guts torn out. It easily could have been Virginia. It did not deserve to be anyone. Yet after a season of such achievement, such resiliency, such grit, the Boilermakers were left to reconcile the crushing end of their valiant run.

"It will come, but we're hurting right now," senior guard Ryan Cline said afterward. "We'll look back and we'll be proud, but this team could have made it to a Final Four."

Purdue would not have been playing in the regional final had Cline not carried them there 48 hours earlier. His legend-making 22-point second half was the reason Purdue reached its first Elite Eight since 2000.

Cline is a great shooter, unquestionably, but an infrequent free throw shooter throughout his career. He had made 22 of 31 that season—without attempting one since the regular season finale against Northwestern—before stepping to the line with 16.9

seconds remaining against Virginia. He made the first attempt for a three-point lead but not the second.

"I just missed it," Cline said. "Don't know what else to tell you."

Grady Eifert epitomized the blue-collar, underdog mentality on which Purdue thrived all season. A former walk-on, once thrilled to wear the same uniform his father, Greg, did and battle in practice, became a captain, a starter, and a star.

The free throw that Cline mourned? It was only possible because Eifert—of course it was Eifert—grabbed an offensive rebound. No Boilermaker grabbed more of them over the course of the season.

Yet when asked about one of the most soul-crushing plays in Purdue history, Eifert's voice creaked as Cline's had. How was Mamadi Diakite able to tip Ty Jerome's missed free throw back out past midcourt, where Kihei Clark ran it down, then fired the ball 60 feet to Diakite, who in one motion received the pass and released a touch shot barely outside the paint that would be a low-percentage attempt with no one else on the floor?

How, with Matt Haarms' long arm in his face, did that shot fall at the buzzer and force overtime?

"I missed the box-out," Eifert said. "I'll have to live with that. It will be tough."

Carsen Edwards summoned the performance that head coach Matt Painter must have envisioned when he brought up the scoring star from Texas to bring a new dimension to his offense. Check that. He may not have been able to imagine this.

The Most Outstanding Player of the South Regional pumped in 10 of his signature 3-pointers—many of them aggressive, even audacious in their degree of difficulty. He scored 42 points—tying the career high set only two games prior in a statement-making drubbing of defending national champion Villanova.

Edwards spent the entirety of this four-game NCAA run torching any memory of the shooting inconsistency that plagued him during the season's second half. He scored 139 points (an eye-popping 34.8 per game) while making 46 percent of the 61 3-pointers he attempted. When leaving the perimeter to attack the basket, he either picked his spots more judiciously or simply maneuvered his way to the rim with more dexterity.

In doing so, Edwards cemented his legacy as one of the most thrilling players in Purdue history. That legacy formed over time through growing pains and the patience and prodding of Painter, and it culminated in a tournament run that rivals any in school annals.

Yet with 1.8 seconds remaining in overtime against Virginia, Edwards was visibly distraught in the timeout huddle.

Less than four seconds earlier, with Purdue trailing 78–75, it had to travel the length of the floor to set up a 3-point attempt. Painter, understandably, later affirmed there was no consideration for anyone but Edwards to have the ball in that situation.

Edwards drove the sideline with instructions to give up the ball if he was about to be fouled. As he approached midcourt, Virginia's Clark closed. On replay, it appeared Edwards beat Clark, but he gave the ball up anyway, passing ahead to Cline on the 3-point elbow.

At that speed, with no margin for error, the pass sailed, and Cline could not make the catch.

"I was trying to kick it ahead before he fouled me, and I just, just kind of—I kind of—it was a tough catch," Edwards said. "It was a tough catch for Ryan, and that's just how it happens. Game of basketball. Game's moving quickly. It is what it is. I felt like the play was able to work. It's just kind of how things ended up."

How close did Virginia come to being the team struggling with those moments? With under a minute to play, Edwards forced a turnover by De'Andre Hunter and scored on a floater in the lane at the other end to put Purdue ahead for the final time at 75–74.

But Hunter came right back with a basket—the game-winner, as it turned out. A few minutes later, he celebrated the Cavaliers advancing to the Final Four.

One week later, Virginia, which a year earlier had been the first No. 1 seed to ever lose to a No. 16 seed, beat Texas Tech to win the national championship.

"The other night was pretty cool, and today stinks," Painter said, in reference to the 99–94 regional semifinal overtime victory over Tennessee. "These guys have been great. They've battled. They didn't let other people's opinion tell them how good they were going to be this year, and I think that's what it's all about."

Purdue Intercollegiate Athletics Hall of Fame

Class of 1994
Keith Carter: Swimming
Terry Dischinger: Basketball, Baseball
Ray Ewry: Track & Field
W.P. "Dutch" Fehring: Baseball, Football, Basketball
Bob Griese: Football, Basketball
Leroy Keyes: Football
Ward "Piggy" Lambert: Basketball, Baseball
Guy J. "Red" Mackey: Football, Administration
Jack Mollenkopf: Football
Rick Mount: Basketball
Jane (Neff) Myers: Volleyball
Arnold Plaza: Wrestling
John Wooden: Basketball

Class of 1995
Joe Barry Carroll: Basketball
Lamar Lundy: Football, Basketball
Orval Martin: Track & Field, Cross Country
Charles "Stretch" Murphy: Basketball
Mike Phipps: Football
Chris Schenkel: Honorary
James H. Smart: Honorary
Sam Voinoff: Golf, Football
Carol (Emanuel) Young: Basketball

Class of 1996
Lawrence Burton: Track & Field, Football
Len Dawson: Football
John DeCamp: Honorary
Frederick Hovde: Honorary
William "Pinky" Newell: Administration
Dave Schellhase: Basketball
Bill "Moose" Skowron: Baseball, Football
Hank Stram: Football, Baseball

Class of 1997
Otis Armstrong: Football
Dr. Loyal "Bill" Combs: Football,
Administration
Joy (Holmes) Harris: Basketball
Mark Herrmann: Football
Elmer Oliphant: Football, Basketball,
Baseball, Track & Field
Fred Wampler: Golf

Class of 1998
Tim Foley: Football
Noble Kizer: Football, Administration
Duane Purvis: Football, Track & Field
Dave Rankin: Football, Track & Field
Cathey Tyree: Basketball, Track & Field
Jeanne (Wilson) Vaughan: Honorary
Jewell Young: Basketball, Baseball

Class of 1999
Bernie Allen: Football, Baseball
Bob DeMoss: Football, Administration
Jim Everett: Football
Paul Hoffman: Basketball, Baseball
Marianne (Smith) Orr: Volleyball
Joe Patacsil: Wrestling

Class of 2000
Adam Abele: Tennis
Tom Bettis: Football
Andrea Marek: Track & Field
Claude Reeck: Wrestling
Joe Rudolph: Honorary
Joe Sexson: Basketball, Baseball
Elmer Sleight: Football

Class of 2001
Joe Campbell: Golf, Basketball
Sybil (Perry) Caruthers: Track & Field
Edward Elliott: Honorary
Cecil Isbell: Football
Bob King: Basketball, Administration
George King: Basketball, Administration
Dale Samuels: Football, Administration
Fred Wilt: Cross Country, Track & Field

Class of 2003
Carol Dewey: Volleyball
Bernie Flowers: Football
Charles Jones: Wrestling
John Konsek: Golf
Ralph Welch: Football
Debbie (McDonald) West: Volleyball
Rod Woodson: Football, Track & Field
Corissa Yasen: Track & Field, Basketball

Class of 2004
Jim Beirne: Football
Dave Butz: Football
Casey Fredericks: Wrestling
Becky (Cotta) Kirsininkas: Cross Country,
Track & Field
Amy Ruley: Honorary
Darryl Stingley: Football
Harry Szulborski: Football
Jim Young: Football, Administration

Class of 2006
Mike Alstott: Football
Steven C. Beering: Honorary
Herm Gilliam: Basketball
Kim (Fritsch) Morstadt: Swimming
Dick Papenguth: Swimming
Glenn Robinson: Basketball
Leo Sugar: Football
Carol (Pence) "Penny" Taylor: Honorary
Keena Turner: Football
Stephanie White: Basketball

Class of 2007
Don Albert: Golf
Darrel "Pete" Brewster: Football, Basketball
Ray Eddy: Basketball, Administration
Ukari Figgs: Basketball
Billy Keller: Basketball
Bob Kessler: Basketball
Ed Langford: Track & Field
Felix Mackiewicz: Baseball, Football
Ned Maloney: Football, Administration

Class of 2009
Erich Barnes: Football
Denny Blind: Baseball, Basketball
Drew Brees: Football
Boris "Babe" Dimancheff: Football
Dave and Joe Lilovich: Wrestling
Jamie McNeair-Reese: Track & Field
Jo-Ann Price: Honorary
Dave Young: Football

Class of 2010
Jeff Bolin: Track & Field
MaChelle Joseph: Basketball
Gene Keady: Basketball
Carl McNulty: Basketball
Henry Rosenthal: Honorary
Jerry Shay: Football
The "Three Amigos": Troy Lewis, Todd
Mitchell, and Everette Stephens: Basketball

Class of 2012
Fred Beretta: Basketball
Gary Danielson: Football
C.S. "Pop" Doan: Baseball, Football,
Administration
Lin Dunn: Basketball
Walt Eversman: Swimming
Jerry Sichting: Basketball
Toyinda (Smith) Wilson-Long: Track &
Field
Jeff Zgonina: Football

Class of 2013
Tony Butkovich: Football
Alpha Jamison: Football, Baseball, Track &
Field, Basketball
Matt Light: Football
Stacey Lovelace: Basketball
Willie Merriweather: Basketball
Carol Mertler: Field Hockey, Administration
Serene Ross: Track & Field
Joe Tiller: Football
Dick Walbaum: Administration

Class of 2015
Mike Birck: Honorary
Brian Cardinal: Basketball
Yvonne Netterville Carter: Track & Field
John Charles: Football
Katie Douglas: Basketball
Andrea Hillsey: Softball
Vilmos Kovacs: Swimming
Taylor Stubblefield: Football
Howie Williams: Basketball
Robert Woodworth: Administration

Class of 2016
David Boudia: Diving
Rosevelt Colvin: Football
Norman Cottom: Basketball, Track & Field
Travis Dorsch: Football, Baseball
Frank Kendrick: Basketball
Joe McCabe: Baseball
Carrie (McCambridge) Karkoska: Diving
Noel Ruebel: Track & Field
Shauna Stapleton: Soccer

Class of 2018
Jermaine Allensworth: Baseball
Gregg Bingham: Football
Clifford Furnas: Track & Field
Stephanie (Lynch) Harpenau: Volleyball
Maria Hernandez: Golf
Ryan Kerrigan: Football
Kara (Patterson) Winger: Track & Field

Class of 2020
Ariel (Turner) Gebhardt: Volleyball
Shaun Guice: Track & Field
Robbie Hummel: Basketball
Chuck Kyle: Football
Bruce Parkinson: Basketball
Casey (Matthews) Spitz: Diving
Shereka Wright: Basketball

Acknowledgments

My heartfelt thanks to Jim Vruggink, who hired me fresh out of Ohio Wesleyan University in 1990 for a 10-month internship with the Purdue athletic public relations department. It turned into an incredible three-decade career with the Boilermakers, during which time I worked with so many wonderful people, including Morgan Burke, Nancy Cross, Barb Kapp, Jay Cooperider, and Alan Karpick. It would be a nearly impossible task to list all the amazing coaches and student-athletes whose accomplishments I was fortunate to publicize, so I won't even try. I am honored to have crossed paths with each of them.

A tip of Purdue Pete's hardhat to Kevin Messenger, who methodically reviewed the manuscript for *100 Things Purdue Fans Should Know & Do Before They Die* and offered tremendous feedback, and to Tom Campbell for assisting with the photography selection. My longtime loyal assistant Marcia Iles was unfailingly gracious in helping me navigate the vast Purdue Athletics archives for all the paramount facts and figures, stats and stories.

I owe a debt of gratitude to Josh Williams, senior acquisitions editor at Triumph Books, for the opportunity to take on this project where Nathan Baird left off and run with it, and to editor Michelle Bruton for her keen proofreading eye.

Last, but certainly not least, thanks go to my wonderful wife, Jane, and to our amazing sons, August and Sam, for their everlasting love and support.

—T.S.

Bibliography

Collins, Bob. *Boilermakers: A History of Purdue Football.* Lafayette, Ind.: Haywood Printing Co., 1976.

Fitzgerald, Francis J., and Alan Karpick. *Greatest Moments in Purdue Football History.* Birmingham, Ala.: Epic Sports, 1999.

Griffiths, Doug, Alan Karpick, and Tom Schott. *Tales from Boilermaker County.* Champaign, Ill.: Sports Publishing Inc., 2003.

Griffiths, Doug, Alan Karpick, and Tom Schott. *Tales from the Purdue Boilermakers Locker Room.* New York, N.Y.: Skyhorse Publishing, 2015.

Karpick, Alan. *Boilermaker Basketball: Great Purdue Teams and Players.* Chicago, Ill.: Bonus Books, Inc., 1989.

Karpick, Alan, et al. *Relentless Pursuit: The Story of Purdue's 2000–01 Rose Bowl Season.* Lafayette, Ind.: Boilers, Inc., 2001.

Keady, Gene, and Jeff Washburn. *Gene Keady: The Truth and Nothing but the Truth.* Champaign, Ill.: Sports Publishing Inc., 2005.

Most Memorable Moments in Purdue Basketball History. Champaign, Ill.: Sports Publishing Inc., 1998.

Purdue University Alumnus magazine

Purdue University Men's and Women's Basketball Media Guides and Game Programs

Purdue University Football Media Guides and Game Programs

Schott, Tom. *Purdue University Football Vault.* Atlanta, Ga.: Whitman Publishing, LLC, 2008.

About the Author

Tom Schott worked in the Purdue University athletics department from 1990 to 2019, rising from a graduate intern to senior associate athletics director for communications. A noted historian, he is author of *Purdue University Football Vault* and co-author of *Tales from Boilermaker Country* and *Tales from the Purdue Boilermakers Locker Room*. He has also written extensively about the St. Louis Cardinals and San Francisco Giants. Tom and his wife, Jane, have two sons, August and Sam, and make their home in West Lafayette, Indiana.